HOW TO STOP A WAR

BY JAMES F. DUNNIGAN

A Quick and Dirty Guide to War: Briefings on Present and Potential Wars
(with Austin Bay)
How to Make War: A Comprehensive Guide to Modern Warfare
The Complete Wargames Handbook

BY WILLIAM MARTEL

Strategic Nuclear War: What the Superpowers Target and Why
(with Paul L. Savage)

HOW TO STOP A WAR

The Lessons of Two Hundred Years of War and Peace

JAMES F. DUNNIGAN

and WILLIAM MARTEL

Doubleday

New York

The views expressed herein are those of the authors and do not represent the views of the RAND Corporation or any of its sponsors.

Library of Congress Cataloging-in-Publication Data

Dunnigan, James F.
  How to stop a war.

  Bibliography: p. 275
  Includes index.
  1. War. 2. Military history, Modern—19th century.
3. Military history, Modern—20th century. 4. Pacific
settlement of international disputes. I. Martel,
William C. II. Title.
U21.2.D828 1987   303.6′6   87-5278
ISBN 0-385-24009-0

To my uncle, John Joseph Dunnigan, Jr., who taught me about persistence, getting the job done and doing it with a sense of humor and compassion

—James F. Dunnigan

To Dianne and William Jr.

—William Martel

ACKNOWLEDGMENTS

We wish to thank the following people for their help and advice in the research and preparation of this book: Robert Brown, Glenn Buchan, Alison Brown Cerier, Stuart Glennan, Sterling S. Hart, Ken Hoffman, Ray Macedonia, Doug MacCaskill, Albert A. Nofi, Steve Patrick, Paul Savage and Jim Simon.

Contents

General Observations on Two Centuries of Mayhem

All wars end. Some wars never start. And some wars that might grow, stay small.

The best way to prevent or stop a future war is to follow the lessons of the past. We wanted to know whether there are patterns in how wars have been prevented and stopped, so we dissected over four hundred wars and non-wars of the past two centuries. Because we are military-simulations types, we have looked at peace in an unorthodox way. We've assigned numerical values to every aspect of these conflicts so we could compare them and spot trends. And we have included in the formula the complex histories of each conflict.

We've found many trends indeed. Getting right to the point:

Wars frequently start by accident.

Miscalculation is the most common cause of war. While many wars are started deliberately, few of these turn out as their instigators planned. For example, in the 1930s the Nazis got the Rhineland, Austria and Czechoslovakia through a combination of audacious diplomacy, growing military power and the reluctance of the other major powers to risk open warfare. Hitler thought he could dismember Poland the same way. He was wrong, and World War II began.

Ignoring the possibility of war is one of the easiest ways to get involved in one.

A nation that has ignored the possibility of armed conflict tends to panic when this possibility becomes real.

Unstable governments are the most prone to warfare.

A stable, well-run government rarely has to resort to warfare. Internal disorder encourages other nations to indulge in military adventures. Also, stable nations are more successful when they participate in a war.

Governments must encourage people to enter a war "voluntarily."

Remember Pearl Harbor, or the *Lusitania,* or the *Maine,* or Alsace-Lorraine, or Versailles or Mukden? These were all rallying cries governments used to justify getting their nations into major wars. Governments make war, but the population fights them. One of the dirty little secrets of government is that the population must be mobilized into fighting a war.

The military usually recommends against a military solution.

Truly professional military personnel are not eager to get into a war. This is a historical truth that is often overlooked. In both World War I and World War II, the military staffs of the aggressor nations generally recommended against going to war. They were overruled by the politicians. A professional soldier is aware of the great risks and uncertainty that accompany any war. You have to be stupid and/or callous to go looking for a fight.

Ignorance of "the enemy" is usually a primary basis for a war.

It is rare that an aggressor believes it can defeat a victim and then proceeds to do just that. Usually, aggressors miscalculate their own combat power, that of their victim or both. The result is a far bloodier war than expected. This century abounds with examples. Starting at the turn of the century, we have the Boer War, in which forty thousand South African irregulars tied up over half a million British troops. This came as a shock to the British. In the Russo-Japanese War of 1904–5, Japan emerged as the first non-European nation to defeat a European power in several hundred years. This did not enhance Japan's military reputation as much as it diminished Russia's. The Second Balkan War in 1913 was a classic case of overestimation, with Bulgaria taking a severe beating because of its over-optimism. World War I got started in 1914 primarily because everybody thought they could win and everybody, including the nominal winners, proved to be wrong. World War II saw Germany gaining some unexpected initial victories, and proceeding to draw the wrong conclusions. The result was the dismemberment of Germany in 1945. Japan was a similar case in that it did not expect to be so successful in 1941, nor suffer such a massive defeat by 1945. In 1950 Russia and North Korea miscalculated the resistance South Korea and the United States would muster. Within a year, the United States was equally incorrect in its estimation of China's resolve in keeping American forces from its border. And then there were Vietnam, Iran-Iraq, Afghanistan. Believing what you want to believe is a difficult habit to break.

American ignorance of war is feared by allies and enemies alike.

To date, the only major wars the United States has fought on its own soil are its revolutionary struggle against Britain and a civil war. After both conflicts the military was quickly disbanded. In 1917, the United States rapidly mobilized and fought in the final year of World War I. The American ground forces were just as rapidly disbanded. After World War II American armed forces maintained an uncharacteristically high manpower level.

With the exception of World War II, there has been little carryover in professional military experience from one war to the next. American armed forces are regarded as massive and amateurish by most of the world's experienced military professionals. Worse yet, the American people are woefully ignorant of the reality of war. This combination is seen as quite dangerous.

Really large wars are difficult to get started, which is why there are so few of them.

There have been three megawars in the last two centuries (the Napoleonic Wars, the Taiping Rebellion, World Wars I/II), which have accounted for nearly half the deaths in all wars.

An important cause of large wars is faulty memory.

People, and especially their leaders, forget how horrible war is and how difficult it is to win one.

Truly major wars provide a degree of immunization against any inclination to start another one.

This resistance to warlike behavior lasts only a few generations. The favorable aspects of a war, like winning one or simply surviving, seem to glow more favorably with time. The nasty aspects, like most bad experiences, diminish with the years. World Wars I and II were not exceptions to this rule. World War II began in 1939 to far less enthusiasm than World War I did in 1914. We still live in the shadow of 1939, but the shadow fades as the memories grow dim. New generations are ignorant of the fear and terror, but not of the sweetness of victory. The world wars began just like the vast wars of the past, out of ignorance and false hope. The next major war will begin the same way.

Victory is a poor bargain, often costing more than anyone wanted to pay.

Worse yet, most wars do not even resolve the grievances that started them.

Major wars often begin because of errors in judgment.

These errors occur most often because of inaccurate information.

As is usual between megawars, there is today an increase in little wars.

One theory is that each major war is preceded by little wars that simply raise the tension level and it is followed by several more smaller wars that clean up loose ends.

Increasing worldwide wealth and population have also fueled the number of armed conflicts.

Nuclear weapons have so far prevented major wars.

Since 1949, when Russia became the second nation to obtain nuclear weapons, the fear of seeing such weapons used has restrained the major powers. This is nothing new. Before nuclear weapons, conflicts were prevented when some nations were seen as unstoppable military forces. But major powers could lose their military edge while nuclear weapons are with us for good.

It is very likely there will not be a nuclear World War III.

This isn't a guarantee that we will not eventually find ourselves fading away beneath thousands of mushroom-shaped clouds. A major world war is always possible, even though the trends are moving away from it. One purpose of this book is to help keep the trends going in the right direction.

WHAT THIS BOOK IS ALL ABOUT
IN ONE HUNDRED WORDS OR LESS

The book is divided into three parts. First we describe what the various types of wars are, what stages all wars go through from start to finish, what the primary causes are and what problems participants encounter trying to avoid a fight. We also cover the unfought nuclear wars. The second part gives the lessons of history on how to stop a war, by exploring both wars and wars that never happened. The third part provides techniques for using the past to predict future wars. By implication, this means we give you techniques to halt or prevent wars. We also present the data we collected on the last two centuries of war.

THE TWO HUNDRED YEARS OF WAR DATA BASE

At the end of the book are the highlights of the data base from which we have drawn our conclusions. There are three charts, one for the wars that happened, one for the wars that were avoided and a third for those that may yet occur. Here in brief is how we compiled the numbers.

We first put together a list of the wars that occurred during the last two hundred years. We then pulled together every aspect of each war that might suggest how wars are stopped.

From the beginning we realized that the lack of sufficiently accurate information would prevent us from doing a scientifically precise study. However, we thought we would find trends. In any case, this approach is more scientific than much of what currently reaches the general public as war and peace research. By using a computer to sort out all of our information, we did indeed find a large number of trends, interesting situations and useful tips on how to avoid wars large and small.

We quickly found that it was better to think by participant than by war. We focused on one thousand warring groups. Because our information was collected for each participant of the war, it was also possible to gather information on a war by adding the data on all participants in a war.

The data base items break down into five groups:

War Description includes the name of the war, when it began and ended, the name of the participant and how large it was.

War Resources describes war-fighting capability. Some of these elements are reasonably self-evident—type of government, population size and the number of people in the armed forces, for example. Other items estimated: quality of armed forces, relative military strength and support from more powerful allies.

War Causes itemizes the reasons that the participants went to war. We covered grievances and how they were handled. Each participant's historical record was reviewed to establish how conflicts were usually handled. This is a shadowy area. Nations are usually vague about why they go to war. After the war is over, history is typically rewritten. We attempted to overcome these problems by creating many measures of motives and imperatives, so inaccuracy with a few would be mitigated by more accuracy elsewhere.

War Termination is one of the more interesting areas. Ending a war is ordinarily simpler than starting one. A few key decisions are usually brought about by compelling events. We looked for the key decision point during the war that led to the selection of peacemaking over continued fighting.

War Results is one of the more easily found categories of information. By the time a war has ended, everyone is paying attention and taking meticulous notes. Here we cover who was the nominal winner and what was lost.

One third of the items in the data base are calculated from other items. For example, the duration of the war is measured by subtracting the start date from the end date (and adding 1, for wars that start and end in the same year). Combat power is calculated by multiplying the number of troops by a quality factor.

On both calculated and entered data, we performed a number of simple calculations and cross tabulations. Acknowledging the crude nature of our information, we did not attempt elaborate statistical analysis.

We spent a lot of time probing the data base for patterns that made some sense and revealed new perceptions of how wars begin and end. Many of our insights may not appear earthshaking. Taken together, they do provide a very revealing look at a subject about which we talk a lot but do very little.

Such intense techniques as factor analysis (or components, cluster or discriminant analysis) might have plucked some interesting gems from our piles of numbers. But the math behind these techniques is rooted in econometric theory and you would have had to become familiar with terms like varimax rotation and eigenvectors to fully appreciate it. Also, given the basic fuzziness of the historical record, we might have been tempted to assign more validity to these phantom facts than they deserved. Besides, most people don't trust mathematical techniques they have a hard time spelling or pronouncing, much less understanding.

Keeping in mind that there are three types of lies (lies, damn lies and statistics), we have striven to keep the numbers understandable. We don't mind disagreement, we just want to make sure we are disputing the same points.

A detailed list of all the data base items appears at the end of the book.

Finally, the numbers are there not to overwhelm, but to illuminate. You can perform simple arithmetic on the material found at the back of the book to confirm our own findings, or come up with some of your own.

Part 1

The Anatomy of War and Peace

We have to start someplace on the road to peace, and that place is with a description of war. War's not all that simple, but it's not a mystery either. The following chapters slice up the many ideas of what a war is and lay them out so you see the details clearly.

2

What Is a War?

War is organized violence caused by national governments.

VARIETIES OF WAR

Traditional Wars. What we usually think of as wars. Two nations gather up their armed forces and go after each other. Perhaps there is even a formal declaration. Not many wars fall into this category, certainly not the majority. But the really big and memorable wars are of this type, and they generate the majority of wartime death and destruction.

Colonial Wars. A broad category of conflicts best described as a major power going to war with a significantly weaker power on the defender's own territory. This does not always involve actual colonies, just big guys beating up on little guys. There were dozens of these during the 1800s, and quite a few since. Vietnam, Afghanistan, Korea and even the Falklands are this type. The major distinguishing characteristic is the great disparity in military power between the two combatants. This does not always mean that the minor power will lose. Vietnam is the most recent example of the lesser power coming out on top. What is most important about this type of war is that only one side, the major power, can escalate the war to include nuclear weapons or other combat between superpowers.

Civil Wars. A nation at war with itself, with both sides deploying organized armed forces. This category includes insurrections, separatist movements, persistent terrorism and rebellions in general. Since 1945, it has accounted for over half the wars. If these affairs are left to themselves, normally the warring factions will sort themselves out and things will settle down. However, in the timeless tradition of such conflicts, one side or the other will often call upon an outside force. The major powers are often eager to join in, particularly if there is any chance that one major power can become, or already is, involved.

Civil Terrors. A nation goes to war against its own people. Many of these wars are very similar to civil wars, except that the "rebels" are not organized well, if at all. Often the population is not looking for a fight. The most prominent examples are the Stalinist Terror in Russia during the 1930s, the Communist Terror in China during the 1950s, the Red Guard Terror in China during the 1960s and '70s, and smaller terrors in Uganda and Argentina. Wars of this type have been waged throughout history, but because modern technology puts so much more power in the hands of the state, civil terrors have become bloodier than most traditional wars. Of the four wars in this century that caused more than ten million deaths, two were civil terrors—Stalin's actions in the 1920s and '30s and the Chinese Communist actions against the population from 1948 to 1975. The most prominent recent example was the Khmer Rouge assault on the Cambodian people that caused several million deaths. In the 1970s, the Indonesian army began slaughtering the restive population of East Timor. Over a hundred thousand have died since then. Part of the Russian campaign in Afghanistan is a civil terror, deliberate assaults on the population that have caused over a million noncombatant deaths.

These war types can be placed on a continuum of violence and world danger. On the most perilous end we have the traditional wars. These are the wars major powers indulge in. These are also the types of wars that generate maximum violence no matter what the military might of the opponents.

Next come the colonial wars, which are generally mismatches between a major power and an unfortunate minor one. This type of war can generate a major war if two major powers take an active interest in the same minor country. Usually, the major powers are prudent enough to check with the other big boys before they invade a weak neighbor. Misunderstandings of this sort were a major cause of World Wars I and II.

Colonial wars are by definition major-power wars. When the colonies are thousands of miles away from the major powers, these conflicts are less dangerous. Today, however, major power colonies are often not colonies in the conventional sense but rather "areas of (self) interest." Russia considers Eastern Europe an area of Russian interest. Four times in the last thirty-odd years Russian armies have mobilized to keep order in these colonies (East Germany—1953, Hungary—1956, Czechoslovakia—1968, Poland—1980). In the last case, Russian divisions were mobilized but did not cross the border. This was only because Russia convinced the Polish Army that it would be less painful if Polish troops put down the unrest.

The United States has, for over one hundred fifty years, publicly proclaimed the Western Hemisphere to be an exclusive area of interest. American armed forces have been dispatched numerous times to enforce this doctrine. In the past twenty-seven years Russia has become involved in military and political affairs in the Western Hemisphere. This is not as dangerous as it sounds. Russia has no resources for moving significant armed forces to the Western Hemisphere. Despite its enormous armed might, Russia is still primarily a land-based power. The considerable Russian Army is fully committed to defending Russia's vast borders. United States military involvement in its own backyards (by our definition, colonial wars), and the nominal involvement of Russia, may sell newspapers, but they are unlikely to start World War III.

Civil wars tend to be less dangerous because normally no one else wants to get involved. Domestic disputes of all degrees tend to be extremely unstable and unpredictable. Vietnam and Afghanistan are examples of domestic unrest in which the major powers learned too late to avoid involvement. Generally the major powers are more interested in maintaining the status quo and keeping the peace. The major powers have more obligations and distractions. They also have more to lose and more enemies eager to see them lose it. While civil unrest in a foreign nation may offer temptations to an opportunistic major power, the risks of things getting out of hand are generally too great to warrant intervention.

Even less tempting to major powers are civil terrors in another nation. Civil terror occurs when the government in power possesses considerable military power and is willing to take extreme measures to see that this condition does not change. Such a government is obviously ruthless about keeping things as they are. So there are few easy pickings for any outside power. Examples of such civil terror are the Khmer Rouge in Cambodia in the 1970s, China in the 1940s and '60s, Russia in the 1920s and '30s, Turkey during the 1910s, Germany during the 1930s and '40s and Argentina in the 1970s. Most measured their casualties in the millions. (The

German terror, primarily against Jews and Slavs, is generally assumed to be part of World War II. It was not, in that the Nazis were committed to this terror with or without a war going on.) Civil terrors are not as widely recognized as the more conventional wars, even though they rank among the most destructive wars of this century.

Many traditional and colonial wars also contain a component of civil terror. We often just think of civilian casualties inflicted by enemy soldiers, but civilian losses from friendly troops are also often substantial. Russia probably suffered over ten million civilian dead during World War II. A large portion of those deaths was inflicted by Russian troops, often long after the Germans had been driven away. Military planners now believe that many of the deaths from nuclear war will occur as a result of civil disorder after the bombs have dropped. Government breaks down under such conditions, and the resulting anarchy causes substantial deaths. There are nonnuclear examples of this in Lebanon and Uganda, which suffered higher losses after their central governments fell apart. Warfare does not have to be highly organized to be deadly.

BIG WARS, LITTLE WARS, MULTIWARS

Most of the dozens of wars going on at any moment are minuscule compared to the major wars that define our ideas of what a war is. Of the over four hundred wars we have examined, fewer than fifty would be considered "large" (as in Korea, Vietnam, Afghanistan or Iran-Iraq). The truly massive wars (World Wars I and II, the Napoleonic Wars, the American Civil War) are fewer than ten in number. (The large wars also tend to involve the same groups, primarily Russians and Chinese.)

The majority of wars are civil wars—revolutions or separatist affairs. In other words, domestic squabbles. This pattern of warfare has existed for as long as humans have engaged in organized violence. There was a momentary change during the 1800s, when a handful of European nations laid claim to large portions of the planet. Instead of fighting neighboring tribes, the colonies fought their foreign overlords.

From 1914 to 1945 most Europeans were busy slaughtering each other. While the colonial peoples were licking their wounds from a hundred years of oppression, the Europeans were exhausting their interest in war. After 1945 the Europeans gave up and let most of the colonies become independent nations again. As befits sovereign states, these former colonies proceeded to resume warring with themselves and their neighbors. Most of the wars since 1945 have been among the former colonies. These nations are still poor and cannot afford to sustain long periods of high-intensity warfare. Their conflicts often break down into banditry, rape and pillage. The colonial powers were no longer around to keep the peace, so the level of warfare increased considerably.

This low-budget type of conflict is warfare at its most basic level. The major powers attempt to influence the outcome by backing one faction or another. Sometimes a major power will even switch sides in the middle of war. It's all a rather gruesome game, with no one gaining much from it. As long as these wars do not involve the armed forces of a major power, there is usually little threat of escalation. Some of these wars, however, are fought on or near the borders of a major power. In this case there is a greater threat that things will get out of hand. Afghanistan and El Salvador are two examples of risky minor wars. Most major power leaders today seem to agree that no one should risk nuclear war over Afghanistan or El Salvador. But if some major power leader were to up the ante, the risk is there.

Minor wars can become regional wars. Many Afghanistan rebels operate from sanctuaries in Pakistan and Iran. Should Russia become convinced that peace can be achieved only by closing down these sanctuaries, then a war in one Middle East nation could spread to three or more. This could tempt the United States to intervene more actively. Add a few more crises around the world and you have a very tense situation. Similar tensions are possible in Vietnam and adjacent nations. Such tension could set off nuclear weapons.

It is also remotely possible for the wars in Central America to escalate to neighboring countries. There is less risk of a superpower confrontation here simply because only the United States has the ability to quickly move substantial armed forces to any part of the world. The Russians are much less capable of intervening far beyond their borders. Despite all the hype about the Russian Navy, there is little doubt in the minds of most sailors about who rules the oceans. The Russian Navy is still largely a defensive force with a secondary mission to defend its ballistic missile submarines. Launching overseas amphibious operations is not what the Russian Navy is all about. Not for now, anyway. The Russian Navy steadily improves, and its airlift capability regularly surprises many in the West.

Most of the very big wars have actually been collections of many wars that happened to take place at the same time and had something tenuous in common. World War II is a good example. The fighting in Europe consisted of a series of wars, of which the one between Russia and Germany was by far the largest. The fighting in the Pacific was really two separate wars. In China a three-way war between Chinese Communists, Chinese Nationalists and the Japanese had been going on since the early 1930s. Before that there had been a civil war in China since 1912. The other war in the Pacific was between the United States and Japan. The Japanese-American war was related to the Chinese war; Japan attacked American, British and Dutch possessions in the Pacific in reaction to Western pressure to get Japan out of China. But the two Pacific wars were fought largely independently of each other. The war in China did not end until 1949, when the Communists defeated the Nationalists. Similarly, the Russia-German war did not really end until the 1950s, when the Communists finally defeated the last remaining nationalist guerrillas in the Ukraine.

These "multiwars" arise partly out of the ability of the major powers to restrain their smaller neighbors from settling disputes through violence. The grievances pile up and are resolved all at once in an orgy of wars once the major powers go at each other. Every major war during the past several centuries has followed this pattern.

A major war requires a major effort. Not just in terms of manpower, but also in terms of an enormous economic undertaking to keep the armies going. Few nations can wage a major war. Nuclear weapons have made warfare between the major powers even more expensive. The high cost of war restrains even the United States and Russia from using their military power.

Smaller nations continue to fight their smaller wars. Fortunately, minor country wars are limited by a lack of resources to keep a war going. There are rare exceptions. One was the Taiping Rebellion in China from 1851 to 1882. Over twenty million died. China was not a wealthy nation, so most of the fighting was "paid for" by living off the land. This destruction of the fragile civilian economy resulted in the murder and starvation of millions of civilians. The social unrest ignited by the Taiping Rebellion set the stage for the forty-year Chinese civil war which caused millions of additional deaths. All of this could also be described as the decline and fall of the Chinese monarchy and the feudal social organization that supported it. Similar upheavals were taking place in Russia and Eastern Europe and are more well known, although they were much less destructive.

An example of a truly horrendous war between smaller nations occurred in South America during the 1860s. Paraguay, led by a capable but fanatical dictator, took on Argentina, Brazil and Uraguay. The result was the death of over 80 percent of Paraguay's population, plus over 100,000 fatalities among the other three combatants. Nearly half a million dead in six years of fighting. All because of one man, and a fanatical sense of nationalism shared by all participants.

Major wars of this nature are still possible. The Iran-Iraq War of the 1980s has the potential for this scale of slaughter. Israel also fears a horrible war. That Israel probably possesses nuclear weapons merely makes an astronomical death toll more likely should the Arab states gain a military advantage.

Fortunately, the poverty of most minor power combatants prevents their conflicts from spreading worldwide. Unfortunately, as nuclear weapons proliferate, it becomes increasingly possible for a poor nation's war to go nuclear. This is currently considered the most likely occasion for the next use of nuclear weapons.

Lesser military powers, often very poor nations, have such desperate wars because you don't need wealth to be angry with your neighbors. Indeed, wealthier nations have more incentive to be peaceful; they have more to lose.

FOREVER WARS

In many parts of the world a volatile combination of factors creates wars that rage perpetually. Some recent examples of these Forever Wars are Lebanon, Iran-Iraq and Vietnam. All are but the latest chapters in wars that have persisted for hundreds or thousands of years. These wars endure for the same reasons: different ethnic groups living intermingled, intolerance between the groups and a tendency toward long memories and little compassion.

A classic example occurred in the late 1970s while an American journalist was interviewing a Druse fighter in Lebanon. When asked why he was fighting, the Druse replied, "To avenge the Christian atrocities against my village in the sixties." Later, the reporter sought additional detail about this incident in the sixties. He could find none. He went back to the Druse and asked for more detail about this incident in the 1960s. The Druse looked at him quizzically and said, "No, it was the 1860s."

TRUE BELIEVERS AND RELIGIOUS WARS

If you are dealing with true believers, of either the religious or political variety, you are going to have a difficult time preventing or ending the conflict. Combatants lacking ideological motivations are more open to negotiation. True believers often believe in fighting to the death.

Widely accepted religious beliefs are the most difficult to cope with, especially if the faith is partial to martyrdom. It is difficult to reason with an opponent who feels a divine inspiration to slay you and looks forward to getting killed in the process. A holy warrior's death means eternal salvation. Classic examples of holy warriors and terrorists are the Shiites in the Middle East, comprising most Iranians and several groups in Lebanon. Their eagerness for martyrdom in combat is legendary, and real.

Secular religion can also be a troublesome ideological opponent. Newly minted teenage Communists are often fearless in the face of death. For this reason, older Communists often jail or shoot their younger compatriots after a revolution. Fanatics are useful for overcoming the enemy, but get in the way of running a government. The older Chinese Communists unleashed young fanatics in 1965 to overcome internal opponents. Much death and misery were caused before the young true believers were defeated.

Revolutions also have problems because they give guns to the masses. What happens when the people are armed and have become accustomed to war? They kill the revolutionaries after the war is won. Meanwhile, the rebel leadership has a hard time getting these do-or-die warriors to calm down. Bloodthirsty youth are nothing new. The Viking berserkers, European crusaders, Turkish bashki-bazouks, Cambodian Khmer Rouge, Lebanese militia are but a few examples. The average age of soldiers in most ancient armies was under twenty years. It's still a young man's game. Beware teenagers with heavy weapons.

On the bright side, many ideologies are but a thin veneer. The Nazi ideology (1934–45) was never completely accepted by the majority of Germans. The majority of the German Army consisted of adherents to non- or anti-Nazi political beliefs. This made the defeat of Germany more a struggle against nationalism than a fight to the death with Nazi fanatics. Most Germans fought to defend their country against a Russian invasion, a danger the Nazi propaganda machine preached all along. Japan, during the same period, was a different story. The Japanese national ideology was based on being Japanese. Religion and nationalism were combined in a way unknown in the West. It took total military defeat, great slaughter among the civilian population and the prospect of annihilation to bring about a surrender.

When ideology is not involved, and this is the case with most wars, peace is much easier to achieve. Keep an eye out for true believers.

Another form of religious fervor is generated when one nation invades another. When Germany invaded Russia in 1941, the Communist government quickly appealed to Russian nationalism. Although Russia had been renamed the Union of Soviet Socialist Republics twenty years before, the religious image of Mother Russia (complete with priests and religious icons) was quickly mobilized.

Wars are easier to terminate if the major adversaries are fighting in someone else's territory. If the war is inconclusive, it is politically easier to simply declare victory and leave the battlefield. Although an invaded nation may toss the attacker out, often roles reverse then. Invasion brings out the worst in all concerned. Revenge gets out of hand and the bad blood lingers long after the fighting has died down. When such invasions are ended by one side prevailing militarily, the peace is often fragile. Wars between neighbors must end with major grievances settled; otherwise, you only have a temporary cease-fire instead of true peace.

The most difficult wars to end result from one ethnic group being ruled by another. This problem is widely recognized, but few nations are willing to give up any of their territory and population simply because some of the occupants look different and talk funny. Africa and the Middle East can trace many of their wars to this type of situation. Unfortunately, there are only two permanent solutions to this problem. Either you give each ethnic group an acceptable form of self-rule, or you destroy the minority populations. In most cases the latter solution is applied. For some reason, persistent slaughter is easier to achieve than meaningful negotiations.

CIVIL DISORDER

When identifying and measuring wars we often come to gray areas where civil disorders and more organized warfare intermingle. Many wars begin, or end, in a muddle of disorganized civil strife. Often a truly chaotic war is fought entirely in a style best described as civil disorder.

We define civil disorder as widespread civilian violence that cannot be controlled by the usual peacekeeping authorities. The peacekeepers are often just the regular police. In many countries the regular police are augmented by paramilitary and auxiliary forces (riot police, border guards, militia, secret police) plus, when things really get desperate, the armed forces. Most of the wars in the past two hundred years have involved some civil disorder. Often it is the cause of the war, or a result. Either way, the patterns of civil disorder in a society play a large part in determining the kinds of war that society is capable of. The less civil disorder a country has, the more lethal it is when it goes to war. A really destructive war requires a high degree of organization and discipline.

Nearly every society has a certain amount of civil disorder, ranging from individual criminal acts to large-scale disturbances. In stable societies, this criminal activity does not form the basis for serious opposition to the government. However, in many countries the criminal activity is so pervasive, or government police forces so weak, that the bandits determine directions and decisions of government. Disruptive acts can include a lot of nonviolent, but very destructive, crime. Large-scale embezzlement, corruption of public officials and other white-collar crime are major reasons for most revolutionary and civil wars in this century.

Often this civil disorder is not ideologically motivated. When there is ideology involved, civil disorder can grow into what we think of as war. Nonideological violence is based on individual need or greed and rarely mobilizes large numbers of people for a sustained effort. Nonideological violence is often a by-product of warfare, as opportunistic people take advantage of the wartime disorder. Sometimes the original ideological motivations decline, leaving only random criminal acts. This, in turn, can produce a backlash of vigilante activity.

A particularly vicious form of civil disorder is the large-scale plundering of a nation's wealth by government officials. This is nothing new, but because a lot more wealth is available in this century, enormous damage can be done when government officials abuse their fiscal responsibilities. Public officials making off with massive amounts of the nation's resources causes much misery, and often death. These thefts are also liable to create armed civil disorder and often conventional wars. Examples abound, the most obvious ones being third world nations whose government officials siphon off national wealth and foreign aid. When these governments fall, their leaders often fly off to luxurious retirement. Even Communist governments, which claim the moral high ground because of their more diligent adherence to fiscal integrity, have known significant examples of government looting for private gain. The unrest in Poland in the late 1970s was partially caused by the corruption in the Communist government. When the new Communist regime came into power, it punished many former officials for abuse of fiscal responsibility. Several governments in Africa (Ethiopia, Chad, the Sudan, for example) handled 1980s' starvation relief funds more for their own benefit than for that of their suffering citizens.

Plundering the public treasury has become more risky as an integrated worldwide financial system has developed. All those billions are no good if there is no place you can hide them from your former subjects. The trend is for soon-to-be-deposed tyrants to negotiate with their rebellious subjects. Marcos in the Philippines, Duvalier in Haiti and Bokassa in the Central African Republic are examples. This haggling comes down to how much the oppressed are willing to pay to be free. The process of government does indeed take some strange twists and turns.

When you look at wars closely enough, you will discover that they invariably arise out of a long string of disputes and provocations. One must measure both material and ideological dissatisfactions when calculating where peace will break down into warfare and at what point civil disorder turns into the more commonly accepted notions of warfare.

Six Stages of War

All wars go through stages from peace to war and ultimately back to peace again.

Stage 1—Situation Under Control

This is the prewar state. No war is in the works, and the nations eventually involved are in whatever state passes for peace in their part of the world. Peacetime in some areas includes a fair amount of internal disorder. Your first task is to make sure you are not confusing a rambunctious peace with a prewar crisis.

Stage 2—Instability

Events that can lead to war appear. The defending nation is not always going to go through this phase. Most wars are induced primarily by the attacking side, without intentional provocation from the victim, although instability often invites attack. Iraq attacking Iran in 1980 is a recent example. Revolutions and civil wars feed on the growing instability of the ruling government. War can be prevented at this point, even though events are rapidly going out of control.

Stage 3—Losing Control

Otherwise known as "going to war." At this point, wartime rules of behavior take over. This is where most people start keeping track of a war. If you really want to know what is going on in a war and you start at this point, you are too late.

Stage 4—Waging War

A series of decisions determine how long and violent the war will be. The first decision is whether or not to consider the initial war plans successful. The second decision is whether or not a fight to the death will be conducted. The third decision is whether or not to begin negotiations to end the war. Let's consider each decision in some detail.

Decision 1. Were the initial plans successful? Usually at least one side has thought hard about how it expects the war to proceed. Customarily, the attacker has a plan that it hopes will end the fighting early, on its terms and with minimal losses. Rarely is the attacking side's population promised anything but a short, glorious war. Frequently, the war starts out badly and the attacking nation's leaders feel compelled to maintain the illusion that the original plan, with a few regrettable exceptions, is playing itself out as anticipated. One reason a democracy has a hard time fighting guerrilla wars is that these are long, painful wars. Just look at Vietnam.

Decision 2. Fight to the end? Individual soldiers and units usually show a more highly developed sense of self-preservation than embarrassed national leaders sitting at a distance from all the killing. The decision to fight on in the face of certain failure commits a side to massive destruction and injury in return for the possibility of delaying defeat or possibly winning some form of bloody victory. Getting back to one of our favorite recent examples, both Iran and Iraq made this decision. The results are predictable. It has been, and will continue to be, a bloody war.

Decision 3. Negotiate? Deciding to undertake negotiations to end a war, rather than depending solely on combat, is the most critical decision made in wartime. This decision is even more difficult to make than the initial decision to go to war. At least the decision to go to war is made in the tranquil atmosphere of peacetime. Once the shooting starts, decision making is conducted under much more stressful wartime conditions. The attacking leadership is heavily committed to the successful implementation of its attack plans. The government of the defending nation has more leeway in negotiations. Although the defender's leaders may have made some promises, generally their primary responsibility is to extricate their nation from the danger brought about by the attacker.

Stage 5—War Termination

When both sides agree that it would be a good idea to talk about peace, a critical stage of the war is reached. Sometimes it only occurs when one side has its back to the wall. Generally, though, when immediate victory does not occur, both sides' governments feel an urge to talk it over and bring the matter to an end before much more damage is done. Political pressures in both nations usually prevent this initially. The most difficult task a national leader can accomplish is to get peace negotiations going, particularly if the country or the enemy is not thinking peace at the moment. But negotiations to end a war are usually a viable option from the very beginning of hostilities. Often fighting is started primarily to get the other side to talk about grievances; many little wars and nearly all terrorism fall into this category.

Historically, negotiation has been preferred to "unconditional surrender." Americans used to be biased toward unconditional surrender. The United States always had an absolutist attitude toward right and wrong. Since 1945, the United States has been more amenable to negotiating less restrictive peace settlements, such as in Korea and Vietnam. But some people still believe that we should have fought in Vietnam to the bitter end. And the American aversion to secret negotiations with openly declared opponents such as Iran indicates that a bias toward unconditional surrender persists. This sentiment worries United States allies and potential opponents.

Russia, and most other nations that have been in business for a long time, are less likely to insist on unconditional surrender. Russia does become inflexible when the core Russian territories are involved, surrendering them only after it has set the torch to them. However, Russia will negotiate away parts of the empire in order to keep some sort of Russian state functioning. Substantial portions of the Soviet Union were only acquired in the past hundred years and are still inhabited by people who do not speak Russian or follow Russian customs. Russia has not been reluctant to trade these territories for a more important advantage, such as keeping an invader from coming any closer. Russia is even more receptive to using recently conquered territories as bargaining chips. This pattern is the basis of the theory that if the Russians invaded Western Europe, they would be eager to trade back what they had conquered in exchange for peace if they ran into too many obstacles.

Knowledge of how a nation has reacted to war-termination proposals in the past suggests how that nation will react in a future war. But watch for recent changes in that nation. Iran was as willing as anyone to talk things over, until Islamic fundamentalists took over. Inflexibility makes negotiation much more difficult and wars bloodier. In 1980, Iraq knew within a few months of attacking Iran that its original plan for a quick victory was not going to work. It was inclined to withdraw from Iranian territory and forget the whole thing. The religiously inspired Iranians had none of that. They wanted blood, or at least the head of the Iraqi leader and a large pile of cash. Such ideological fervor is the exception, and eventually passes. But while it is in effect, it is powerful.

Stage 6—Aftereffects

After the war is over, it's not over. Wars often fail to settle the original disputes, and they cause new ones. A bad peace can lead to even more destructive wars.

Revenge is the most common culprit, even if it's only an excuse. If you want to see where the next war is coming from, look at how the last one ended.

The Four Causes of War

There are many aspects to getting a war started and keeping it going. Attempts to understand the causes of war often collapse under an enormous number of potential reasons. Our research narrowed it down to four major causes: long-standing grievances, internal disorder, a sense of military superiority and fear of being attacked. Most wars have more than one of these major causes, although normally one predominates.

We broke down the wars in our survey by direct cause, to see what portion of the participating countries was drawn into war by each, and also what portion of all deaths in war was caused by each.

CAUSES OF WAR

Direct Cause of War	Percentage of Participants	Percentage of Deaths
Long Standing Grievances	41	12
Internal Disorder	39	51
Sense of Military Superiority	16	13
Fear of Being Attacked	4	24

Old grudges (long standing grievances) and paranoia (fear of being attacked) account for nearly half the wars; civil disorder (internal disorder) and bullies (sense of military superiority) account for the rest. Note that half the deaths were from wars caused by internal disorder, even though a much smaller percentage of nations was involved in this sort of conflict. Below we explain each cause in more detail.

LONG-STANDING GRIEVANCES

The United States and Canada have the longest undefended border in the world. This border is unique among major nations, which says a lot about how widespread grievances exist and persist between nations.

"Grievances" might appear too broad a term for a single cause of war. But the grievances between nations have much in common. The classic squabble is over disputed territory. Many nations maintain claims on territory that they once ruled centuries in the past. These conflicts generate yet another class of grievances, desire for revenge for past military defeats.

The most persistent irritation is a desire for self-rule. Peoples everywhere insist on rule by leaders culturally similar to themselves. On the other hand, alien rulers are reluctant to relinquish control over populations. Every nation has problems of this type, varying in intensity.

Language, and to a lesser extent religion and social class, has been a major cause of warfare. Conquest or migration caused by natural disaster often mix together populations that speak different languages. Research shows that, despite the common view, different cultures hate each other even more once they get to know each other. When large numbers of a group move across the border from one nation to another the result often is intense animosity. You can generally expect, at the very least, civil disorder and, at worst, war. This pattern has repeated itself throughout history. There are only two long-term solutions to the problem. Either one language group absorbs all the others or the different groups separate and establish their own governments. Sometimes these different governments still exist within a structure with other language groups. Important examples are Canada, Belgium, Switzerland, India, Vietnam, Yugoslavia, Spain, Sri Lanka, numerous African and South American nations, China and Russia. In all of them, when there are no external threats to enforce unity, the less powerful groups that do not control the central government are always tempted to try to secede. The majority of revolutionary activity in the world is based largely on ethnic differences. Such internal disturbances spill over to neighboring nations and are repeatedly the cause of even larger wars. Most of the warlike mayhem in the world today can be traced, at least partially, to internal cultural differences.

A powerful nation that acquires and controls a number of different populations through military force or economic enticements is an empire. There aren't too many empires left—Russia, and to some extent China,

Vietnam, Iran and India. Each consists of a number of populations that speak different languages and, to one degree or another, would prefer autonomy. Because of this underlying disunity, empires are continually at war with themselves. If they lack natural borders, they frequently find themselves at war with their neighbors, many of whom are related to its subject populations. These regular applications of military force tend to make empires potent military powers and often quite durable entities.

China has existed as an empire for over two thousand years, disrupted only by occasional periods of disunity and internal strife. India has been an empire nearly as long as China, but has been more often unstable and torn by civil strife. India, unlike China, is afflicted by deep religious differences and a strict caste system. India is unified today because Britain conquered the independent Indian states in the 1700s and 1800s.

Of the three major empires, Russia is the most lacking in natural borders and consequently the most prone to border wars. Fighting over disputed borders is the most common motive for wars between two nations, second only to civil wars and revolutions. Borders are disputed most frequently when it is physically easy to pass over them. Major rivers, oceans or mountain ranges make for less easily disputed borders. Find a border that is just a line on a map and has a significant number of people living along it, and you will find a border that has been disputed sometime. As people have long memories, past border disputes are easily revived.

Russia has existed, and continually expanded, for over five hundred years. Of all the examples, Russia is the most unstable. Russia has none of the advantages of China. China is not adjacent to many powerful neighbors, it has a more homogeneous population and its military does not play such an overwhelming political and social role.

Russia has been aptly described as an army that happens to possess a country. Russia exists to provide whatever the armed forces desire. And its armed forces believe as a matter of official principle that the best defense is a strong offense. This policy has gone a long way toward cultivating a very impressive list of enemies. In the West there are the restive nations of Eastern Europe, occupied by the elite units of the Russian Army. To the south is Turkey, an ancient opponent, and an active war in Afghanistan. To the east lies China, actively seeking the return of territory taken by force during the 1800s, when China was wracked by internal disorder. Japan also has grievances, and South Korea holds Russia responsible for its partition. Russia feels, like many empires before it, that to cease expansion is to risk disintegration. But actually the economic and diplomatic strain of this policy is weakening the empire.

There are numerous minor empires. Iran has been in the empire business for about as long as China. The ethnic Iranians (Persians) comprise the majority of the population and occupy the center of the country. But in the border areas there are significant numbers of Azers, Turkomens and Kurds in the north, Baluchis and various Afghans in the southeast and Arabs in the west. Vietnam has a similar situation, with Thais, Cambodians and several other ethnic minorities in the border areas. As an example of how bizarre population arrangements can be, the Chinese-Vietnam border has few Chinese or Vietnamese inhabitants, except for the Chinese and Vietnamese troops shooting at each other.

Empires are unstable entities held together by military force and a single ethnic group determined to maintain its power, no matter what. Empires are wars waiting to happen.

INTERNAL DISORDER

Every nation in existence is in danger of civil disorder. Every nation has had at least one instance of severe internal unrest. At any time, at least 5 percent of the planet's population is engaged in violent resistance to their governments. Worse yet, several times that number are being savagely oppressed by their own governments.

Peaceful relations with one's neighbors and internal prosperity are the best ways to avoid internal mayhem. Maintaining favorable economic conditions is difficult for most governments. Rulers often find it easier to build a strong police force. Thus we have the familiar pattern of poverty-stricken citizens closely watched by an overindulged constabulary.

Most of these well-policed but desperately poor nations eventually slide into civil disorder. The danger of significant violence is much less, as you need wealth to get a properly dangerous war going. These poorly financed wars become dangerous only if the superpowers provide resources.

Such intervention will continue, particularly into poor nations on or near superpower borders. It is not practical for one superpower to get too involved on another superpower's frontiers. Picking a fight in the other fellow's backyard puts you at a disadvantage. Stir up trouble on the other nation's frontier, but don't allow it to develop into a serious confrontation. The Russians learned this the hard way in Cuba during 1962. For the same reason, the United States backs off from supporting Eastern European rebellions. Afghanistan is a little different. Afghanistan was long perceived as a neutral zone between Russia and Britain. Moreover, the Western nations have a stronger interest in this oil-rich region than Russia. Despite this, restraint is exercised. Over time, restraint tends to erode. In the long run, civil disorder subsides to what passes for normal conditions in the area. Otherwise, escalation sets in and peace returns only after a bloodbath.

Most nations are too poor, or cost conscious, to go to war over civil disorder. Instead, police and paramilitary forces are increased to cope with the violence. Where the population is not progovernment, the last thing you want to do is send in the army. Regular troops tend to get carried away, and the population responds by getting carried away too. Committing the army is tacit recognition that the civil disorder is edging toward civil war.

Nations rarely indulge in regular warfare unless attacked or otherwise strongly provoked. Nations living on the edge of starvation are thus restrained from throwing away their tenuous hold on survival by engaging in organized combat. Countries that already have large and well-equipped armed forces are more likely to go to war. The attitude appears to be, "We got it, we might as well use it." Such well-endowed nations are also eager to support violence in foreign nations. A wealthy population is less likely to miss the money. But it would miss dead citizens, so it tends to use mercenary forces. Russia uses Cuban soldiers in Africa and Central America. Britain uses Nepalese (Gurkhas), and many Middle Eastern nations employ soldiers from a variety of nations.

The purpose of mercenaries and foreign adventures is to limit the unsettling effects of wars on the folks at home. People are driven to violence reluctantly. Rulers learn soon, or at great cost, to limit the use of organized violence.

There is a large pool of unhappy people in the world. A quarter of the world's population is in various states of agitation. These unhappy populations provide fuel for potential wars. It's bad enough that prudent rulers in these nations may stumble, frequently they are gamblers. The ultimate horror is that one of these risk takers will come to power in a heavily armed nation. It's happened before. Hitler, Stalin and Napoleon are not unique. Mixing such leaders with tense populations is like throwing a lighted match into a fuel tank.

Unstable governments are always in danger of falling into internal or external violence. Rebellion, civil war and secessionist disputes are the most common forms of strife. Nations weakened by such internal conflict make tempting targets for ambitious neighbors. Disorder breeds disorder and major wars often develop out of internal conflicts. All the major wars of this century evolved in this fashion. Most of the minor wars developed the same way.

For all of history, major powers have promoted internal order within their allies and disorder within their enemies and the allies of their enemies. This must change if nuclear war is to be avoided. Trying to influence the internal affairs of a foreign nation is a tricky business. Misunderstandings and embarrassments often occur between stable, friendly nations. When the two nations are not too friendly toward each other, and one is in a state of disorder, the confusion level goes up.

When a nation is plagued by internal disorder, its decision making becomes erratic. Relationships with other nations become more difficult. If war breaks out within such a nation, the possibility of external war increases considerably.

Nations often use external aggression to address internal problems. In the last decade we have seen such vivid examples as Argentina attacking the British in the Falklands. Iran continued its war with Iraq partially as a solution to internal problems.

A nation that is undergoing radical social change will often become involved in external wars. Iran is again an example, which makes its Arab neighbors very nervous. The bloodiest example is Lebanon. Here the introduction of a large population of Palestinians on top of an already shaky situation provoked a lengthy civil war. This, in turn, led to invasions by neighboring Syria and Israel.

Beware disorderly nations.

A SENSE OF MILITARY SUPERIORITY

Some wars happen because a nation gets greedy, and thinks it is strong enough to get away with it. The more power a nation thinks it has, the more it is inclined to abuse it. But most of the time, aggressors miscalculate the strength and resolve of the nations they attack.

In late 1941, the Japanese underestimated the resolve of the United States. Because of Japan's aggression in China, America and several key European powers cut off Japan's oil supply. Faced with a choice of withdrawing from China or seeing its economy collapse, Japan instead elected to attack the United States. Many Japanese leaders knew full well that America was many times stronger militarily and economically. The Japanese convinced themselves that if they struck an emphatic enough blow against American forces, the United States would willingly negotiate a settlement. They were wrong.

In 1950, North Korea thought it could rush troops into South Korea and unite the country under a Communist government. Russia and China backed North Korea, the United States appeared to have pulled out of South Korea. America quickly dealt itself back in and the result was a three-year slaughter with over a million dead.

Another prominent example is the 1967 Arab-Israeli war. Arab nations mistakenly believed their own propaganda about their military strength. Forces were massed for an attack on Israel. Israel attacked first and proved devastating.

Then there was the United States in Vietnam during the 1960s. The involvement began as a military-assistance operation to a friendly government. It escalated to one of the more costly and traumatic wars in American history.

Another recent example is Iraq's attack on Iran in 1980. Iran was supposed to be too weak to resist. Iraq planned to seize a few border areas, overthrow the unfriendly government in Iran and then return to peace. Years of bloody combat followed this miscalculation.

In 1982 Argentina, apparently learning nothing from everyone else's recent experience, grabbed the Falkland Islands from Britain. The enormous distance from Europe to the Falklands did not deter the British, as Argentina thought it would. Argentina suffered a humiliating defeat as well as an unscheduled change of government.

Why this big gap between illusion and reality? Completely ignoring the possibility of war is dangerous to a leader's domestic image. People expect their leaders to prepare for possible wars. Yet contemplating participation in a war is not high on most societies' list of favorite activities. The usual compromise is to maintain an armed force that looks effective, or, at the very least, satisfies domestic concerns about security.

This is all very well when things are peaceful. If war breaks out, several unpleasant events develop. First, there is the enemy. If your adversary's forces are more capable than your own, peacetime illusions of military security are rudely shattered. Next to go is domestic tranquility. Realizing that all the peacetime expense has not bought security, supporters tend to become unruly. These unpleasant surprises are responsible for the mental shock experienced at the outbreak of a war.

Wartime reality is followed by peacetime illusions, eventually followed again by more wartime realism. There are some compelling reasons why nations so diligently ignore their vivid wartime lessons.

The most likely cause for this cycle is the lack of reliable information about what is likely to happen in a future war. Armed forces have to guess what they will have to do once the fighting starts. Consider the following:

- Armies spend most of their existence under peacetime conditions. Of the last hundred years, the United States has been "at war" for fewer than thirty. This is typical for major powers.
- Even when there is a war, actual fighting occupies only a very small portion of the time. During major wars, combat units may be "in contact" and "under fire" for sustained periods of time; most of the time they remain in one place and spend most of their energy staying out of danger. A deliberate battle, in which troops actually advance upon each other and "fight," occupies only a very small percentage of their time.
- Only a very small portion of any armed force actually gets involved in combat. Five percent is common and 20 percent is tops among major power armed forces.
- Finally, those that do engage in combat don't last very long. After two hundred to four hundred days under combat conditions, a soldier is disabled by either physical injury or "combat fatigue." In longer periods of intense combat, the troops waste away even faster. Thus most of the people gaining experience don't last long enough to pass it on.

You would think that governments would take action to overcome the above problems. Some try, but most fail to retain enough permanent military knowledge to overcome the tendency to quickly forget the realities of warfare. Nations that are frequently at war develop this "military tradition," although usually at a terrible cost.

The most effective armed forces in the world are in Europe, for the very good reason that the Europeans have been battling each other diligently for the last several hundred years. Those nations that don't regularly go to war are less effective at it.

A nation's wealth and level of technology can compensate for limited military expertise. The United States is regarded by many nations to be inept militarily. At the same time, the United States is seen as able to overcome this lack with superior wealth and technology.

As technology has become more complex and expensive, America's advantage in this area has increased. The United States can not only afford to *have* high-tech weapons, but also to exercise with them. An example is aircraft. First, you must be able to afford to build them (at ten million to over one hundred million dollars each). Then there is the cost of crews using them (over $100,000 per man-year). Only then will you have a significant edge over nations that are not as wealthy and as technically proficient.

The same formula of wealth and practice applies to ships. It is not enough to build them at great expense. You must use them so the combination of men and machines will be deployable at the outbreak of a war. All things being equal, the ship and crew that have been at sea longer will defeat the ships that spend most of their time at anchor. Britain ruled the seas for several centuries because its ships stayed at sea more than they remained in port.

Unlike a ship or aircraft, armies are sprawling, labor-intensive creatures that operate in a chaotic environment. Exercising an army is considerably more expensive and uncertain than maneuvering your ships and planes. Thus fleets and air forces can be brought to a higher degree of skill in peacetime than armies. But the foot soldier still decides wars. Civilians, and many military leaders, often lose sight of this fact. Everyone is quickly reminded when the shooting starts. At that point the armies stumble forward in a bloody exercise that produces proficient ground combat units. Unless, of course, the army is defeated first. Remember, "It's not a matter of who is better, it's more a question of who is worse." This ancient military quip applies primarily to armies. Efficient fleets and air forces can help you win a war, but the army is decisive.

Another consideration for any civilian government is to ensure that the military is not tempted to make war on *it*. The number of military governments in the world shows that soldiers, effective or not, are remarkably willing to seize control of the governments they are pledged to uphold. The army poses the greatest danger, because it is the largest armed force. Most nations can afford only token navies and air forces. The navy and air force often lead the dissent because they have a higher proportion of educated personnel. This makes a loyal army a useful tool in keeping the other services in line. The army thus becomes the most powerful branch of the armed forces, by a wide margin.

One of the most popular ways of ensuring army loyalty is appointing senior commanders more for their political loyalty than military skill. Obviously, the quality of the army declines as its leadership is loaded up with political hacks. The more competent military leaders thus denied promotion are then tempted to seize control of the army and the government. This accounts for the large number of military takeovers led by lower-grade officers or sergeants.

Often a government threatened by a military takeover will weaken its armed forces one way or the other. A military less capable of fighting a war is the price paid for staying in power. Unfortunately, the military's lack of combat power tends not to be admitted by either military or civilian leaders. Appearances can more easily be kept up than reality can be changed. It's easier, and more practical politically, to spend money on uniforms and good-looking equipment than on training and selection of competent combat leaders.

Within a government, it is in everyone's best interest to say that the military is in good shape. Pointing out shortcomings is looked upon as disloyal, disruptive or suspicious. It's easier to make excuses than to set things right. But the military is not just another government bureaucracy. It has to defend the country. When its effectiveness is grossly overestimated, tragic decisions are often made. In a peculiar form of brinksmanship, all concerned ignore the reality of a coming war until it's too late. The military must go with what it has. No one is quite sure what the military can do until the shooting starts. Everyone is usually surprised.

In countries with a military tradition, professional soldiers want to avoid war. They usually know how dangerous and unpredictable it is. Soldiers also have a more accurate appreciation of the military balance between nations. Often, however, soldiers are unwilling to risk the political heat from giving their superiors an accurate appraisal of an unpleasant military situation. Worse, they can become convinced that the popular delusions of relative military power are the reality. It happens, it happens a lot.

Soldiers have to fight when war comes. Given the life and death nature of combat, they want the best chance of victory. Although the most senior military leaders are rarely exposed to enemy fire, they are very concerned with their reputations and place in history. Therefore, the soldier's attitude toward weapons, troops and equipment is "too much ain't enough." But taxpayers can be pushed only so far, so the military often has to go with what they've got. Soldiers tend to conclude that what they got isn't enough and argue against attacking until military spending has been increased sufficiently.

Theoretically, it is possible to avoid optimism toward military power. If the professional soldiers were experienced enough, they could accurately determine what was possible and thus restrain their national leaders. Unfortunately, there are many professional soldiers, but few experienced ones. Most soldiers go through their entire careers without ever having participated, much less fought, in a war. Most who have fought, have done so at a command level far below the one they currently hold. In other words, most professional soldiers have no practical experience in their chosen profession.

The professional military has many reasons for arguing against entering a war of aggression. That there are wars is largely because of overwhelming popular opinion, overly ambitious civilian leaders or military leaders who are confident enough in their own abilities to risk trial by combat. Rarely is the decision to attack made according to a plan that succeeds. Something as unpredictable as warfare does not coexist easily with predictable plans.

FEAR OF BEING ATTACKED

The least frequent, but disproportionately most destructive, cause of wars is when one side invades because it fears attack. Most of the Arab-Israeli wars began for this reason, as have several other major wars. The fear is often justified, and war most often occurs between two antagonists who are heavily armed and inclined to fight.

Inflammatory rhetoric, refusal to negotiate and mobilization are the immediate causes of such wars.

The most dangerous element is mobilization of forces, in which both sides keep pushing their armies closer to wartime preparedness. The ultimate escalation is to mass forces on your opponent's border. This is no trivial exercise. Combat forces are not normally ready to fight, so it takes time to get ready. These preparations must be matched by the other side, or the less-prepared force will be at a significant disadvantage.

Mobilization doesn't occur in a political vacuum. The population must be inspired to support a warlike attitude. Ancient or newly minted grievances must be stirred up to create and sustain a warlike mood.

Few wars begin spontaneously. When you hear of armed forces being deployed, or reserves being called into service, of leaves canceled and bases cut off from normal civilian access, get very worried. Mobilization is an expensive process, and is not usually conducted as just an exercise.

With nuclear weapons, part of the mobilization is done in the laboratories and missile factories. The controversy over nuclear arms control is driven by the fear that one of the nuclear powers will achieve a technological advantage, causing the other side to perceive an imminent inferiority and launch an attack. As absurd as this sounds, such situations have occurred in the past. Britain seriously considered a surprise attack on Germany's growing fleet in the years just before World War I. In 1981, Israel launched an air strike against Iraqi nuclear research facilities. If the attacker in such situations were to use nuclear weapons, the losses would exceed the deaths in all previous wars.

Because of the catastrophic effects of nuclear weapons, war planners devote a lot of attention to the problems of perceived inferiority in nuclear weapons. A lively debate rages continuously over the prospects of one of the superpowers launching a successful first strike. Confusing this issue is the uncertainty of just how effective nuclear weapons will be. Uncertainty is always a major issue when dealing with possible inferiority and the need for a preemptive attack. Those who fear inferiority the most tend to have the most faith in current weapons. Russia has a spotty record of technical proficiency. So they fear inferiority and overestimate the efficiency of Western nuclear weapons. The SDI (Star Wars) program worries the Russians because they, more than most experts in the West, believe it would work. A successful SDI would negate Russian nuclear weapons, effectively disarming them. This is a classic situation in which an inferior power might launch an attack before its inferiority became critical.

Even if SDI were not completely successful, it would be devastating to Russian satellite reconnaissance and communication. An SDI system could blind the Russians and seriously impair their communications. Russia might easily consider this a sufficient inferiority to prompt a serious response. The balance of nuclear terror may be unpalatable, but it is preferable to tempting Russia to make a preemptive attack.

Spy satellites play an increasingly critical role in keeping the major powers informed about their opponent's true state of military preparedness. Blinding one side increases the temptation to launch an attack against a feared aggression by one's enemies.

Less well-informed nations will continue to make unnecessary attacks. Well-informed nations, like the Israelis, will also persist in attacking first to forestall suspected aggression. Although fear of attack is the least-used cause of war, it is becoming the most dangerous.

CAUSES AND GOALS

Causes are one way of looking at war. Looking at it another way, consider the goals. When the most common causes of wars are compared with the most typical goals, there is further confirmation of the deadliest patterns. Internal disorder and disputes over real estate cause most of the wars, and most of the deaths. We defined the major goals of wars as: regaining territory (territorial disputes), changing the government (revolutions), breaking apart a nation (secession) and terrorizing a population into submission (civil terror).

GOALS OF WAR

War Goals	Percentage of Participants	Percentage of Deaths
Territorial Dispute	55	47
Revolution	42	21
Secession	2	.1
Civil Terror	1	32

It Was All a Mistake

In all the causes of war—long-standing grievance, sense of military superiority, internal disorder, fear of attack—there is a common theme. *Most wars start by accident.*

MISUNDERSTANDINGS

Decisions are often made on the basis of what the key leaders believe, not what is.

Recent history abounds with examples. Let us go back to the spring of 1941. German armies were massing on the Russian border. Stalin was receiving reports that Germany was going to invade. Only an extreme act of faith could counteract the evidence. Stalin had the faith, and until the German armies were some distance inside Russia, he refused to believe invasion was happening.

Less than ten years later, American forces were advancing into North Korea. China announced that it would resist any foreign power entering North Korea. Chinese forces began to mass on the North Korean border. The American commander, MacArthur, insisted that the Chinese would not intervene. He was wrong.

Let us move forward another fifteen years to South Vietnam. American forces had been sent to that country to prevent North Vietnam from taking over. The North Vietnamese were not about to confront American ground forces in conventional combat. Time was on their side, they would lay low, resist and wait. The United States decided to unleash an air force bombing campaign against North Vietnam. This ran contrary to American experience with such bombing tactics in World War II and Korea. Surveys after previous bombing campaigns had shown that civilian morale was, if anything, improved because of the bombing. Supply lines could be crippled but not cut. There was always enough capacity to support military needs. The American leaders wanted to believe that the bombing would work, and so the bombing went on. To this day, many believe the bombing campaign was simply not pressed hard enough. History shows otherwise.

Jump forward another ten years to Afghanistan. Russian influence in this nation's internal affairs had become more pervasive during the 1970s. Communist politicians were in control. But the Afghan Communist Party was unreliable. The situation was unreliable. Despite over a hundred years of largely unsuccessful experience in Afghan affairs, Russian leaders felt that a military operation would quickly rectify the situation. It didn't, although it might eventually. Don't bet the family fortune on it. The story circulating in Washington is that the KGB completely failed to predict the high level of Afghan resistance.

There are several variations on how you can misjudge the situation.

Opportunity for easy victory. Special conditions (real or imagined) lead a nation to think that if it attacks at the right time it will win a victory that it otherwise couldn't. Iraq attacking Iran in 1980, Argentina going after the British Falklands in 1982 are some recent examples.

Attacker overestimates own power. Spending a lot of money and effort on the armed forces leads one to overestimate how much bang one is getting for the bucks. Russia believed its very expensive armed forces could easily bring Afghanistan to heel. The initial plan has no doubt been modified many times since. Some very inventive memos are doubtlessly being produced. Not much else is, except coffins filled with Russians.

Attacker underestimates opponent's power. Even if you have a good handle on your own capabilities, you can always err by misreading how well your opponents are coming along. Israel thought a forceful incursion into Lebanon in 1982 would shut down the PLO and eliminate anti-Israeli activity. They were partly correct; they were able to shut down the PLO for a while. Peace and friendship with Lebanon were more elusive. After three years, the PLO is coming back and the anti-Israeli attitudes are worse than ever. You can't trust your opponent to dry up and blow away.

Attacker misunderstands warmaking process. World War I was unique in that practically everyone was attacking. Everyone attacked and just about everyone failed pitifully. Offense requires much more military expertise than defense. For a peacetime army to be successful at offensive warfare it must have very talented people who have been intensively trained. Even the Germans required a few warmups before they got their blitzkrieg act together in World War II. The Israelis follow the "get the best people and train their buns off" approach. There is a catch. A truly professional military will usually advise against offensive wars. United States armed forces have finally learned why. The Grenada invasion and Libyan air raids were both carefully planned and used overwhelming force against a much weaker opponent. Even with those advantages, Grenada was full of embarrassing flaws, and the Libyan air raids revealed a number of troubling problems in the use of modern air power.

Defender believes it can prevail. The attacker is not always solely at fault. Often one nation will bait another, trusting its natural superiority to ward off any attack. Egypt constantly provoked Israel after the 1967 war. Finally Egypt crossed the Suez Canal in 1973. Its plan was to halt and let the Israelis smash themselves on carefully prepared Egyptian defenses. It almost worked. The Egyptians grew overconfident and moved farther than they had planned. The Israelis recovered quickly and eventually prevailed. A larger example of this perverse defense mentality occurred in the Pacific during World War II. The Japanese felt they could inflict a severe blow on European and American forces and then switch to a successful defense. They were wrong, as some of their more perceptive commanders had warned.

Ignorance of potential opponents is often magnified by simple inertia. Change is typically painful, or at least uncomfortable. Obsolete perceptions of potential opponents are more easily maintained than new evaluations can be made. A modern example is the recurring "missile gap" between the United States and Russia. The missile gaps between the superpowers are periodically revealed as illusions.

Errors in sizing up the situation will continue to be a major cause of war. Until leaders stop seeing what they want to see, nations will continue to stumble into disastrous wars.

TECHNOLOGICAL ACCIDENTS

Modern technology has given new meaning to "warfare by accident." The classic terror is that the complicated nuclear attack warning systems will malfunction and start a catastrophe. While considerable attention is lavished on this danger, we forget that similar electronic warning systems can precipitate conventional combat. Ships and aircraft are increasingly dependent on them. The combination of randomly failing electronics and complex weapons could cause tragedy. The users of these systems are well aware of the problems. But what is the point of having formidable weapons if they are not in a position to be used? As long as there have been technically complex weapons, there have been accidents. For example, one sixth of the losses of modern battleships were due to accidental explosions. If such a formidable ship can accidentally demolish itself, it's no wonder users are fearful about the safety of current systems. Most modern weapons require much preparation and user indulgence before they will function as intended. During the 1986 Air Force raid on Libya, two F-111 aircraft were needed for every one that got through in working order to drop its bombs. In the Russian Air Force, the situation is worse. That's one reason they build so many weapons.

Actually, in spite of the growing number and complexity of weapon systems, there have been far fewer accidents once they have been allowed to mature. This simply induces a false sense of security. And anyway, the trend is to replace weapons before the bugs are shaken out.

The most likely instigators of accidental combat are less-developed countries and Russia. The Russians have already had several costly accidents. Several of their warships, including a few nuclear ones, have gone down by accident. Accidental explosions of their missiles are common. Their largest missile-storage and repair facility went up in a series of explosions, depriving about 40 percent of their fleet of missile reloads for most of a year. Similar conditions plague their aircraft and armored vehicles. As Russian equipment becomes more complex, it tends to become less reliable and more accident-prone. Historically, the Russians would keep a weapon system for a very long time, allowing them to become thoroughly familiar with its quirks. As they increasingly go the high-tech route, they are faced with more unfamiliar problems. If there is to be a serious nuclear weapons accident in the air or at sea, it will likely be Russian. Their strategic missiles are likely to cause accidents because they keep these systems at a low level of readiness most of the time. However, as the Russians become more confident, or smug, these weapons are made increasingly combat (and accident) ready. This raises the potential for an accidental firing. The missile may well be brain dead and way off course—but the other side doesn't know that as they prepare to return fire.

Because of the possibility of accidents, all nuclear weapons are equipped with a surfeit of safety devices. An additional reliability problem is that any one of these safety devices may fail, actually reducing the probability of the system's performing as advertised.

Less-developed nations equipped with high-tech weapons are prone to accidents. Not really trusting their somewhat magical devices, their soldiers often misinterpret the instructions. The dismal performance of Russian weapons in the hands of Arab soldiers is partially attributable to this. The 1986 American air raids on Libya generated spontaneous firings of Russian-supplied air defense weapons many hours after the attack was over. On the other extreme, ill-trained infantry equipped with automatic weapons are prone to shooting at each other in confused circumstances. Certainly, this occurs in all armies and most wars. It happens much more frequently when the troops are less confident of their abilities. Many a "border incident" has occurred when tension plus insecure troops plus modern weapons equals a spontaneous firefight.

INTENTIONAL ACCIDENTS

In addition to real accidents, there are intentional accidents. One nation tricks another into fighting. This is a large-scale version of the "Let's you and him fight" gambit. This has been known to backfire. One of the more ghastly boomerangs was the system of alliances that France devised before 1914 to get Russia and Germany to fight each other. France planned to grab back the two provinces Germany had annexed in 1871. France did get the provinces back, at a cost of over nine million dead Europeans and the destruction of the European social system. As a bonus, France and the rest of the world also incurred World War II.

Russia, not learning from France's experience, signed a nonaggression pact with Nazi Germany in 1939. Less than two years later, German armies streamed into Russia. Until that moment, Russia thought that *Germany* would be trapped by a surprise *Russian* invasion.

The lesson is, if you start a war, don't expect to escape the nasty side effects. And watch out for accidents.

Propaganda and the Willingness to Fight

Even though most wars are really accidents, nations always want to proclaim some indisputable reason for going to war.

One reason is that most people are not generally in the mood to go off to war. They require encouragement. Propaganda is the most common solution. History is brimming with examples of propaganda being used to get people in the mood to fight.

The 1898 explosion in the United States warship *Maine,* in Havana harbor, was apparently an accident. At the time, it was called sabotage and became the excuse for the United States to declare war on Spain.

The 1941 Japanese attack on Pearl Harbor got the United States into World War II. America was more worried about Germany at that time. The Germans came to Japan's aid and declared war on the United States before America could declare against Germany. Although Germany was always the more dangerous adversary, it was the Pearl Harbor incident, and the propaganda it generated, that got the United States into a properly warlike mood.

The 1915 sinking of the *Lusitania* by a German submarine was the trigger that got the United States into World War I on the side of the Allies.

Germany's seizure of Alsace-Lorraine in 1871 was the French rallying cry as they entered World War I in 1914.

The 1919 Treaty of Versailles ended World War I and stripped Germany of much of its territory and wealth. This was a major factor in Germany's aggressive activity up until 1945. The Nazi Party made the recovery of Germany's territory, population and "honor" the excuse for a long list of atrocities.

The 1931 Mukden Manchuria Incident was apparently a fabrication by the Japanese Army but was used as an excuse for Japan going to war against China.

Even the most reprehensible nations wish to occupy a morally superior position before sending their troops into battle. Nazi Germany staged a border incident with Poland before invading that nation in 1939. Russia made a big diplomatic fuss with Finland before invading that country in 1940. The invasions of Korea in 1950, Afghanistan in 1980 and Iran in 1979 all were preceded by loud cries of anguish and hurt by the attacker.

Whenever a government begins making noises that the national honor, territory or other asset has been put upon, head for cover. A population is being prepared for war.

The Nazi government in the 1930s continually complained that Germany needed space *(Lebensraum)* and had to expand toward the east to fulfill its destiny. The honor of Germany was at stake. Although few paid any attention to Hitler's cries for living space, Germany started World War II to get that land. A recent example is Russia's invasion of Afghanistan. Russia claimed that it must come to the aid of a socialist state threatened by a revolution. Actually, Russia did not want a Communist government on its borders overthrown. Russian noises about socialist brotherhood were cover for a geopolitical imperative to keep its borders secure.

RALLY ROUND THE FLAG

Once shots are fired, a remarkable psychological change happens. Wartime mentality is quite different from peacetime mentality. The immediate effect of war is to turn nearly every citizen into a rabid patriot. Some citizens cool off faster than others, and populations often do rise up against warlike leaders. Eventually. It all depends on how successful the war is and how effective a control the government has over its citizens.

Governments entering a war voluntarily will attempt to prepare the population through propaganda and patriotic cheerleading. Even without this preparation, it is rare for a population not to show initial enthusiasm for the fighting. When a war begins, heroes quickly appear, even if some of them have to be invented. Many nations often designate every dead soldier a hero. After all, who's to protest? Hope, often without much basis in fact, becomes a common currency of the government and the population. Just as we involuntarily pump adrenaline when threatened, a society assumes certain traits when a war begins. One characteristic that is not common is any strong desire to end the war on unfavorable terms.

After the initial enthusiasm for a war has worn off, a desire to be done with the conflict grows. Reality rapidly overcomes the exaggerated claims and promises customarily made at the beginning of hostilities. The government then modifies its assurances of the war's rapid conclusion. This rewriting of the government's position can go on for a long time. Eventually the armed forces and/or the population will rebel, if defeat or victory does not occur first.

When the initial flush of patriotism has worn off, warring governments must take measures to keep the population in a properly warlike mood. The government and mass media will hammer away repeatedly that the war was the right decision, that "we" are on the right side of the issues and that retribution must be made for the wrongs committed by the enemy.

When things get really desperate, leaders make blatant appeals to nationalistic pride. In the past, and today in the Middle East, the appeal to righteousness was made in religious terms. Nonreligious dogma is increasingly replacing religion. The gods invoked elsewhere today are Socialism, Democracy, Communism, Racism, Nationalism and other isms.

How to Negotiate

Nearly every war is preceded by negotiation, ranging from sincere discussions to resolve differences all the way to demands for immediate surrender. Rarely are these negotiations conducted without some hope of avoiding violence. But it is difficult for negotiators to make progress in the middle of so much misinformation and so many political pressures, unrealized goals and unrealistic demands.

As passions rise, it is natural for issues to become complex. The pressure for results intensifies. It is easy for the participants to lose control of the negotiations. It is difficult to remain evenhanded when surrounded by paranoia. To negotiators locked in passionate discord, each suspecting that the other is not entirely forthright, normally trivial events take on a sinister meaning. Unplanned gunfire at the border, a terrorist attack on a prominent politician, an accidental explosion on a warship or inflammatory speeches by politicians, religious leaders or journalists can quickly turn peace into war. Too many unexpected and accidental events at the wrong time, and the situation becomes uncontrollable. It's no accident that the term "crisis management" has entered our vocabulary as our society has become more complex.

RULES OF THE GAME

To better understand how one nation is bested by another in diplomatic negotiations, consider the following points that skillful diplomatic negotiators pay careful attention to. Failure to adequately deal with them will lead not only to diplomatic defeat, but also to war.

Keep your eye on the goal. It is easy to lose track of what the negotiations are really about once the heavy-duty bargaining begins. The other side may raise a lot of bogus issues to divert your attention. It's bad enough if you get flim-flammed; it's worse if you realize that nothing was really settled and that all you have to show for all that negotiating is another grievance.

Be patient. It may have taken years, decades or even centuries for the disputes to reach the point where warfare is a possibility. Don't expect to resolve a lot of discord in a short time.

Don't underestimate protocol. Diplomats observe a number of commonly accepted, although seemingly silly, customs. Protocol's function is to diminish tensions created by cultural differences. Use it, make sure that the other side does and watch out for attempts to misuse it.

Keep it confidential. Some nations prize secrecy more than others. Whatever the case, secrecy is almost always desirable when conducting diplomatic negotiations. Unless you want to make the press and public opinion a part of the negotiating process, observe secrecy. Eventually, history will judge you, but first you have to accomplish something that can be judged.

Don't forget the differences between them and us. Diplomats often spend most of their time with other diplomats, creating a separate society. Protocol and good intentions can mask fundamental cultural differences between the nations the negotiators represent. This is a dangerous illusion. Diplomats represent nations, they don't run them or reflect the true nature of their nation's society.

Know the other fellow's history. Never mind what they say they will do or what they may have done lately. Past patterns are more revealing, and more likely to be repeated in the long run.

Watch the fine print and the press releases. Ultimately, the negotiations must be reduced to print. Spelling errors, clumsy syntax, inaccurate translations and vague wording can be potentially troublesome accidents or deliberate attempts to deceive.

Be aware of the national game. In Russia, chess and vodka are national passions. In the United States, baseball, football and consumerism are followed avidly. In the Orient, the popular game is Go, which uses indirect strategy—you surround the other guy's pieces rather than attack them directly as in chess. The nature of these games is reflected in the way people negotiate. Be aware of the influence of these national passions. Each reflects different approaches and interpretations of subtlety. Chess players and Russian negotiators calculate every move, and wait for their opponents to make a mistake; they also value an inspired play. Americans believe that you should play by the rules—and they love to trounce their opponents (notice how many of our politicians use sports analogies).

Know the meaning of words. Good diplomats attempt to become fluent in the other side's language. This is not just a convenience, but a way to gain valuable insight into how the other folks think. Knowledge of any foreign language makes one aware of how differently one can view the world simply by using different words and syntax. When negotiations proceed, such nuances can easily become sources for misunderstanding and distrust. When the agreements are reduced to print, there is even more opportunity for squabbles. Watch your words.

Beware new friends. A diplomat's primary function is to appear friendly, not necessarily to make friends. Don't confuse adroit use of protocol with a desire to forge a lifelong friendship. You must know someone from a foreign culture much more thoroughly than one of your own in order to form an effective friendship. Don't be fooled by the good acting of an experienced diplomat.

Count your change. Concessions and agreements can be packaged in many different ways. Make sure that you aren't given a booby-trapped gift.

Resist last-minute "adjustments." This is a common negotiating technique used by those with good bargaining skills. These proposals may sound impromptu, but a clever negotiator will plan them far in advance.

PROFESSIONALS AND AMATEURS

Unfortunately, not all negotiators are good at their jobs. Some nations pay closer attention to the skills of their negotiators than others. European countries have long cultivated their diplomats and lavished rewards and honors on those who enter the profession. Other more insular nations, particularly Japan, Korea and the United States, have not developed their diplomatic resources.

There are several reasons why the United States has always been handicapped in diplomacy. First, its people want to avoid constant foreign entanglements with the "old countries" they or their parents immigrated from. Second, because the United States is physically isolated, its leaders feel no imperative to deal efficiently with troublesome foreigners. Third, the United States has always been the major military and economic power in its neighborhood. There's no need to be terribly diplomatic when you can easily throw your weight around. Also, in the United States many potential diplomats become lawyers. The reward system favors winners of commercial conflicts, not diplomatic ones, and the talented people go where the rewards are. So the United States has an overabundance of skilled lawyers yet is often caught short in diplomatic conflicts.

Countries with strongly entrenched and professional civil services develop longer diplomatic memories. In Russia and most European nations, diplomats and intelligence professionals retain their positions for decades. Whatever other faults these systems might have, forgetting past experience is not one of them. When any of these nations deals with the United States, it must face American counterparts driven more by short-term political demands than long-term planning. This makes the Europeans and Russians nervous. In deference to America's superior military and economic might, Europeans must follow the United States's lead in diplomatic policy, particularly with regard to Russia. But both Europe and the Russians think that American foreign policy is too subject to domestic politics and popular emotion. Unpredictability and volatility are common causes of wars. With nuclear weapons available to most of the nations involved, there is more to be lost should a dispute get out of hand.

The United States' history accounts for its curious diplomatic performance. Europeans often lose sight of the fact that America was populated by people fleeing the disorder and violence of the Old World. Although the United States has enormous military power, much of the population is descended from people so antiwar that they were willing to move thousands of miles to an alien culture to escape military service. Americans are not adverse to fighting strenuously to defend their enviable way of life. But Americans are much less willing to support peacetime military ventures. As has often been repeated by Americans and their battlefield adversaries, "Americans make good fighters but lousy soldiers."

Immigrants to the United States were also running from totalitarianism, and they embraced American-style democracy with fervor. To most Europeans, this form of democracy seems close to anarchy. Russians fear its "lack of order." To Russians, law and order is a minor religion. Thirty years after his death, Josef Stalin is admired by many young Russians as a strong leader who maintained order. Given these stark differences in backgrounds and attitudes, it's a minor miracle that Russians and Americans are able to negotiate at all.

In turn, European democracy appears a bit odd to those few Americans who bother to study it at all. European governments exercise much more control over their citizens than America's does over its. Internal passports, more regulations and far fewer lawyers make life in a European democracy seem very confining to Americans. Europeans (and Russians) tend to view Americans as a bunch of undisciplined cowboys. This attitude is tinged with envy and fear. The concept of such extreme personal freedom seems attractive. Yet the thought that these same free spirits command the world's largest arsenal of nuclear weapons is a constant theme in the European press. As long as the Russian threat exists, Europeans can't live without American military protection. Often Europeans feel caught between two unpleasant giants. This situation makes for some very strange diplomacy.

The largest peacetime concentration of armed forces in history currently resides in Europe. If there's another massive nonnuclear war, it will be fought in Europe. This situation inclines European diplomats and national leaders to act with caution and circumspection. Americans do not face the same array of dangers as Europeans, and American foreign policy reflects this.

Another reason American foreign policy is volatile is the use of political appointees in key diplomatic posts. Sometimes the United States finds some very talented diplomats with this approach. But nearly always, America ends up with an envoy who has very little experience in diplomatic affairs and is often an inept diplomat in the bargain. To European diplomats, American foreign policy appears both volatile and arrogant. American diplomats regard European diplomats as cynical, manipulative, world weary and arrogant. This is often true, but the Europeans come closer to what a diplomat must be to get the job done.

Americans are taken advantage of because of their form of government. Unlike most other nations, the United States government has no real central authority. Well-sponsored initiatives come from many directions. The President can do many things on his own, the Congress is frequently overruled or second-guessed by the Supreme Court. Special interest groups are capable of wielding substantial power.

And then there are some sharp differences in ethics. Some nations believe that the ends justify the means. This negotiation style is known as Byzantine diplomacy. The Byzantine Empire, which had once been the eastern half of the Roman Empire, occupied what is now Turkey and the Balkan Peninsula for a thousand years until the 1400s. Surrounded by many powerful enemies, the Byzantines used bribes, assassination, treachery, marriages, showmanship, religion, hostages and, when all else failed, military force to achieve their aims. They had a very effective army and navy, but waged relatively few wars. Because Western Europeans were often on the losing end of diplomatic dealings with the Byzantines, in the West the term "Byzantine diplomacy" came to mean something less than honorable. However, to give the devil its due, the Byzantines maintained the peace and their empire, even if they were not always gentlemen.

The Russians consider themselves the heirs of many Byzantine traditions, including their style of diplomacy. Over the years, most European nations came to accept the Byzantine style of diplomacy, perhaps not publicly, but definitely in their actions. The United States has been less keen on following in the Byzantine tradition. This has caused still another set of misunderstandings between the United States and other nations in diplomatic dealings. Not surprisingly, American diplomats are coming around to the acceptance of Byzantine diplomacy, even though American society is still far from accepting it. In 1986, Americans accused European nations of Byzantine diplomacy in trying to free hostages in Lebanon, while President Reagan's National Security Council staff was indulging in some unauthorized Byzantine operations of its own. Russia shows that it still knows how to play the game. When some Russian diplomats were kidnapped in Lebanon, they were soon released, and there is evidence that KGB operatives took their own hostages and employed other Byzantine techniques.

CRAZY FOREIGNERS

The difficulty of understanding another nation's internal affairs can also jeopardize negotiations. And nations that use Byzantine diplomacy make things even tougher by being deliberately deceptive on what is going on at home. Americans tend to misunderstand the nuances of events in foreign nations. Part of this is because the United States is isolated culturally. Except for Mexico, the United States has no culturally dissimilar neighbors. Most Americans rarely have to deal with foreigners on a regular basis. This ignorance is compounded by a lax attitude toward professionalism in the diplomatic service.

The United States has had more than its share of diplomatic problems, such as being ill informed about radical changes in foreign countries. For example, although some elements of the American diplomatic/intelligence community knew of the import of Khomeini and radical Islam in Iran, none of the senior American decision makers believed it until after the Shah was overthrown. Much noise was made in the United States about our ignorance and, by gosh, we really ought to clean up our act. American government institutions are not overhauled that rapidly, so the United States is still in the same shape. For example, in 1986, the government attempted to deal with nonexistent Iranian moderates. Old habits persist. After all, the Korean and Vietnam wars can be traced to self-imposed cultural blindness. We neglected the political changes in North Korea after the Communists took over in 1946. Similarly, the United States ignored friendly overtures from the Vietnamese Communists *and* nationalists in the late 1940s. After the Korean War ended in 1953, the United States did pay constant attention to political developments in Korea. After the Vietnam War, more attention was paid to ongoing developments in Southeast Asia.

The embarrassing developments of events in Korea, Vietnam and Iran have not caused the United States to be be more diligent and responsive to ongoing changes in foreign nations. To be fair, many other nations suffer from the same problem. But no other nation possesses the military, diplomatic and economic power of America.

No matter how attentive a nation's diplomats are to conditions in foreign nations, there may always be bizarre developments. And if a crisis develops too rapidly, adroit diplomacy cannot turn the situation around. Especially when religion or ideology enter into play, matters can outpace observers within and without.

Modern communications have made mass hysteria a major component in world diplomacy. In less-developed nations, for example, radio, and to a lesser extent TV and newspapers, can mobilize large numbers of people to a particular point of view. The media can give focus to grievances that have been long repressed. The billions of dollars spent each year to broadcast and jam propaganda show how important nations consider electronic media. Even the most poverty-stricken populations can obtain portable radios. Literacy is not required, and they are addressed in their own language or dialect. Nearly every revolutionary movement in the past half century has been aided by radio broadcasts. A new wrinkle in the Iranian revolution of 1979 was the distribution of tape cassettes full of radical Islamic speeches.

On the dark side, governments can use mass communications to make conditions appear other than they are. "Propaganda," "doublespeak" and other terms hardly do justice to the ability of mass media to mold a population's outlook and opinions. If a population is sufficiently upset, it can be rapidly aroused by the right message. Media allows that message to be quickly and widely broadcast. The result is that situations may brew over a long period, as they always have, and then suddenly burst out of control. Before the age of mass communications, a central government could suppress disorder before it spread. No longer. No army can move as fast as a radio broadcast. The transistor radio is mightier than the sword.

COMMUNISM IS GLORIOUS

Most cultures have a saying that recognizes the futility of arguing about politics or religion. What we often forget is that, despite our belief that most governments are not heavily influenced by the supernatural, religious-type doctrine still plays a significant part in diplomacy.

There was a time, not too long ago, when the clergy was responsible for the body as well as the soul. Over the last several hundred years, the responsibilities for the material and spiritual needs of populations have become separate. Yet the combining of spiritual belief and economic allegiance is too powerful a concept to be abandoned. Communism has seized upon this ancient concept by inventing a religion that did away with the supernatural and put "priests" back in charge. From a historical perspective, communism is remarkably similar to the ancient theocracies in which the head of state, and his assistants, are revered as sources of the only valid truth. These priests represented gods that owned everything in the kingdom. In theory, this priesthood acted for the public good. For this type of government to be successful, there had to be a certain amount of thought and action devoted to the population's welfare. But the rulers were only human, and their success varied with the abilities of the priests.

The Communist gods Marx and Lenin laid down laws that are interpreted and enforced by the cadre (priesthood) of the Communist Party. Opposition and dissent is heresy, and punishable as heresy has always been, with the most severe retribution. Tens of millions of heretics to Communist doctrine have perished. Those who are somewhat lax in their spiritual purity are known as the apparatchiks in the party. They are the least trusted. But all who wish to survive, toe the party line. The path to wealth and power is through joining and being active in the Communist Party.

As a relatively new religion, Communists are eager to convert nonbelievers to the true way. This is nothing unique with new religions. Christianity swept the Western world in the first thousand years of its existence. Likewise Islam spread from the Atlantic coast of Africa to the Pacific islands of Indonesia in its first five hundred years. Communism has grown unpalatable for many who have tried it. Yet there are new adherents to whom the slogan "Communism Is Glorious" still has meaning. Any Communist official, whether still a true believer or not, will negotiate in the defense of Communist dogma.

Nuclear War

For the moment, the mere presence of nuclear weapons has restrained the major powers from military adventures they once would have casually entered into. It remains to be seen if the risk of accidental or unintended nuclear war is worth fewer incidents of gunboat diplomacy. Indications are that the inhibiting effect of nuclear weapons is wearing off. The major powers are getting more involved in traditional demonstrations of military power. Gunboat diplomacy was risky enough in the past when major power military units confronted each other in far-off places over minor issues. Today, the gunboats are increasingly armed with nuclear weapons. Accidents do happen.

In the past, terrifying new weapons caused wars, and so potential victims showed restraint. Sometimes this moderation went no further than a reluctance to use the weapon. For example, ever since the first large-scale use of poison gas from 1915–18, there has been a reluctance to use it on a wide scale. However, chemical weapons have not disappeared. Many nations, particularly Russia, devote considerable resources to maintaining chemical weapons in their arsenals. As time goes by, the memory of using these weapons fades. There is less reluctance to using them again.

There is a reasonable fear that the same pattern will occur with nuclear weapons. Something along the lines of "familiarity breeds contempt." In the forty years since nuclear weapons became available, the announced strategies and tactics for using them have changed several times. Initially, the strategy was to consider nuclear bombs a doomsday weapon. The goal was a "balance of terror." Of late, nuclear weapons are considered less a weapon of last resort and more just another weapon in the arsenal. Military planners have been spending more time studying the fighting of a protracted nuclear war. The first use of nuclear weapons is no longer a sign of final despair but simply selection of another military option. Unlike similar decisions, such as unleashing submarines against merchant shipping or the use of chemical weapons, nuclear weapons can escalate to massive destruction of entire regions, and possibly the world.

Most civilians are very much against any use of nuclear weapons. However, there is not as strong a desire to eliminate them. Perhaps this is simply a tacit recognition of the historical fact that once a weapon is introduced, it is never withdrawn from the arsenal.

The official attitudes toward nuclear weapons may eventually be accepted by the population. That is a function of a government's constant defense of its position and gradual convincing of the population that it is correct. As nuclear weapons come to appear less horrible, there use becomes more likely and their ability to forestall war is diminished.

This trend will be brought up short as soon as someone uses a nuclear weapon again. Nuclear weapons will probably never lose their ability to terrify a population. One can only hope that the next use of a nuclear weapon is restricted and does not escalate to an exchange of strategic missiles.

While the military looks forward to trying out their conventional weapons in little wars, no one is eager to see even limited use of nuclear weapons. Nuclear weapons thus present a unique situation in military history. No one really knows how to handle them.

Nuclear weapons are truly too terrible to be used. There are three schools of thought on the meaning of nuclear weapons:

Armageddon. The world as we know it will come to an end.

Pragmatic. The world will not end, but another device will have been added to the arsenal of regularly used weapons.

Deterrence. The most likely and least painful of these terrible possibilities is that we will be so horrified by the use of nuclear weapons that we will avoid using them.

Unfortunately, history is rife with wars in which horrible weapons were used. Poison gas during World War I is a good example because it was used despite a general understanding that it harms the side using it as much as the intended victim.

Nuclear weapons are different. One nuclear weapon can destroy an entire city. War in the nuclear age can cause hundreds of millions of casualties within hours, destroying friend and foe alike. Nuclear war is likely to destroy everything the combatants are fighting to preserve.

TYPES OF NUCLEAR WAR

After the invention of nuclear weapons a new breed of military analysts was born, the nuclear strategists—political scientists, physicists, mathematicians, historians and engineers. Their business is to figure out what will happen in a nuclear war. The only data they have is from two explosions in Japan and hundreds of tests.

These high priests of nuclear strategy fall into several schools of thought on how nuclear wars will be fought. Some see nuclear war as one gigantic burst of destruction: One side will launch its missiles first, and the other will retaliate immediately. In the basic city-busting scenario (strategist talk for urban-industrial-area attacks) thousands of today's nuclear warheads, vastly more powerful than the nuclear firecrackers that exploded over Japan, will explode in the U.S.A., Russia, Europe, Japan, China and the Middle East. Hundreds of cities will be vaporized, and up to one hundred million Americans and Russians, not to mention millions of Europeans and Chinese, will die almost instantly. Later, between two and four times as many people will die from starvation, disease, lack of shelter and psychological depression. This kind of nuclear war will be quick, painful and uncontrollable. This scenario of nuclear war reminds us of a chain-reaction car accident: Once it begins, it happens very fast, and the occupants have no control over their fate.

Thinking about nuclear war in this way led early nuclear strategists to argue that nuclear war would mean mutual assured destruction (MAD) for nations foolish enough to start one. They said there was no way to fight a nuclear war without getting millions killed. Even now there is a popular theory that all life on the planet will be destroyed in a mammoth ice age, called nuclear winter, following a nuclear war. In any case, just one nuclear war will cause more destruction than the last two hundred years of warfare combined. And it will happen in less time than it will take you to read this chapter.

Rather than seeing nuclear war as a sudden volley of nuclear explosions that kill millions instantly, other strategists think it will be fought in steps. The key concept is escalation. Some believe a country would edge slowly up the ladder of escalation in order not to cause more destruction than necessary. This also leaves time to signal your resolve to the enemy. A few nuclear explosions tell the enemy forcefully that you are willing to fight a nuclear war. So these strategists think escalation is a political tool for expanding a nuclear war in steps.

Today, the foremost theory of nuclear war is the counterforce attack, which involves massive strikes against land-based missile silos, leadership bunkers, bomber bases and submarine bases. Even submarines on patrol hundreds of feet underwater can be destroyed by land-based ICBMs, if you can find the subs. In a counterforce nuclear war, about six thousand warheads will explode in the U.S.A. and Russia. Theoretically, the victim of that attack will retaliate against the same type of targets in the enemy's homeland. Some think, maybe we should say hope, that at this point the war will stop before hundreds of cities are annihilated.

Even if cities are not destroyed, radioactive fallout will kill millions of civilians. Effective attacks on silos, which are hardened to withstand the effects of nuclear explosions, require surface-bursts. Each of the thousands of nuclear warheads explodes just before it touches the ground, which digs an enormous hole and kicks millions of tons of radioactive dirt into the atmosphere. For example, a one-megaton warhead will dig a crater roughly one quarter of a mile in diameter and over one hundred feet deep. The highly radioactive fallout in this limited nuclear war, in which cities are not targeted, will kill millions who live downwind of the nuclear craters. Government studies in the 1970s estimated that in the United States, this would be between ten and forty million dead, depending on the season. In Russia, it would be between fifteen and forty million victims. In China, which is even more densely populated than Europe or the United States, it could mean hundreds of millions dead.

The theory of limited nuclear war appeals to some strategists because it leaves open the possibility that cities will not be destroyed. If we can avoid attacks against cities, there is hope nuclear war will not automatically sentence one hundred million or more people to a horrible death.

There are five general types of nuclear war. Each has a different objective, and each has to be stopped in a different way.

TYPES OF NUCLEAR WAR

Nuclear War	*Objective*
Counterforce Preemption	Destroy nuclear forces
Counterforce Retaliation	Destroy nuclear forces after preemption
Countermilitary Attack	Destroy conventional forces
War-Supporting Industry/ Urban-Industrial Attack	Destroy economy
Nuclear Terrorism	Destroy population centers
Decapitation Attack	Destroy leadership

Counterforce Preemption (infamous first-strike attack)

This involves a first-strike attack by one nation against nuclear forces. The targets include ICBM silos in the American Midwest and in a crescent-shaped belt across Russia. United States ICBM silos number around 1,000, the Russians' approximately 1,400, not including the new mobile ICBMs like the SS-X-25 and SS-X-24. Other targets are bomber bases and submarine ports.

The purpose of counterforce preemption is to cut down the enemy's ability to retaliate. The victim then has to decide whether it is worth it to retaliate against the attacker's larger reserve forces.

One problem with the theory of counterforce preemption is that on any given day the United States has 3,000–4,000 nuclear warheads on its submarines on patrol in the Atlantic and Pacific. The Russians have 300–500 warheads on their submarines. These submarines are virtually invulnerable. If submarines retaliate, they will kill half the population and destroy the economies of Russia and the United States.

Counterforce Retaliation

In this case, the victim of preemption launches its nuclear forces against nuclear targets in the attacker's country. For instance, if the Russians launched a counterforce preemptive attack, the United States could retaliate against Russian ICBM silos, leadership targets, bomber bases and submarine ports. But if the United States waits for Russian warheads to strike, then most of its nuclear forces, except submarines on patrol in the oceans and bombers in the air, will be destroyed.

Retaliation is a political hot potato. There are two ways to retaliate—Launch on Warning (LOW) and Launch Under Attack (LUA). LOW means that the United States retaliates after Russian missiles are launched, but before the warheads, sometimes called NuDets (NUclear DETonationS), explode on U.S. soil. If the United States knew precisely which Russian missiles were launched and from which missile fields, then it could target the remaining ones. But to do this, the United States must be certain that a Russian attack really is happening and be able to track missiles from specific missile fields. Fundamentally, LOW depends on satellites and radars to warn of the attack.

LUA is retaliation only after confirmation by several types of sensors that an attack, called a raid, is coming your way. Unlike LOW, the nation gets confirmation of the attack from multiple sources, like satellites and radars. LUA also means more detailed information about the exact nature of the attack, including the size of the raid and probable targets. But the risk with LUA is that there may not be enough time to retaliate before enemy nuclear warheads explode over missile fields, bomber bases, submarine bases and command posts. Still, it is doubtful that a nation will launch nuclear forces on the basis of warning alone. In such circumstances, people prefer unmistakable evidence of wrongdoing. Detection of missile launches by satellites or early warning radars or nuclear explosions on your territory provides pretty good evidence by any standard that your enemy has started a nuclear war.

Countermilitary Attack

This option involves attacks against conventional military forces. Armies and their logistical supplies (at army bases), naval bases and airfields all around the world are prime targets. The reason for destroying these forces and matériel is to prevent the enemy from winning a conventional war that began before or started after a nuclear war.

Surprisingly, an effective countermilitary attack involves thousands of nuclear warheads. For example, a typical army division is spread out over hundreds of square kilometers. To destroy just one typical division requires as many as fifty small, or tactical, nuclear weapons (with yields between 0.1 and 50 kilotons). To conserve warheads, you can destroy just the bases where tanks are stationed or ammunition storage sites. While this tactic uses fewer nuclear warheads, a full countermilitary attack involves as many or more warheads as counterforce preemption. When you count the number of countries with potential targets, the list gets quite long. No one escapes this kind of war.

War-Supporting-Industry (WSI) or Urban-Industrial (UI) Attack

For this option there are thousands of potential targets: factories, power-generating stations, oil refineries, high-technology industries and all the economic centers that are necessary for supporting a war. In this type of nuclear war, targets can number in the tens of thousands. But because many targets are located near one another in cities and towns, several can be destroyed if one nuclear warhead is exploded in just the right place, called a DGZ, for Designated Ground Zero. Nuclear targeters use computers to figure exactly where a nuclear warhead should be aimed to destroy as many targets as possible.

But there is a problem with WSI attacks. Targets are located in the same places as people. These attacks are sometimes called urban-industrial attacks because they will kill or wound tens of millions of civilians who live in urban areas. Most experts estimate collateral civilian casualties, a euphemism for dead people who happen to live near WSI targets, between fifty and one hundred million dead in the United States and in Russia. In fact, except in the most narrow technical sense, WSI attacks are attacks against people, regardless of intent.

Nuclear Terrorism

Suppose a terrorist group gets a nuclear weapon. With today's technology, you can put a small nuclear weapon in a suitcase. A nuclear suitcase bomb with a yield of 5 kilotons will destroy many city blocks. If it is planted in a parking garage beneath a building, the explosion would collapse the building, even a hundred-story skyscraper. The blast wave would knock down other buildings and blow out windows for many blocks. Expect a small terrorist nuclear weapon that explodes in a crowded city at noon to kill tens of thousands of people and create a long-term radioactive "hot zone."

How does one prevent nuclear terrorism? The best way is to prevent terrorists groups or unstable nations from getting nuclear weapons. One reason Israel bombed the Iraqi nuclear reactor in the spring of 1981 was its fear that the Iraqis might give weapons-grade uranium or plutonium to terrorists or nations that support terrorism, like Libya.

Once a nuclear weapon is in the hands of terrorists, you must destroy the weapon or get it away from them. Against nuclear terrorists, the U.S. NEST (Nuclear Emergency Search Teams) use sophisticated equipment for detecting the radioactive material in nuclear weapons.

No government wants to start searching for a nuclear weapon after being told it will go off in twelve or twenty-four hours unless terrorists demands are met. Do you think terrorists will tell you in which city the weapon is hidden?

The only defense against nuclear terrorism is to restrict the availability of nuclear weapons. This becomes more difficult over time. On the bright side, terrorists have not yet obtained or used chemical weapons, which are far more available.

Decapitation Attack

Who decides to stop a nuclear war? The same people who decide to start one. In the United States, authority to use nuclear weapons is vested in the National Command Authority or NCA.

Decapitation is the destruction of the leadership that controls a nation's nuclear forces. In recent years a growing number of people have argued that at the outset of a nuclear war it might be a good idea to destroy that leadership. In theory, a perfectly successful decapitation attack might prevent the enemy from retaliating. If the leadership is destroyed, it cannot order its commanders, missile-wing officers, submarine commanders or bomber crews to launch nuclear weapons in retaliation. Besides destroying the leadership, a decapitation attack seeks to destroy command, control and communication (or "C^3") sites: commercial telephone centers, microwave antennae, satellite earth stations, satellites in orbit and dozens of other locations.

But even a perfect decapitation attack does not guarantee that the order to release nuclear forces will not be given, because the political and military leadership can delegate authority to fire nuclear weapons. Specific people in the political chain of command or military commanders in various theaters may be given authority to order nuclear retaliation. Unless you get all of the people who can order nuclear retaliation, which is highly unlikely unless you know exactly who and where they are, then decapitation will do no more than shake the hornet's nest. But if it is successful, retaliation might be prevented altogether.

The targets of a decapitation attack are the President of the United States, the Vice President, Congress, most of the cabinet secretaries, Joint Chiefs of Staff and many senior military officers who are in Washington, D.C. If a Russian submarine launched a missile from the Atlantic that exploded ten minutes later over Washington, virtually all of the U.S. political leadership and some of the military leadership would be destroyed, probably before they even knew what happened. In the Carter administration, National Security Council adviser Zbigniew Brzezinski ran a mock exercise to see how long it would take to get the President from the White House to Andrews Air Force Base to board the National Emergency Airborne Command Post (NEACP). After this unscheduled helicopter landing on the White House lawn was almost shot down by the Secret Service, everyone discovered that with eight to ten minutes of warning the President could not possibly escape. Later, the NEACP was moved to Grissom Air Force Base in Indiana because it could not help the President. And in a crisis, what do you think the Russians would do if they learned the President got on the NEACP? They just might figure that the United States was ready to launch an attack, and then launch an attack of their own.

The United States leadership also has a command post in Colorado. Cheyenne Mountain is the home of NORAD, the North American Air Defense Command. It monitors United States warning radars and satellites that alert the United States to a nuclear attack.

The United States also has aircraft continuously on airborne patrol. One is always flying somewhere over the United States. Commanded by an Air Force general, it can order retaliation if all of the other command centers and aircraft are destroyed in a surprise attack. However, it has considerable technical difficulties. It trails a five-mile-long antenna for long-range communication, and antennas can break. Another problem is that a Russian counterforce attack against U.S. ICBM silos in the Midwest would throw enormous amounts of dust and debris into the atmosphere. Jet engines do not work very well when they eat lots of dirt. If there are no problems the aircraft can fly for only a couple of days, even with refueling, because jet engines need oil. Assuming no other problems, it will have to land at some point, which is when it becomes vulnerable.

For the Russians to launch an effective decapitation attack, they would have to destroy underground command posts, aircraft and, shortly, mobile command posts. If only one target survives, then U.S. retaliation will destroy a reasonable part of Russian civilization.

In peacetime, Moscow is the center of the Russian government and military. A United States preemptive attack against Moscow in peacetime would destroy a large part of the Russian leadership. The Russians also have deep underground command centers, aircraft and mobile centers for their leadership. Some think that the Russian leadership is far more protected than the U.S. leadership. The Russians, like the Americans, presumably would disperse their leadership to many locations. In effect, decapitation is unlikely to destroy all of the people that can order retaliation.

One problem with being a leader is that you know the enemy wants to destroy you the moment nuclear war begins. In fact, leaders will be the first people to die in a nuclear war. Some feel there is justice in this: The ones who start a nuclear war are the ones who die first. If you are a leader the prospect of dying first is a powerful reason not to start a war. As a leader, then, you certainly will want to avoid all of the known or obvious places where the enemy might think you are. But are there safe havens or sanctuaries for leaders in a nuclear war?

The answer depends on what the United States and Russians think about decapitation and stopping a nuclear war. If they believe the benefits of decapitation are worth the risk of unrestrained retaliation, then they may target all known leadership sites. If they believe that decapitation is not likely to prevent enemy retaliation, then leadership targets could be very safe places. But how do you know what the other side is planning? If you even suspect the other side is more concerned with preventing or reducing retaliation than stopping a nuclear war, then you must plan for decapitation.

Is it desirable to kill the leadership in a nuclear war? The probable answer is no. If the leadership is destroyed, the chain of command falls to lower-level military commanders in the United States and Russia. It seems unlikely that they won't retaliate. Stopping a nuclear war is difficult enough in the best of circumstances, but in the absence of leadership nuclear war is likely to wind down of its own accord. And that means more destruction.

HOW NUCLEAR WAR STARTS

Perhaps the only way to determine how to stop a nuclear war is to think about how one might start. Always keep in mind, though, that we have no real experience with nuclear war. The explosions over Hiroshima and Nagasaki, which had yields of 12 kilotons (thousands of tons of TNT) and 22 kilotons, respectively, are very small weapons compared to today's nuclear weapons that have yields from 40 kilotons to 20 megatons (million tons of TNT). Neither the attacks against Japan in 1945 nor the hundreds of nuclear weapons exploded between 1945 and today in U.S. and Russian test programs show us what nuclear war is like.

There are two general views about how a nuclear war might start: crisis escalation and surprise attack.

The most prevalent view is that a nuclear war will be the result of a crisis. The classic case is a superpower confrontation over sensitive political issues that leads to a regional crisis. The 1962 Cuban Missile Crisis escalated because both sides had their national interests and prestige on the line. The Russians were attempting to balance U.S. nuclear superiority by basing missiles so close the United States would have no warning of a Russian attack. The United States wanted to keep this hemisphere free of Russian influence. In future conflicts, the nations may not feel they can back down. Each may fear the other will take advantage of its weakness in the future. In a future crisis, the United States or Russia may make military moves that the other matches as both sides spiral closer to direct military confrontation.

Each side escalates a crisis to show resolve, to show a willingness to use nuclear weapons, hoping the other will back down. As the crisis escalates, an accident or misinterpretation can start nuclear war. Leaders also should fear that subordinates may take unauthorized actions that cause a war. In the Cuban Missile Crisis, President Kennedy was afraid that the American Navy might attack a Russian sub with one of the new nuclear depth charges and cause a war. Democracies are especially dangerous because leaders may act to placate public opinion and the media. Leaders never forget they are elected, even in a crisis. And successfully managing a crisis is sure to get votes.

At some point in the escalation duel, one adversary may decide a nuclear war is imminent. It will calculate the advantages of preemption versus the advantages of letting the other side shoot first. To reach this conclusion you calculate the balance of nuclear forces, loss of economic assets and estimate how many casualties each side will have if you launch first, and then if the other side launches first. Although few really pay any attention to these exchange calculations, they make for great drama. The way to come out best, of course, is not to shoot first. If you don't shoot first, chances are the other guy won't either. But if one party really thinks the other is going to shoot, and if it believes that it comes out better by going first, then you have a nuclear war.

If we are to prevent nuclear war, the crisis period must be managed carefully. Each nation must act very carefully not to provide the other with a crisis. One foolish action, such as evacuating the leadership, can be seen by the enemy as preparing for nuclear war. In the spring of 1984, the Russians practiced evacuating its leadership from the Kremlin and Moscow. Reports on CBS News said hundreds of Russian officials had been seen leaving the city. What if the Russians tried that during a crisis? The United States might increase the alert level of its nuclear forces and evacuate its leaders. In response, the Russians could move more nuclear missiles closer to U.S. coasts. Then the United States might put more bombers on airborne alert. This vicious circle of escalation can lead to nuclear war. Avoiding actions that make the situation worse is the heart of crisis management.

The second view of how a nuclear war will start is the surprise, or bolt-out-of-the-blue, attack. Imagine that the United States or Russia thinks that it cannot prevail in a nuclear war that starts from a crisis because both sides already anticipate a nuclear attack. Any advantage from preemption is lost already because at the beginning of the crisis, ICBMs, submarines and bombers are put on high alert. For missiles, this means they can be launched within seconds of being ordered to do so. For submarines, this means putting more than the usual 60 percent of U.S. submarines and 15 percent of Russia submarines out to sea. And bombers can be dispersed to remote bases or even put on continuous airborne patrol to orbit the enemy's borders. There is no such thing as a surprise attack when both sides are alert and ready to respond instantly to an attack.

So a nation would be foolish to pick a crisis for starting a nuclear war. Instead, a nation could attempt a surprise attack. While the other side would have ICBMs and some submarines and bombers on alert in peacetime, it would be caught at a disadvantage. If the Russians wanted to start a nuclear war, which few think they do, they would come out a lot better if they launched a surprise attack. To buy this logic, however, you have to believe the Russians or Americans might wake up one morning and say, "Hmmm, this seems like a good time to start a nuclear war."

Here are some scenarios of how a nuclear war might start.

Use It or Lose It (Imminent Inferiority)

In this case, a nation starts a nuclear war because it fears the adversary is about to gain military superiority. The debate over the Strategic Defense Initiative, or Star Wars, is about this issue. If the United States or the Russians were preparing to deploy ballistic missile defenses, then it could preempt before the other gained superiority. Even moderate defenses for destroying satellites or protecting against attacks by small countries give an enormous political and psychological edge. The fear of being inferior must be ranked among the most likely causes of nuclear war.

Shoot First Before the Other Guy Does (Anticipatory Preemption)

If a nation thinks it is about to be attacked with nuclear weapons, then it may try to destroy enemy nuclear forces before they strike. A general rule is to avoid actions that look like preparations for a first-strike attack. Evacuating the leadership or civilians from cities or dispersing bomber forces away from their bases are good examples. An enemy cannot tell if the intent is to strike first or to deter him from striking first.

Up the Ante (Escalation Trap)

Escalation occurs when each combatant, knowingly or unwittingly, raises the ante in a crisis to show the other that it has the political resolve or guts to risk nuclear devastation, it views the stakes as important and its prestige is on the line. If neither side can escape this vicious circle, then a confrontation in Central America, Cuba or the Persian Gulf can escalate to nuclear war.

A basic rule of international politics in the 1980s is: Do not become entangled in areas of vital interest to a superpower. If the United States encourages Eastern European separatism or the Russians endanger Western oil supplies in the Middle East, we could have a nuclear war.

Let's You and Him Fight (Catalytic Nuclear War)

The nuclear club includes the United States, Russia, England, France, China and probably lately Israel and South Africa. They fear that small nations, like Libya, for example, could use nuclear weapons to start a nuclear war between the nuclear giants. Suppose Libya exploded a nuclear weapon in a major U.S. or Russian city or port facility during a super-power crisis. Would the United States or Russia blame the other, and then retaliate in kind? Libya then would be the catalyst for a nuclear war. Today, the superpowers keep close tabs on potential nuclear powers. Knowing who has weapons, and what kind, is critical information in a crisis.

Accidental Nuclear War

Nuclear arsenals have systems that prevent unauthorized or accidental use. Most United States warheads, such as those on ICBMs and bombers, are controlled by the PAL (Permissive Action Link) system. If you do not have the right electronic code, you cannot detonate the warhead. Most United States nuclear warheads are controlled by the PAL system. The Washington *Post* has reported that warheads on submarine-launched ballistic missiles, or SLBMs, are not under the PAL system. This is because radio communications to submarines on patrol, which are how PAL codes are transmitted, are unreliable, vulnerable to disruption and extremely slow. On a submarine, the commander and his officers must agree jointly to use nuclear weapons. It is actually extremely difficult to use nuclear weapons without an authorized order. This still leaves the possibility of nuclear weapons being used during a civil war, which is a horror no one has a cure for.

There are many kinds of accidents. One of the rights of passage for Russian submarine commanders is trying to slip in and out of Swedish territorial waters. Sometimes the Swedish Navy detects one of these Russian submarines, and once it fired depth charges at a Russian submarine hiding on the ocean bottom. If a Russian submarine commander were to fire a torpedo, perhaps even a nuclear one, in retaliation, accidental nuclear war might start.

There are fifty thousand nuclear weapons in the world. Nearly one thousand have been set off since 1945, all but two in tests.

The Madness Factor (Irrationality)

Generally, the leaders of major nations are stable people. The process of becoming a leader in a democratic or totalitarian state tends to weed out unstable individuals. Still, an unstable, even potentially psychotic person could become the leader of a nuclear power and start a nuclear war for irrational reasons. If Hitler had been armed with nuclear weapons, would he have started a nuclear war? While he might have been more reluctant to start a war, he just as easily might have taken risks believing that England, France or Russia would not respond for fear of unlimited nuclear war. We can take some comfort that, when told that he had nerve-gas bombs, he refused to use them because he *thought* his enemies *might* have them and retaliate. Even maniacs are brought up short when confronted by weapons of mass destruction.

Still, in an international or domestic crisis we should worry about any unstable or irrational side of a leader's personality.

ALLIES, THIRD PARTIES AND NEW NUCLEAR POWERS

Most thinking about nuclear war focuses on what the United States and Russia will do. Yet most strategists believe nuclear war will escalate from a regional conflict involving the allies of the superpowers. Most scenarios of nuclear war begin with a war in Europe between NATO and the Warsaw Pact, or in the Persian Gulf.

Once a nuclear war started, some nations might be drawn in. Europe, for instance, probably would, especially if the war began with attacks against theater targets in Eastern and Western Europe and Russia. Nations in Central and South America, Africa and Asia might be able to stay out of the fray. If you were a Russian planner, would you ignore Chinese ICBMs that could strike you at any time? The Russians would probably destroy Chinese nuclear forces right from the start.

Third parties would do best to stay out of the war. To become directly involved probably guarantees that some nuclear weapons will land on your soil. This may happen anyway if you are close to a United States or Russian military base that may be attacked to prevent its use in a conventional war. The ability to stay neutral in a nuclear war depends on where you are and how important you are to one side or the other. A good guess is that other nations will find themselves involved in the competition between the United States and Russia *after* the nuclear war. When nuclear forces are pretty much gone after a nuclear war, conventional forces around the world will determine the balance of power.

Could allies and third nations be used to stop a nuclear war once underway? Theoretically, other nations could be intermediaries if the United States and Russia found it difficult to talk with each other. But practical problems make this involvement unlikely. Would there be means of communication or even governments left in the United States or Russia? Which nations would the superpowers trust with negotiations? Are the risks of involvement for other nations worth the gains?

Suppose you are the leader of a nation in Africa, Asia or Europe. What does the future hold for your country after a nuclear war? Even if military bases in your nation are not attacked with nuclear weapons, radioactive fallout may contaminate your cities and agriculture. Unless you can intercede immediately and prevent a nuclear war or significantly reduce it, there is little you can do to reduce its effects. And the risks of immediate involvement are considerable. You may be suspected of being allied with one of the nations fighting a nuclear war and find yourself under attack. The more you look at the prospects for third parties attempting to stop a nuclear war, the more dismal they get.

If there is one region in the world that cannot escape nuclear war it is Europe. American and Russian nuclear forces and armies in Europe would be prime targets in a war, and the tensions between East and West are focused on Europe. However, Europe could still play a useful role in a crisis. In the Cuban Missile Crisis, British and French support of the United States helped to deter the Russians. Aside from lending support to the superpowers, nations can exert pressure on the superpowers to avoid a war. It goes without saying that actions before a nuclear war are more important than actions during or after a nuclear war.

Still, the leaders of other nations should think about whether their best course would be to risk involvement or to sit out the war.

The spread of nuclear weapons to more countries will continue, and it will change the balance of power. The effect will be analogous to the impact of the invention of firearms. Firearms equalized the military power between wealthy professional warriors and poor, untrained troops. With firearms, a farmer could bring down an armored knight. Nuclear weapons in the hands of smaller nations will have a similar effect. Even though the nuclear forces of the superpowers could quickly obliterate any other nation, a smaller state (Libya, South Africa, Israel) could bring enormous pressure on a superpower simply by having a few nuclear weapons. This has already happened between Russia and China. Before China obtained nuclear weapons, Russia seriously considered several military "solutions" to whatever dangers they thought China posed. Now, Russia treats China with more care.

It's also likely that a nuclear weapon will eventually be used by a minor power with an unstable government. Many governments already have more military technology than they can handle.

The techniques for manufacturing nuclear weapons are no longer secret. The technology for making the weapons and skilled personnel are less widely available. As the years go by, the chance that all three elements will exist in the same place increases.

Some nations that obtain nuclear weapons choose not to officially admit it. They do this to spare themselves diplomatic and political problems. Best guess is that Israel has two hundred or so low- to medium-yield weapons for delivery by fighter. It is commonly believed that South Africa detonated its first weapon in September 1979 in the South Atlantic. American VELA satellites detected the explosion, according to press accounts.

If a minor power set off one nuclear weapon, the target area would rank with the worst natural disasters. A greater danger, however, is that the explosion might be misinterpreted by one of the other nuclear powers. If a superpower somehow got involved in an accident of this sort, the results would obliterate civilization.

The lesser powers are aware of the leverage they can obtain by possessing, or seeming to possess, nuclear weapons. The traditional warning signs for wars will change as lesser powers exercise an influence over greater powers that has rarely existed in the past.

THE MECHANICS OF STOPPING A
NUCLEAR WAR ONCE UNDER WAY

Some currently popular theories of nuclear war call for fighting until termination is in your best interests. This means that you do not stop a nuclear war as soon as possible because you still want to destroy certain targets. But if one believes that nuclear war signals an utter failure of foreign policy, then the sooner it stops, the better it is for the nations fighting it.

The mechanics of halting nuclear war involve command, control and communication (C^3). You have to be able to control nuclear forces and to talk with the enemy.

The most basic function of C^3 is talking and listening to your nuclear forces. The United States, Russia, Britain and France have elaborate systems for sending messages to ICBMs, submarines and bombers. In a nuclear war the forces will be told when to launch nuclear weapons and what targets to hit. For the United States the targets and options are in the SIOP, which stands for Single Integrated Operational Plan.

While C^3 can order nuclear forces to launch their missiles or drop their bombs, in theory it also can be used for talking and listening to the enemy. Stopping a nuclear war means that the combatants must communicate. But what do you say to the enemy that is killing millions of your people, contaminating huge areas with radioactive fallout and destroying the basic fabric of your society?

First, communicate why the war started because it is important for each side to know why the other attacked. A corollary is who started the war. While it may seem clear to the Russians that the United States started the war, the United States may think the Russians are to blame. Just because a Russian submarine fired a nuclear torpedo first does not mean the Russian leadership is to blame. It is possible the submarine commander launched the torpedo on his own.

Each side will suspect that the other is lying, especially if what they hear differs from their own account. Leaders also should be aware that what they are told by advisers will be tainted. No adviser wants to admit mistakes in the best of times. Who will want to tell the U.S. President or the Russian General Secretary they made a mistake that contributed even slightly to the start of nuclear war?

Each side will want to establish as clearly as possible what happened to start the war. There may have to be cooperation between the intelligence services, or what is left of them. Unfortunately the CIA in Virginia, the Defense Intelligence Agency, or DIA, in Washington and the National Security Agency, or NSA, in Maryland probably are prime targets in a nuclear war. Similarly, the KGB headquarters in Moscow and the GRU (Russian military intelligence) are likely targets. If the intelligence agencies are destroyed, then the United States and Russia may have to agree blindly on who started the war, or failing that just agree the war must be halted immediately.

The real issue is when to stop a nuclear war. If nations behave normally, which means with a close eye on their national interests, they will want to know that there are equal numbers of civilian losses or nuclear forces destroyed. If this seems callous, put yourself in the position of the U.S. President or Russian General Secretary. Would you want to stop a nuclear war if you believed that you had come out far worse? What if your casualties were fifty million and the other side's were a couple of million? Or if most of your land-based missiles, bomber bases and submarine ports were destroyed, while the other side had lost only a small fraction? Would you say end the war, or would you want to "even things up" first?

Unfortunately, history shows that nations seek advantage in peace and in war even if it means incurring large losses. The French in World War I fought to keep Verdun, though it cost them 350,000 dead in six months. Verdun was not worth 350,000 dead in an area of several square miles where the mud turned red from the blood of so many dead soldiers. Nations will act ruthlessly even if more people die unnecessarily.

Nations think about the balance of losses to influence what the world will look like after nuclear war. Neither the United States nor Russia wants the other to have a significant advantage in the postwar world, so they may continue fighting to make sure there is a rough balance of power in the future. No one wants the other side to have significantly larger nuclear forces, conventional armies, air forces and navies, or greater economic power. Nuclear war is bad enough without letting the other side dominate the world after the war.

When both sides want to stop, there are many ways to handle the mechanics. Each side can agree not to launch more nuclear strikes. They could agree that whatever happened is over and that there will be no further nuclear attacks. To accomplish this, both sides can "standdown" their nuclear forces by returning bombers to their bases and decreasing the level of alert. For instance, each side may reduce the alert level of forces over several days. Suppose both sides standdown their forces all at once, but one nation is deceitful: It waits for the right moment to destroy the other nation's nuclear forces in a surprise nuclear attack. Because nations will be very uneasy about steps that are sudden or major, slow, incremental steps toward halting the war will work better than radical actions to defuse the crisis. Nations will be very paranoid about actions that are not deliberate and cautious.

One problem with stopping nuclear war is that both sides will be extremely suspicious. Even if both sides act in good faith, each distrusts the other. After your nation was attacked with nuclear weapons, you might wonder whether this talk of termination is just a clever ruse. Because there is no way to avoid these emotions, they should be kept in mind when trying to understand how to stop nuclear war.

Skeptics will ask: Is stopping a nuclear war before it runs its course realistic? Possibly, but only after counterforce preemption and retaliation but before attacks against cities. This possibility depends on U.S. and Russian restraint, and partly on how automatic their war plans are. If C^3 works as promised, each side would probably retain control of its forces throughout a nuclear war. That's a big if.

But we probably couldn't stop a nuclear war fast enough to make a difference. Even a limited nuclear war, involving attacks against missile silos and military targets, would kill tens of millions in the United States, Russia and Europe.

Governments like to invent protocols they would observe in cases like these. But planned protocols may be worse than nothing. First, they may not work because they depend on the cooperation of nations, who may fear a loss of secrecy if they do, in essence, what the enemy knows they will do. Worse, governments may think they will work, and take chances.

Are there better and worse types of nuclear war? The question is hard to answer without sounding macabre. It is indisputable that the "best" type of nuclear war is a limited one that fizzles immediately. For example, only a few nuclear weapons are exploded, preferably out to sea where there is no damage to national homelands. The worst type of nuclear war is one that destroys cities, killing tens or hundreds of millions of people.

Nations may not be as tough as they sound. Once the first nuclear weapon explodes, even a small one like at Hiroshima, national leaders may be so horrified they stop all hostilities immediately. We can never know just how leaders will behave in a crisis, but it is certain that few leaders today have any idea what a nuclear explosion will do. Seeing films of nuclear explosions on television is not the same as seeing detailed satellite photographs of nuclear devastation.

The effects of the release of radioactive fallout from the nuclear meltdown at Chernobyl in 1986 are trivial compared with the consequences of even a limited nuclear war. The accident contaminated water and soil in the Ukraine and crops in Scandinavia and Europe. There are several signs that Russian leaders were badly shaken by the aftereffects of

Chernobyl. First, they immediately unleashed a torrent of internal publications on how horrible nuclear war would be. The Russians do not initiate this kind of discussion unless they are willing to live with it. The most obvious result of this discussion, for the West, was the 1986 Russian proposal to eliminate all nuclear weapons. Even this tiny example makes us wonder how many leaders actually will fight a nuclear war without looking for a way out as soon as possible.

HOW TO AVOID OR HALT
A NUCLEAR WAR

Today, the United States and Russia know well enough to avoid crises that could lead to nuclear war. Avoiding confrontations in certain world regions is the basic recipe for avoiding a crisis. Another rule is not to play in the other superpower's backyard. For example, the Russians know that putting troops in Central or South America could cause a nuclear war. Putting missiles in Cuba in 1962 came close. The United States knows that instigating a revolution in Eastern Europe could have the same effect. But some of the gray areas, like the Persian Gulf and the Far East, are up for grabs. In these areas, foresight and caution will go a long way toward preventing a nuclear crisis.

Any confrontation between the superpowers can lead to a major international crisis. As nuclear war may be inevitable in certain crises, all sides must use caution in international politics. This certainly does not mean that the United States or any nation should abandon its vital national interests, only that nations should exercise extreme caution. Better hot lines to ensure easy communication in a crisis would go a long way toward lessening the danger of a nuclear war. The present communications system would be easily disrupted by the effects of nuclear weapons (the electromagnetic pulse). There should be several means of communication—each with elaborate security precautions—so there is a greater chance that one will survive. Now we use two communications satellites; with a little agreement, we could use several satellites, several cable links and several radio frequencies. The other way to lessen the danger of nuclear war is for all major powers to constantly monitor all nuclear forces.

Here is a summary of the steps a nation can take to avoid or halt a nuclear war:

No first-strike attacks. If this sounds simple, it is. The best way to prevent a nuclear war is not to start one. All scenarios of nuclear war assume one side shoots first, usually for unexplained reasons. Just about everyone agrees that no rational person would shoot first. But everyone firmly agrees that if someone else launches a nuclear attack, then they will retaliate. Deterrence is based on retaliation, so all sides must be secure about the ability to shoot back.

Communicate what to do if nuclear war starts. Communication in the nuclear age means deterrence. Both sides know, or certainly believe, that a nuclear attack will be met in kind. As long as this rule is sound, nuclear war probably won't happen. Once a nuclear war starts, both sides will follow specific doctrines. From what targets to hit, to when those targets are attacked, nuclear options are excruciatingly exact. Once nuclear weapons start to fly, it is like a movie script: Everyone follows a well-rehearsed part, and when the movie is over, so is the world.

Nations should have some understanding of what others will do in a nuclear war. If not, then a nuclear war will rage on without each side being able to influence what the other does. There is no way to change the nature of nuclear war plans or how nations communicate with nuclear forces. But communication channels or procedures established in peace might make it easier to stop a nuclear war—or at least, stop a nuclear war sooner.

The termination option. There are options for all conceivable kinds of nuclear attacks. A termination option should be one of the options. It may mean limiting retaliation to only the kinds of targets that the other side hit. Or delaying retaliation to slow the tempo of the war. Or expressly refusing to hit certain kinds of targets, like command centers, unless the other side does first.

Target only by necessity. Everyone knows that potential targets range from missile silos to oil refineries and cities. Halting nuclear war involves limiting the type and number of targets that you hit. Unless there is an overwhelming reason to hit a certain target, it is best not to.

Slow and deliberate, not hasty and automatic. One reason why nuclear war seems so automatic to some is that under stress decision makers may overreact. Destroying one or two targets may be sufficient to send a message. In a crisis people may destroy one hundred or two hundred, or one thousand or two thousand because of flawed decision making or pressure to capitalize on the moment. A cardinal rule of nuclear war is severely limit the targets you attack. If the other side is reckless, then yours may have to be also. But the chances are that each side will be as horrified as the other. If yours shows restraint, maybe the other side will too.

Don't target cities—all things being equal. Unless the other side decimates your cities, chances are that cities can be spared. There is no military utility to bombing cities. The only thing it may do is spark the other side to do the same. Use restraint. The other side may be looking for any sign of willingness to stop the madness before it goes any further.

Preserve the leadership. If the leaders are dead or unable to communicate their decisions, what happens from then on is a matter of planning and accident. Most people will follow plans, a few will improvise. There are basically two groups that determine what happens: the American and Soviet leaders. Kill them, and chances are the war will be worse.

Worry about other nations later. Nuclear exchanges against the American and Soviet homelands are catastrophes. But a global nuclear war is worse. If possible, do not immediately escalate the war to third parties. Destruction of third nations will not change the outcome, but only make the outcome worse.

Worry about your people now. In the past, nations could play nuclear brinkmanship. In the Cuban Missile Crisis, Americans supported their government because they believed almost unanimously in the threat posed by the Russians. Today, things are very different. No longer can nations enter a nuclear crisis thinking they will have the unanimous support of their people. Demonstrations against the Vietnam War changed all that. Governments today should expect massive opposition to their policies in a nuclear crisis. Rioting, demonstrations, in some cases near anarchy may occur if people think a nuclear war is even a remote possibility. If governments do not carefully craft their policies, they will face two opponents: their people and another nation.

Part 2

The Lessons of History

Everything that will happen, has happened. Well, not exactly, but close enough so that if you are familiar with the history of war and peace you have excellent prospects for seeing what the future will bring.

A Quick Run Through Two Hundred Years of Military History

Over one hundred fifty million people have died in wars since 1787, while the global population has grown from seven hundred million to five billion. This equals a loss rate of less than 1 percent. Warfare is the most common manmade cause of death.

There's a saying in business that 15 percent of your customers account for 85 percent of your sales, or 85 percent of your problems. Likewise, a few wars represent the majority of the carnage. Six wars have caused most of the damage, each of them resulting in over ten million deaths. These were the Napoleonic Wars (1792–1815), the Taiping Rebellion (China, 1851–82), World War I (1914–18), the Russian Communist Terror (1927–37), World War II (1939–45) and the Chinese Communist Terror (1949–75). The interesting trend here is the increasing frequency of large-scale killings in recent times. Even adjusting for a larger population, we live in a historically violent time.

More effective armed forces have made bloody-minded tyrants more deadly. Mass killings like those in Cambodia and Uganda would not have been possible without the easy availability of modern weapons. An unarmed population of millions can be easily annihilated by ten thousand heavily armed thugs. Make that several hundred thousand thugs and you have a massive bloodbath. Add to the weapons some modern communications equipment and administrative training, and you have the modern police state.

The horror reached a high pitch in Nazi Germany and Russia. Propaganda, ruthless police forces and concentration camps made control and murder more efficient than ever before. More recently Cambodia was turned into a slaughterhouse. Less than a hundred thousand heavily armed and fanatic young people exercised ruthless control over a population of eight million. Over two million Cambodians were killed in a classic case of civil terror.

Another trend during the last two hundred years has been the decline in formal wars with declarations and organized armies. There is a lot more money for weapons. There are a lot more unemployed teenagers. And there is a lot less military and political control.

Wars come in many shapes and sizes. Most of them are local disputes that are unlikely to escalate to world-threatening proportions. While this may provide some peace of mind in the middle of all those worrisome headlines, nearly every war has the potential for leading to something larger. Every major war has been spawned from a smaller one.

Wars that involve one of the major powers are, logically enough, the most potentially dangerous. Any armed conflict involving two or more of the major powers shooting at each other is a high-risk event, particularly when nuclear weapons are available. This has led to an encouraging development—major powers are getting directly involved in far fewer wars. Up until 1945, about half the wars of any size involved troops of the major powers.

The fear of nuclear war has impelled the major powers to keep their forces out of minor countries' wars. But economic and diplomatic assistance, as well as arms, continue to be fed into other people's conflicts around the world. A case can be made that there are more minor power wars now that the major powers no longer have much direct control over the fighting in proxy wars. Nevertheless, lack of direct involvement by major powers has reduced the total number of deaths, even though not the *overall* number of conflicts.

WARS AND LOSSES BY HISTORICAL PERIOD

Period	Percentage of Wars	Average Losses Per War in Thousands
1787-1815	11	75
1815-1900	43	64
1900-1945	12	496
1945-1987	33	140

Although there has been much change in the past two centuries, some aspects of war have not changed much at all. Technology has changed enormously, human nature has not. Nations still go to war for the same reasons. National leaders still ignore implications of the new weapons as they did two hundred years ago. Leaders are still more concerned with results than with means.

Communications have improved. Leaders may immediately contact each other directly, if they choose to. But leaders do not usually stoop to use a telephone or radio to contact their opponents. They want to safeguard their dignity, so they invoke protocol. Diplomats and other subordinates draft memoranda to be sent, often by hand, to the enemy leadership. Weapons technology has advanced far more quickly than the abilities of national leaders to effectively communicate with each other.

There are many important differences between the societies of the 1780s and those of the 1980s. On close inspection, though, the differences haven't helped the cause of world peace.

In 1786 most of the world was ruled by authoritarian governments. Royalty ruled by divine right. Nobles often owned most of the wealth of the nation. There was no democratic voting. The ruling class formed a consensus, under the leadership of its ruler. The king/emperor/kaiser/tsar/sultan/emir or whatever had to worry about losing the support of a small ruling class. The rest of the people were less of a concern. Totalitarian nations of the 1980s operate much like the authoritarian nations of the 1780s. The buzzwords have changed, the practice of government has not.

There have been some significant developments. Two events in the 1700s demonstrated to all but the slow learners that things were about to change. First, there was the revolution in the British North American colonies. The colonies then established a democracy. The basic concept of democracy had been around since antiquity but had never really caught on in a big way. The United States had a large population for the period and the largest land area ever ruled by a modern democracy. The second event was the French Revolution. One of the most powerful kings in Europe was executed and the then most powerful nation in the world became a republic. This caught everyone's attention. Then the French Republic self-destructed in a fit of paranoia and petty squabbling and was transformed under Napoleon into the French Empire. Napoleon turned out to be one who had and was spreading some decidedly antimonarchist ideas.

From 1792 to 1815 Napoleon and the French dominated world events. But all the monarchs of Europe united against and defeated Napoleon. Conventional monarchy was reintroduced into France and intense negotiations were undertaken by the major powers to prevent another major war. Thus from 1815 to 1914 there were no cataclysmic wars in Europe.

The European nations put their energies into conquering other parts of the world, a task they had been warming up for during the previous four centuries. The Western Hemisphere had been put off limits by the rapidly growing United States. No matter, the United States was too feisty and far away to bother with and South America was a largely unpopulated wilderness. Latin America was not worth fighting the United States over, particularly since Britain controlled nearly all the trade with the region.

This left Africa and Asia. Africa was close and open for the taking. Throughout the 1800s European nations fell over each other establishing claims to Africa. A large number of wars with the primitively equipped inhabitants kept many Europeans busy and out of each other's way.

In Asia, there was more resistance from more sophisticated inhabitants, and it was farther away. But the rewards were greater and the carnage matched that in Africa.

In 1800, Asia held over two thirds of the world's population. Yet the 20 percent of the world's inhabitants who lived in Europe now dominated the planet. They did this without any striking technological advantages. Technical superiority would come in the next hundred years. For three hundred years prior to 1800, Europeans had simply been more aggressive and, when it suited their purpose, more ruthless and brutal. During the 1500s, several thousand European soldiers conquered millions of people in the Americas, including several highly organized empires. By 1800, European soldiers and sailors controlled access to Africa and Asia. European soldiers, diplomats and merchants had picked apart the Indian subcontinent and were making inroads into the Chinese Empire. The victims of this ambitious behavior did not realize that the Europeans were just getting started.

During the 1800s, the Industrial Revolution went into high gear in Europe. Most of the basic products and ideas we take for granted were invented: electricity, steam power, oil-based fuels, concrete, steel ships, the telephone, mass media, advertising, computers, income taxes, modern police forces, universal education, the voting machine, dynamite, the machine gun, antiseptic medicine, heroin, psychoanalysis, recorded music, microbiology, genetics, labor unions, communism, morphine, photography, electric motors, the typewriter, painless surgery, nightclubs, the sewing machine, the hypodermic syringe, synthetic fibers, cocaine, numbers theory, self-help books, linoleum, the internal combustion engine, refrigeration, championship golf, paper dress patterns, scientific weather forecasts, ice-making machines, bicycles, plastic, canned food, artificial sweeteners,

Bingo, health insurance, submarines, hydroelectric power plants, insulin, rubber gloves, skyscrapers, automobiles, radio, the safety razor, professional football, magnetic sound recording and many more.

Before the century was out, most of the world's manufactured goods were pouring out of European factories. The military superiority of European armies was even more enhanced by mass-produced, highly destructive weapons. Steel warships, machine guns and automatic cannon overwhelmed non-European armies. Wealth on a previously unimaginable scale was being produced by machines. The rest of the world provided raw materials, and markets for what the Europeans could not consume themselves. Non-European cultures that had changed little over thousands of years found themselves overwhelmed by European merchants, soldiers and, in many cases, colonial governments.

It seemed that nothing could stop the Europeans. But two developments laid the groundwork for a catastrophe that would bring down the European colossus. One was the expansion of the Russian Empire. The other was the unification of Germany.

Unlike the other European powers, Russia did not look beyond the seas for lands to conquer. Russia went after her Asian neighbors. This was done for three reasons. First, Russia had been invaded from the east many times and was always afraid of the next incursion. Second, Russia's eastern neighbors were weak at the time. Third, Russia's western neighbors were not weak. So Russia methodically marched toward the Pacific.

At the same time there was a developing potential for disputes with Austria. The Turkish Empire was falling apart, and both Austria and Russia were going after the pieces. In addition, Austria also ruled many slavic cousins of the Russians. But for the time being, Russia went out of its way to maintain good relations with Austria, even sending Russian troops to help put down rebellions in Austrian territories.

The other sinister event of the 1800s was the unification of Germany from a collection of feuding tribes and minor states. In the mid-1800s, the spirit of unification reached a crescendo. A war with France was contrived to create an external threat that argued for unification. It also prevented France from interfering with the unification; France had nothing to gain and much to lose from a unified Germany.

The Franco-Prussian War of 1870 was short and Germany victorious. But the Germans got greedy. They took the provinces of Alsace and Lorraine from France. The French vowed revenge. The stage was set for a major war.

Germany, now actively threatened by France, allied itself with its Austrian kinsmen. In another major diplomatic blunder, Germany refused to renew its treaty of friendship with Russia. Russia, feeling threatened by a unified Germany, which was now allied with Austria, arranged for an alliance with France. The 1800s were drawing to a close, as was an age of relative peace.

By 1900, colonialization of Africa and Asia was largely complete. The European nations began to venture once more into their own backyards. What they found was World War I, set off by a dispute between Austria and Russia over the fate of the declining Turkish Empire. The fighting of World War I and associated wars raged from 1912 to the 1920s. This war ended with the dismemberment of the German, Russian and Austrian empires. The Germans and Austrians, like the French before them, vowed vengeance. Their desire for revenge was made more desperate by a worldwide economic depression that began in the late 1920s. The world economic system had never fully recovered from the 1914–18 fighting. The wars resumed in the 1930s, first in China, then Spain and finally Europe. Fighting continued on and off until the early 1950s.

Over forty years of recurring combat exhausted the European nations. When the fighting ended, the United States was clearly the most powerful military and economic nation in the world. Starting in the late 1940s, there were thirty years of economic and technological growth on a scale never before seen. The United States was generous in aiding the economies of its allies and former enemies. This helped prevent the economic stagnation that followed the 1914–18 fighting.

The formerly expansion-minded European powers now put most of their energy into their own affairs. The colonial empires began to fall apart and over a hundred new nations were born.

These new nations were often artificial entities whose borders were created at the whim of colonial administrators. Most of the populations still lived under preindustrial conditions, just as they had before colonialization. But their leaders often had acquired expensive lifestyles during the colonial period. The combination of disputed borders, poverty and corrupt leaders created instability, both internal and external. The resulting conflicts were doubly tragic because the nations involved were so poor. The major powers have used these wars to expand their influence. Their successes have often proven illusory because the nations afflicted were often too unstable to be reliable allies.

For the first time in history there developed truly enormous differences in the quality of life between populations. The average lifespan of populations once varied only from the low thirties to high forties. The low end is still with us, but many industrial nations now have average lifespans over seventy years. Because the more developed societies have fewer children, there are also differences in birthrates. The poor countries are becoming much more populous than the wealthier nations.

This population imbalance has some insidious aspects. The colonial period improved public health in undeveloped societies, thus lowering the death rate, particularly among children. However, much less was done for the local economies. The false hope of industrial jobs caused farmers to head for the cities. Food production fell as population grew. Starvation and malnutrition increased. Populations were kept alive through massive food imports from the wealthier nations. But the poor nations often could not afford the food and had to depend on charity. Another aspect of this charity was that the needy nations played the major powers off against each other in a quest for greater aid.

The larger and better organized low-tech nations quickly addressed the problem and concentrated on agriculture. China and India, holding over 40 percent of the planet's population, eventually managed to become self-sufficient in food. Most of the smaller nations, particularly in Africa, were less successful and have become chronic problems for themselves and the wealthier nations that support them.

The latter part of the 1900s has been a period of peace among the major powers and incessant warfare among the numerous poor, recently minted nations. It has been several centuries since the major powers have been at peace with each other for so long.

The wealthy nations have become wealthier and the poor ones have not improved their economies rapidly enough to close the gap.

Over half the planet's nonnuclear military power is split between the two superpowers, the United States and Russia. The other first-world nations hold most of the remaining armed strength. Only highly populous, but relatively poor, India and China possess any significant military power without possessing a large and highly developed industry.

For the first time in several hundred years, the bulk of the world's military power is no longer found in Western Europe. America and Russia have most of the combat forces, yet Western Europe and Japan each has more economic power than Russia. Things were simpler when Europe had it all. Now you need a scorecard to tell who has what.

The big question mark is how the bulk of the world's population, living in poor and undeveloped nations, can coexist with the wealthy and more heavily armed high-tech nations. Everyone fears a nuclear war and the greatest fear is that nuclear weapons will next be used by a nation that thinks it has nothing to lose.

During the last two hundred years, the social, economic and political changes have been far more dramatic and far ranging than those in warfare. Military developments are barely able to keep up with changes in society.

Wars That Never Happened

History is full of wars that never happened. These non-wars do not get the attention they deserve. More than the wars that occurred, the non-wars are examples of what to do when you want peace.

An example: The Polish Worker's War (1980)

Poland and Russia have been at each other's throats for over a thousand years.

In 1980, labor unrest in Poland was taking on a nationalist tinge. Russia expected three things from Poland: adherence to a Communist form of society, subjugation to Russian direction in defense and foreign diplomacy and order.

The growing Solidarity labor movement threatened all three. Since 1945, Russia had sent troops into any East European country that strayed from these principles. During the summer of 1980, Russian troops began mobilizing on the Polish borders.

The situation was critical for Russia. Should Russia lose control of Poland, land access to East Germany would vanish. In addition, the Warsaw Pact bloc would forfeit nearly half its non-Russian military strength. Poland possessed the largest and most powerful armed forces of all Russia's allies. Worse yet, the Polish Army was full of conscripts who were infected by the new political winds sweeping across Poland. The armed forces' professional cadre of officers and senior NCOs was more devoted to

Poland than to communism. The Poles had a long military tradition and had always been tenacious and resourceful fighters. Russia did not look forward to yet another war with Poland.

In East Germany in 1953, Hungary in 1956 and Czechoslovakia in 1968 the Russians had shown no hesitation about sending in troops. But this situation was obviously different. The Polish Army might well put up a stiff fight, and the population was aroused. There is little doubt that the Russian Army would still have prevailed, so long as no Western powers got involved. But there was a risk of escalation if the Poles held out too long, established a "free Poland" and appealed for aid. More serious were the long-term results of such a war. Poland's armed forces could not be trusted for some time afterward. Russia would have to send additional forces to occupy the country. Finally, Poland's economy would be damaged, placing a fiscal burden on Russia.

Calmer heads prevailed. To prevent a war with Russia, the Polish Army was allowed to take over the government. This was risky, as the population might still rise against its own army. (Also, there was a risk that the army takeover would give the Russian Army ideas about taking over *its* government.) The uprising did not happen, compromises were arranged with the Polish workers, arrests were made and large-scale violence was averted.

In the last two hundred years, such has not always been the case in Poland. Poland was a major or contributing cause of several major and minor wars. Russia has intervened with a heavy hand several times in the recent past. Few people outside Poland and Russia are aware of just how close war was in 1980. One of the notable wars of the late twentieth century became a nonevent.

WHAT TURNS A POTENTIAL WAR INTO A NON-WAR?

A tolerable number of disputes between nations. If enough effort is spent on controlling the disagreements between two nations, issues worth going to war over will not develop. Unfortunately, this is more easily attempted than accomplished. Grievances of one form or another are the root cause of all wars. Disputes between countries and within nations are ever present. People and nations often don't realize that their complaints are adding up until it's too late.

No illusions about military capabilities. If both potential opponents estimate that neither is significantly more powerful, there will be one less temptation to wage war. But it is difficult to calculate accurately both your own and your potential opponent's power. It's even more complex if you or your opponent has superpower patronage. Here is where the superpowers can use their military power to maintain the peace. A treaty of mutual assistance between a minor power and a superpower provides an insurance policy against unwanted military entanglements. Few nations want to take on one of the superpowers. Living under such a nuclear umbrella has its disadvantages, too; the minor power is constrained from military adventures. This does not harm the cause of peace, and so is a minor price to pay for protection from aggressive neighbors. On their part, superpowers have to be careful whom they make serious military pacts with. Become a partner with a maniac and you could find yourself in a war you could have avoided.

Government stability. Civil disorder in one or both nations is the most common cause of wars. Anything that contributes to domestic peace and harmony does the same for international tranquility. Power is a drug with bad side effects. Remember that a politician's primary objective is to stay in office. To achieve this often difficult task, unseemly risks are taken and dangerous compromises are made. The upkeep of a ruler's position usually requires that several other power blocks be catered to. These other groups must be bought off, neutralized or destroyed. Not everyone will stay bought. Neutralizing competing groups by keeping them from participating in the government is by definition temporary. So ruthless leaders prefer to destroy competition instead. This is not always possible. The competition may be too strong, or local custom may not permit such severe measures. If competing groups base their power on popular support, you may have to kill a lot of people to stifle them. The democratic nations avoid destruction of opponents. The nondemocratic nations do not. Communist nations, in particular, have indulged in massive slaughters to suppress competing power groups. And even democratic nations will resort to massive killings if the victims are not voters. This was particularly the case during the colonial period. Even Britain, one of the more enlightened colonial powers, was not adverse to solving colonial unrest with lethal force. The United States slaughtered hundreds of thousands in the Philippines at the turn of the century to maintain American rule. Internal power struggles often go beyond national borders, if not initially, then eventually. War is like fire. It burns on as long as the fuel lasts.

THE NON-WARS

Many wars don't quite come off. They are rarely noticed or studied. But non-wars are more important than wars. If we are going to prevent wars we must pay closer attention to the successes and less to the failures. Every war is a failure of peacemaking efforts. These failures are examples of how *not* to do it.

We identified dozens of tense diplomatic situations over the last two centuries. We analyzed each one's potential for war, just as we did each war that actually happened. In the data base, our calculated value appears as the RISK. Here are the non-wars that came closest to being real wars.

United States and France—1790s

War was avoided because of a wide ocean and recent good relations.

Although France's aid had been critical in America's revolution, these two former allies nearly went to war in the 1790s. The critical element in this near-war was France's own revolution, which was partly inspired by its recent experience in America. Unfortunately, France's revolution was not against a colonial power three thousand miles away. The French people rose up against their own government and incurred the wrath of Austria and Germany. The French people established a new government and promptly found themselves in a series of wars that continued for over twenty years. America was involved largely because it refused to cease trading with France's enemies and resisted France's attempts to expand its colonial holdings in North America. The same policies got the United States into war with Britain.

In France's case, calmer heads prevailed, after some naval skirmishes. Mutual sympathy with each other's revolutionary background and the former alliance played a part in avoiding a full-scale war. A more tangible cause of the settlement was the presence of large French territories in North America. Much of the territory along the Mississippi as well as islands in the Caribbean were still French. Britain and the United States had designs on these territories. Eventually, France sold the Mississippi territories to the United States. Had a war occurred, the United States or Britain might have gotten these lands anyway. However, the cost would likely have been much higher. War is an expensive way to settle disputes.

Britain and France—late 1800s

Ancient grievances and late-nineteenth-century colonial disputes fade to insignificance in the face of the threat of German aggression.

Only in the last hundred and forty years have Britain and France been allies. Before, they had been enemies for as long as they had been unified nations—over nine hundred years.

The last time Britain and France nearly went to war was in the late 1800s over colonial matters. Ultimately, the colonial disputes were not deemed as important as other conditions closer to home. France was feuding with Germany. Britain and France had even united against Russia in the 1850s to defend Turkey. In the late 1800s, for the first time in many centuries, France saw Britain as a less dangerous enemy than Germany. Britain had long maintained a policy of supporting the weaker European powers to maintain a "balance of power." France was no longer the strongest European power, Germany was. Britain and France put aside eight hundred years of hatred and warfare, became allies and kept the peace. Amazing.

Britain and Germany—late 1800s, early 1900s

Centuries of good relations mollified current disputes and prevented war.

Britain and the German States have been allies, or at least friends, for most of Britain's history. Only in this century have they found themselves in serious conflict. Britain and Germany nearly went to war in the late 1800s over colonial, trade and naval matters. These issues never existed earlier because the German nation did not exist until 1871. The new German Empire was going through a period of explosive economic growth, which concerned competing British industries. To make matters worse, Germany was flush with new nationalism. Germans wanted their "place in the sun." They wanted what the long-unified nations had and Germany didn't—colonies.

Initially, Britain cooperated with Germany in colonial matters. There were good reasons for this initial cooperation. The royalty of Britain and Germany were blood relatives and there had long been friendly commercial and cultural relations between the Germans and Britons. The British were initially understanding about the growing German nationalism. However, what worried the British the most was Germany's construction of a modern battleship fleet. Britain had long been dependent on seaborne trade and had been the premier naval power in the world since the early 1700s. But Germany was becoming the dominant industrial power and was looking for overseas markets. This trade depended on a large merchant marine and a navy to secure the sea lanes. The new German Navy and growing competition from German industry became a political issue in both countries.

War between the two nations became a popular topic. Several times during the 1800s, Britain had dealt with potential naval rivals by paying a midnight visit to sink their warships. As an island, Britain was immune to reprisal by land forces. However, open warfare was avoided until 1914, when Britain's grievances against Germany resulted in a military alliance between Britain and France.

France and Germany—1871 to 1913

French military inferiority delayed war, but not long enough to forge a lasting peace.

Germany and France have been enemies from the moment Germany finally moved toward unity in the mid-1800s. Germany's final unification was consummated with a military victory over France in the 1870–71 Franco-Prussian War. The armed rivalry between the two nations did not cease for seventy-five years. In addition to the military buildups along their mutual borders, there were other sources of conflict in their respective colonies. What prevented war from breaking out before 1914 was Germany's attitude that there was nothing to fight over and France's calculation that Germany could not yet be defeated to regain France's lost provinces. What finally brought on war in 1914 was a series of miscalculations about what could be accomplished with military power.

Britain and India—1858 to 1948

Adroit use of diplomacy and military force kept the peace in a normally strife-torn subcontinent.

Starting in the 1600s, Britain began to acquire commercial and then political control over large portions of the Indian subcontinent. One of the major wars avoided in the 1800s was between Britain and the large population of India. The ratio of actual or potential Indian military force to the British forces in India was not very promising for the British. But Britain kept the peace, despite numerous potential outbreaks of warfare, by using very adroit political, military and commercial diplomacy. Britain's initial ventures with India were purely commercial, and it was only after 1850 that a trading company turned control of India over to the British government. The stockholders of the British East India Company did not want wars or other wasteful operations eating up their profits. The government treated India like a commercial venture, too. Diplomacy was always conducted from an accountant's perspective. The skirmishes fought were small and easily handled by the available British and British-led Indian forces. Except for one major mutiny, the Sepoy Rebellion in 1857–58, Britain held the upper hand and generally kept the peace right up until 1948, when it voluntarily gave up control of India.

The peacekeeping was an amazing achievement, for no one had ever conquered all of India and made it stick. The moslem Moghuls came close during the 1500s and 1600s. The British wandered by in the 1600s and outmaneuvered French and Dutch competition, as well as the numerous Indian potentates. With a minimum of violence and a maximum of political adroitness, Britain demonstrated an alternative to purely military conquest. Previous invaders of India had eventually inspired serious rebellions and civil wars. Britain managed to avoid them by following a prudent and opportunistic military policy. They did not fight unless they had to and then no more than they had to. Most British activity was conducted as a commercial venture. Perhaps governments should give their accountants more authority.

United States and Canada—1800s

Goodwill and common interests gradually dissolved any possibility of war.

From its very inception, the United States wanted to incorporate Canada into one large North American nation. Too many Canadians refused the offer during the American Revolution in the late 1700s. However, during the 1800s, the possessiveness toward Canada was revived by anti-British Irish immigrants to the United States who thought that an invasion of Canada would be a splendid way to strike a blow against Britain. (The Irish did not care much for Britain's occupation of their country, which was one reason so many had emigrated to the United States.) Several haphazard and halfhearted invasions by private citizens were attempted in the late 1800s. They caused a good deal of ill will between Britain and the

United States. Competent diplomacy on both sides prevented this ugly situation from turning into a major military activity. Mutual respect and a strong desire by the governments to maintain the peace made the diplomats' jobs much easier.

Latin America—1900s

Reaction to the bloody excesses of the 1800s and sometimes-smothering attention by the United States keeps the peace.

The 1800s had been a particularly bloody century for Latin America. Latin American wars created several times more deaths than conflicts in more populous North America. Latin America was also much more politically divided. Surprisingly, the 1900s saw a substantial reduction in warfare there. With the exception of the Chaco War in 1932, the only significant violence was internal. This can be attributed to several factors.

First, the warfare of the 1800s resolved many of the major political disputes between nations.

Second, the intensity of the warfare during the 1800s made large-scale war much less acceptable to leaders and the population. People now knew for certain just how extraordinarily violent their wars could be.

Third, the United States had begun its reign as policeman of the Americas. Large-scale commercial, diplomatic and, implicitly, military dominance of Latin America helped to defuse several potential wars.

Eastern Europe—1945 to the present

The presence of Russian armies keeps the lid on a normally volatile area.

Although there have been several military altercations in Eastern Europe since 1945, others did not materialize and those that did take place could have been much more violent.

The basic cause of civil unrest in Eastern Europe is the armed control of these nations by Russia. Eastern Europeans have long feared Russian influence in their affairs. From the late 1700s to 1917, Russia occupied and ruled a large segment of Poland. Russia learned how to rule a foreign population that consistently demonstrated a preference for self-rule. This experience was severely tested after 1945 when much of Eastern Europe fell under Russian control. To insure that these nations maintained a properly subservient attitude, substantial garrisons of Russian troops were brought in. East European governments were thoroughly saturated with

Russian advisers and the local functionaries were carefully screened to eliminate those who were not able to contain their anti-Russian sentiments. The Russians did not expect to be loved, they only wanted to be obeyed. Russia could not afford the expense of staffing all the military and police forces in these countries, so they had to leave this in the hands of the locals. Such indirect control was affordable, but not always reliable. Yet in only four instances did this system break down. And in each case a temporary application of Russian military muscle rectified the situation. As time goes by, the Russian position can be expected to worsen—you can't keep people down forever. The chance of a successful, or more successful, rebellion will grow.

The Eastern European situation is a classic case of grievances that can be suppressed, but not eliminated. History has shown that you must either culturally absorb subservient or minority populations or eventually lose them to rebellion. There are many examples of this situation, such as the Celts (Irish, Scots and Welsh) in Britain, Tibetans in China, Catalans and Basques in Spain, everyone in Belgium, Arabs in Israel, Turks in Bulgaria, French in Canada, non-English speakers in the United States, over a hundred minorities in Russia, Chinese in several Asian nations, Germans in (Tyrol) Italy, tribal divisions in African nations, everyone in Yugoslavia and non-Germans in Switzerland.

Some nations are more successful at handling cultural minorities than others. Where an accommodation is reached, everyone can live in peace for centuries. The underlying cultural tensions never disappear, but everyone becomes accustomed to getting along. Switzerland is a good example, as is the United States. To a lesser extent, Canada, Belgium, Britain and Italy keep things calm. But all these combinations are explosive, needing only a spark to arouse ugly passions.

When a heavy hand is required to keep the peace, violent passions are just contained until an uncontrollable explosion occurs. Russia has been subduing minority populations for over five hundred years. They have the experience, but will never find the perfect solution.

Egypt and Libya—1970 to the present

Appeals for Arab unity and Libyan adroitness in pulling back from the brink of an unendurable provocation put off an Egyptian invasion.

Nearly always a province or colony of a larger state, Libya has rarely been independent throughout its several thousand year history. Libya can-

not be certain that its independence will last. Her fragile hold on independence has been further endangered by the rambunctious foreign policies of
Khaddafy. Attempting to assassinate the leader of your strongest neighbor
(Egypt) does little to aid national security. Egypt has many reasons to
invade Libya, too. Egypt has ten times the population and much less
wealth per capita. Libyan oil resources would do much good for the Egyptian economy. Why hasn't Egypt invaded? Egypt has been trying to get
back into the good graces of its Arab neighbors after making peace with
Israel. Libya still remains out there in the western desert, a tempting prize,
waiting for the right combination of cause and diplomatic conditions.

Should Libya appear to lose the support of its patron, Russia, continue
to alienate other Arab states and fall into a state of civil disorder, the
conditions will be nearly ideal for Egyptian intervention.

Algeria and Morocco—1963 to the present

*A combination of reluctance to go too far and limited resources to do so
keeps an insurgency from turning into full-scale war.*

A border dispute over who owns portions of a former Spanish colony
has put Morocco and Algeria into a proxy war that has continued for
many years. The anti-Moroccan insurgency has Communist leanings, and
by providing support for anti-Moroccan rebels, Algeria has kept Moroccan
armed forces in a virtual state of war. Morocco has declined to escalate the
fighting by carrying the war to the source of the rebels' support in Algeria.
This constant insurgency is a severe drain on the primitive Moroccan
economy, and threatens to disrupt its political stability. In turn, Algeria
has not seen the issue as worthy of full-scale war. Unfortunately, Algeria
can afford to let the rebel movement persist because it costs very little. This
is an example of a good old-fashioned, orderly and controlled war. Unfortunately it is rare for nations to keep their cool while their soldiers are
under fire.

United States and Russia—1945 to the present

*Economic problems, fear of American technology and difficulties manag-
ing an empire have kept Russia from going after the United States directly.
Russia has nothing America wants desperately, keeping war fever down in
the United States.*

Russia and the United States have been sparring with each other since

1945. In 1962, they almost came to blows. Only after it was all over, did everyone realize how close the world came to World War III. The United States demanded that Russia remove its nuclear missiles from Cuba. It was a classic confrontation between a land-based power (the Russians) and a naval power (the United States). Both of the superpowers had recourse to nuclear weapons and, in Russia's case, it was their only possible option. In the long term, Russia could have used its ground forces against United States allies. The risks were enormous and the potential danger and probability of mutual annihilation exceedingly high. The situation was defused by a number of U.S. initiatives that were accepted by Russia.

The first United States initiative was a naval blockade of Cuba, to be lifted only when the Russian missiles were removed. The Russians complied and were offered the second United States initiative. The United States promised not to invade Cuba and offered to remove missiles from Turkey. The fact that these missiles were due for removal anyway was irrelevant. The Russians were given a way to save face in a situation they considered a security threat, even though their actions started the commotion. From the Russian point of view, medium-range U.S. nuclear missiles in Turkey are just as threatening to Russia as medium-range Russian nuclear missiles in Cuba are to the United States.

As previous, and subsequent, actions have demonstrated, the Russians are not reluctant to open fire when they perceive their national security to be in danger. A nation that shoots down wayward military or civilian airliners will not hesitate to use stronger measures when the perceived danger is great. However, at the time the stakes were much higher for the Russians than anyone realized in the West. This was the era of the "missile gap." Russia was thought to have a substantial number of intercontinental ballistic missiles. The ones being placed in Cuba were of much shorter range and could not reach the United States except from a location like Cuba. Later we learned that the Russians had no effective intercontinental missile force in the 1960s. Their only reliable means of dropping nuclear missiles on the United States was with slow, World War II–vintage bombers. The missiles in Cuba would have been Russia's only response to America's nuclear capability. Russia could not admit this. (Before the missile gap, there was the bomber gap in the 1950s. To fool American visitors in Moscow watching a May Day Parade, the Russians flew their bomber force in big circles. A few dozen bombers looked like a force of hundreds. The Americans reported this to the U.S. government, the United States built a massive bomber force and the Russians lost all the way around.)

The Cuban Missile Crisis was resolved by adroit diplomacy on both sides. Unfortunately, the Russians and Khrushchev suffered a loss of perceived strength. Russia felt this loss acutely. Much of Russian control over its subject states, and influence over other areas, depends on the perception that Russia is stable and possesses the strongest military force on the planet. They explained their defeat in Cuba by saying they wanted to maintain world peace, but privately they concluded that the cause was insufficient naval forces. Within the Russian military, this embarrassing incident was used to pry loose sufficient funding to build up the Russian Navy to an unprecedented size. The navy might make the Russians more adventurous in a similar situation today, but it would be unlikely to change the outcome. The Russian fleet is spread too thin and would be too far from its home ports to sustain any credible activity off American shores. Russia also built long-range missile and submarine forces that eventually outpaced the Americans'.

That the Russians pushed the Cuban Missile Crisis so far, realizing that they were risking a nuclear war to which they could not respond, shows how important perceived strength is to the Russians. This has been their style in the past, and will be again in the future.

United States and Vietnam—1948 to 1964

Weariness from the Korean War, wariness from the French experience and a willingness to let the 1954 settlement work kept the United States out of Indochina for sixteen years.

Between 1950 and '53, France fought an increasingly futile war in Indochina against Vietnamese nationalists. As one of America's principal European allies and a key member of the NATO defense alliance, France expected considerable support from the United States. America was willing to send money, but not troops, as the Korean War was going on. Americans were not keen on participating in the Korean fighting, and were even less enthusiastic about sending troops to yet another Asian war. Despite the strong desire of many American leaders to work directly with France in making Indochina free of Communist influence, there was too little public support. American participation never went beyond supplying France with weapons and equipment. Subsequent material support of the new government of South Vietnam eventually escalated to full-scale war using American troops.

United States and Cuba—1962 to the present

Castro's diplomacy, Latin American resentment of United States intervention and Russian presence combine to keep the peace.

The United States had never hesitated to take sides, or take part in, Latin American civil wars and revolutions. Such intervention freed Cuba from Spain in 1898. In 1957 there was another revolution in Cuba. In 1959 the new government pronounced itself Communist and the United States declared itself outraged. Cuba was not looking for war with the United States, for obvious reasons.

Many key people in the American government would have been quite happy to send in the Marines to clean out the Communist cancer in Cuba. There was not, however, sufficient public enthusiasm for such a move. The American public had been subjected to much media exposure of the corruption of the former Cuban government. Any move against the current Cuban government risked bringing back the despised former leadership. The unpopularity of the Korean War lingered, and the population was not united in fear of a Communist menace.

The United States government supported an armed movement among Cuban refugees, and this led to an unsuccessful refugee invasion of Cuba in 1961, the Bay of Pigs incident, which received U.S. logistical support. The Cuban Communists, mindful of the U.S. history of military intervention in Latin American affairs, frantically sought allies. The United States had convinced the other Latin American nations to condemn the Communist regime in Cuba. The major European nations continued their historical respect for the U.S.-enforced, 140-year-old Monroe Doctrine and refrained from any interference. This left only Russia, which was keen to obtain a loyal ally ninety miles from the U.S. mainland.

Russia overplayed its advantage and began building nuclear missile launchers. This roused the American public and a confrontation between the United States and Russia ensued. America held the advantage, although Russia made nuclear war noises. A compromise was achieved. Russia withdrew its nuclear forces, the United States pledged not to invade. The Vietnam period followed and Cuba never became a major issue again.

Previously, the United States had done pretty much as it pleased whenever it saw its interests, however minor, threatened. The experience with Cuba changed its policy, because it was the first time that a Latin American country resisted the United States and succeeded. Although the outcome was not catastrophic for American interests, it is unlikely that an American government will ever be able to interfere in Latin American nations' internal affairs with the degree of freedom it had before Cuba. Not only was war avoided in Cuba, but the likelihood of future wars and military interventions was reduced.

French Civil War—1958 to 1963

The rebels, though determined and violent, were unable to generate support from a war-weary population.

France came out of World War II both a winner and a loser. From 1940 to 1944, France was occupied by German armed forces and suffered from the effects of extensive fighting in 1940 and '44 as well a bombing campaign between 1942 and '44. Many French citizens collaborated with the Germans during the occupation, an issue which continued to divide the French after the war. Also, the economy was damaged by the war and subsequent revolts in the colonies. The colonial rebellions dragged on and, one by one, succeeded.

The last major colony to go, Algeria, caused the most disruption. Algeria was actually considered a part of France rather than a colony and contained a large ethnic French population. Algeria also contained a majority Arab population that wanted independence. To further complicate matters, Algeria was home to the French Foreign Legion, the French Army's hope for redeeming a reputation that had suffered mostly defeat and humiliation from 1940 through the late 1950s.

The political divisions between those who favored decolonizing and military unrest and those who did not brought France to the brink of civil war. In the early 1960s, extremists who wanted to keep Algeria French caused military rebellions and terrorism against the French government. The dissent was finally put down by granting Algeria independence and disbanding several mutinous Foreign Legion and parachute units. This was as close as France had come to a military coup in nearly a hundred years. But the conscripts had transistor radios, so they knew that the coup did not have wide support, which dampened their enthusiasm for its continuance.

In the end, most of the rebellious spirit was contained within a minority of the population and the professional military. This time the majority had its way.

Russia and China—1958 to the present

Chinese patience and Russian inability to risk a conventional or nuclear solution provide a tenuous peace.

Russia and China have never been friendly and have rarely had any reason to be. From 1860 to 1904, Russia grabbed Chinese lands. Russia was brought up short in 1904 when it confronted Japan's efforts to grab Chinese territory. Russia lost the war with Japan, and a large portion of the Chinese territory it had seized. Russia was able to hold on to China's former northeastern Pacific coast territory, and China still insists that these lands must be returned.

While enduring revolution and civil disorder during the late 1800s, China deeply resented the incursions of Japan and European nations. Eventually, all of these land grabs were reversed, except for the Russian ones.

Relations between Russia and China have taken several strange turns during the past eighty years. While China was torn by civil war during the 1920s and '30s, Russia backed both Communist and non-Communist factions, another example of Russia's pragmatic, Byzantine style of diplomacy. Russia during this time was the self-proclaimed head of the international Communist movement. During World War II, Russia was neutral toward Japan until a week before Japan surrendered. At that point Russia launched a massive invasion of northern China. Russian forces then aided the Communist faction in the final stages of the hundred-year-old Chinese civil war. Once a Chinese Communist government was established, Russia pledged support.

But the Chinese made the largest contribution to the partnership by saving Russia's position in North Korea. In 1950, Russia urged and supported Communist North Korea in its invasion of American-supported South Korea. The invasion failed and North Korean forces were chased north to the Chinese border. Russia then supported China's intervention, which went on for three years and caused over half a million Chinese casualties. Russia supplied only weapons, equipment and supplies. This caused some bad feelings between China and Russia, particularly since Russia kept political and diplomatic dominance over North Korea.

By the late 1950s, the ancient distrust between Russia and China resurfaced and resulted in a diplomatic break. A large element in this mistrust was Russia's dragging its heels in giving China the technology needed to build atomic weapons. China developed nuclear weapons on its own, and set off its first nuclear explosion in 1964. During the following ten years Russia proceeded to build up its armed forces on the Chinese border. There were several armed clashes between border troops, including skirmishes in 1969.

In the 1970s, China reestablished relations with the United States. Shortly thereafter the Chinese government moved away from orthodox Communist practices toward more efficient, and capitalistic, economic policies.

Under the best diplomatic conditions, relations between Russia and China would not be cordial. Russia is still the nation that seized ancient Chinese territory in the 1800s and is the most powerful neighbor of China. On the other side, Russia harbors a long-standing fear of the oriental peoples. From the 1200s to the 1400s, Russia was dominated by Asiatic nomads. Although this period ended over five hundred years ago, it is not forgotten. Russians can count and they know that China has a much larger population and has never accepted Russian annexation of Chinese territory. Generally unknown to Westerners is the racism of the Russian people, and the Russian government, toward Orientals. Fear and loathing are not the sort of attitudes upon which to build peaceful relations.

Russia is unlikely to give up its far eastern territories, not just because they contain considerable natural resources and give Russia access to the Pacific, but also because Russia does not give back what it has taken unless it has to.

China, in turn, has several reasons for wanting these territories back. The natural resources are much needed. The underpopulated territory is needed by the ever-expanding Chinese population. Finally, there is the security problem. Russia maintains the largest and most powerful military force that China faces on its borders. Russia's historical propensity for grabbing additional territory at any opportunity troubles the Chinese. The Russians could decide to annex more Chinese territory.

Russia has several options on China. It can ignore Chinese pleas for the return of Chinese territory and simply declare the current territorial situation to be permanent. However, China can be expected to keep up diplomatic pressure and to support any separatist movements that might arise, or be stirred up, among Russia's oriental populations. If the opportunity presented itself, China would simply march in and retake the far eastern territories. From the Russian point of view, the most likely opportunity would be during a war between NATO and the Warsaw Pact nations. This realization keeps Russia quite interested in European peace.

What prevents China from simply marching into the sparsely populated far eastern territories are the Russian nuclear weapons in the area. The Chinese are remarkably vulnerable to nuclear attack, because 90 percent of the people live on 10 percent of the land. Imagine a few dozen nuclear weapons exploded on the ground. The fallout would kill hundreds of millions of Chinese. For the Russians, nuclear weapons used to be a very effective, and economical, method of keeping China at bay. However, once China developed nuclear weapons on its own in 1964, the Russians also lived in terror of a "nuclear solution" to disputes along the Chinese border. Even if China could not "kill" Russia with nuclear weapons, they could tear off an arm or a leg.

Russia is said to have seriously considered making a nuclear strike on China's nuclear facilities in western China and Chinese military forces in northern China when the Chinese nuclear program was still in its infancy. There are reports that the Russians approached the United States during the late 1960s, asking if America would oppose a Russian first-strike against the Chinese nuclear testing and weapons manufacturing facilities. The United States government, according to intimations in Henry Kissinger's memoirs, was quite upset, and told the Russians not to try it. Fear of unpredictable repercussions from the United States and the rest of the world, not to mention the Chinese, stopped them. Here is a case of nuclear weapons being the potential cause of a nuclear war, as well as contributing to its prevention.

However, the potential for war between Russia and China remains as long as Russia holds on to its far eastern territories.

One can confidently maintain that there will be a war between Russia and China. One cannot accurately predict just when.

United States and China—1953 to 1975

Fear of repeating the deadly stalemate of the 1950–53 Korean War, plus the involvement in Vietnam, caused the United States to take a more diplomatic approach to the "Chinese problem."

The United States had had a trade and immigration relationship with China since the 1800s. Along with the major European powers, the United States sought special privileges in their China trade. Although America's trade relations with China were not as brutal as many other nations', the

United States gained a certain amount of ill will in China because of racism toward Chinese immigrants to the United States.

Chinese immigrants and racism play a large, and often unrecognized, role in other nations' relationships with China. China has the oldest continually functioning civilization. This long tenure has given the Chinese an attitude of superiority toward other cultures.

For many centuries, Chinese have emigrated to other nations. In most places, they have not assimilated completely, America being one of the few exceptions. Intermarriage is rare and continued contacts with China are common. The "overseas Chinese" have considered themselves still a part of China. The Chinese government has likewise considered these ethnic Chinese, despite their citizenship in a foreign nation, to remain part of the Chinese society. As some Chinese officials put it, "Our daughters are living with their overseas husbands." The "overseas husbands" are sometimes cruel to their Chinese immigrants, who often return to China.

The Chinese liked the fact that the United States is a nation of migrants. Once U.S. racism toward Chinese abated and immigration rules toward Chinese were liberalized in the 1930s, American relationships with China became warmer. China was wracked by revolution, civil war and general chaos, and the United States became one of the several models that reformers wished to impose on it. The other model was communism. The Chinese Communists, because of better organization, greater ruthlessness, less corruption and significant support from Russia, prevailed over the American-influenced groups.

In 1949, after a century of unrest and warfare, the Communists consolidated their control of China. The remnants of the American-backed faction fled to the island of Taiwan. The United States refused to recognize the new regime. Symbolic of American actions was the refusal by Secretary of State Dulles to shake hands with Chinese Premier Chou En-lai. Chou never forgot this, even years later when he pushed détente with the United States, in the 1970s. A little diplomatic discretion would have made later relations much easier.

By 1950, China and the United States were at war in Korea. In three years of combat, China suffered over a million casualties, the United States suffered less than one sixth as many. Twelve years later, during the mid-1960s, the United States was again deeply involved in an Asian war. The Vietnam conflict was heavily subsidized by Russia and China, just as they had supported North Korea in its attempt to seize South Korea. Potential war with China heavily influenced American actions in Vietnam.

Learning from Chinese experience in Korea, Communist Vietnamese forces avoided engaging American forces in conventional combat. Instead, the takeover war in Vietnam was fought on a lower level, generally using guerrilla forces and avoiding the concentrated forms of combat where American firepower would prevail. The Communists took advantage of an important geographical difference between Korea and Vietnam. Korea was a peninsula, making it difficult for the Communists to infiltrate men and supplies into the non-Communist territories. Vietnam had much more extensive land borders, mostly covered by jungles and hills. The Ho Chi Minh Trail was a critical factor in the Communist success.

There were many similarities between the Korean and Vietnam conflicts. Both nations were divided into Communist and non-Communist areas. In both cases the Communists used guerrilla war in the non-Communist portions. In both cases, the Communist governments and guerrillas received support from Russia and China. In Korea, the Communists attempted a conventional military invasion and failed. It was not attempted in Vietnam because the United States had demonstrated in Korea a willingness and ability to defeat a conventional invasion. What was also shown in Korea was an American reluctance to confront Chinese combat units again. This created a set of "rules" in Vietnam whereby China kept its military units out of the fighting as long as America kept its ground forces out of North Vietnam and did not otherwise attack Chinese territory.

Meanwhile, there was Taiwan. Until Vietnam became the focus of American efforts in the Far East, there was a precarious situation on the island to which the non-Communist Chinese factions had fled. The island was fortified by the Chinese Nationalists and the United States assisted in providing weapons and equipment. Also important was the presence of the American Navy between Taiwan and the Chinese mainland. Up to 1962, China continually made serious moves toward invading Taiwan and thus eliminate the last Chinese resistance to the Communist government. The Taiwanese Chinese had built up a formidable ground and air force, making any successful landing extremely expensive. The Chinese Communists had no navy to speak of, so as long as American naval units steamed off Taiwan, an invasion attempt was unlikely.

Chinese attention shifted away from Taiwan and toward Vietnam during the 1960s. This in spite of continued, although diminishing, Taiwanese support for resistance activities on the mainland. In Vietnam the Chinese finally won a victory of sorts over the United States after losing out in Korea and Taiwan. The victory was somewhat meaningless, as China was undergoing another internal battle between two factions within the Communist Party. The radical faction of the Communists was defeated by the moderates. The radicals had supported bad relations with America, primarily on ideological grounds. Despite America's long history of relatively good relations with China, the United States was still perceived as a capitalist nation and therefore a "class enemy" of all orthodox Communists. This attitude was fostered by the Russian Communists, who wanted China isolated from other major power allies. China needed allies with high technology to help it rebuild its economy. The cost of the Korean War, the break with Russia in the late 1950s and the chaos caused by the radicals brought the economy to the brink of disaster in the late 1960s. This set the stage for the reestablishment of friendly relations between the United States and China.

The moderate Communists were still Communists. But they were realists and knew that conditions had changed considerably since 1949. China had come to tolerate the presence of Taiwan. Also, the moderates were aware that the capitalistic Chinese on Taiwan had produced a robust economy. Japan, another capitalist nation, which had suffered relatively greater destruction than China during World War II, was also enjoying splendid economic growth.

Peace in Vietnam, even if on Communist terms, had eliminated the cause which had brought the Vietnamese and Chinese into an unnatural alliance. Vietnam and China had rarely, through the centuries, been at peace. By 1979, Chinese and Vietnamese troops were shooting at each other. Although the fighting was restricted to sporadic border clashes, it showed a reestablishment of the normal state of relations between China and Vietnam. The new hostilities between China and Vietnam were partially instigated by Russian activities. Russia was now Vietnam's principal ally. Thus China was threatened by Russia in the south as well as the north. The Russians now had major naval bases in Vietnam. China was still without a significant navy.

It should be no surprise that the long period of bad feelings between the United States and China came to an end in the 1970s. The alliances reflected a more normal state of affairs. China's traditional enemies, Russia and Vietnam, were now somewhat counterbalanced by China's traditional allies, major foreign powers that did not share a border with China—not just the United States, but also the Western European nations. Japan and South Korea, usually compliant vassal states, became friendly trading partners.

It is unlikely that the United States will find itself in a state of hostilities with China again in the near future because the United States is a natural counterbalance to the Russians.

China and Vietnam—1975 to the present

Problems with the Chinese Army and fear of Russian retaliation, plus combat-seasoned Vietnamese troops, keep an imperfect peace.

China and Vietnam have had a hate-hate relationship for over two thousand years. Until about a thousand years ago, Tonkin (more recently known as North Vietnam) was part of China. It was a very rebellious part of China and eventually the Chinese gave up and only insisted that it behave itself toward China. This it did, in between Chinese invasions.

Once liberated from Chinese domination, Tonkin became Annam and conquered its ethnic cousins in the southern part of what is now Vietnam. The two parts of Vietnam were actually quite different countries. They were separated by mountainous highlands, with travel between them primarily by sea. Moreover, the southern region was more influenced by travelers from India, Indonesia and Cambodia. After about five hundred years of effort, the two areas were more or less merged. But that wasn't the end of the warfare in the area. The Cambodians laid claim to portions of the southern region. Laos was largely a backwater anyone could claim. Burma and Thailand were not really part of all this strife, being separated from Vietnam/China/Cambodia by geography and a tendency to look westward toward India.

Civil war and turmoil were a long-established way of life in the area when, in the late 1700s, French ships appeared and offered assistance to whichever local leader would present the best terms. Within a hundred years France had seized direct control of all Vietnam as well as Cambodia. China, meanwhile, was lurching through transition from a medieval to modern society.

In 1975, for the first time in over a hundred years, China and Vietnam were able to view each other without regard to foreign influences. They promptly went to war over border disputes and mistreatment of Chinese living in Vietnam. There was also the matter of Vietnam invading Cambodia and replacing a Chinese-supported government with a Vietnamese-supported group. The opening move was by the Chinese, and their invasion force was quickly repulsed.

Don't expect to see peace in Vietnam any time soon. The normal state is war. The South Vietnamese still prefer to be separate from the North Vietnamese. The Cambodians don't like any Vietnamese. At the moment, the only things keeping Chinese armies out of Vietnam are a lack of surplus wealth to squander on such an enterprise and the presence of Russian forces in Vietnam and on China's northern border. Meanwhile, several hundred thousand troops glare, and occasionally shoot, at each other across the border.

Yugoslavia and the Balkans—1945 to the present

Tito and his legacy are all that prevent another round of fighting in the region.

Before we had unrest in the Persian Gulf and the Middle East to worry about, there were the Balkans. They were at war for over a thousand years. The Balkan region has been a frontier for most of its history. In ancient times, it was the frontier between the civilized world and the barbarians. Then for five hundred years, until the early years of this century, it was the strife-torn border between Christian Europe and the Moslem Turkish Empire. Despite the Turks' best efforts, the area remained largely Christian.

The mountainous Balkans have been a homeland for many different ethnic groups. Most of these groups are Slavic, although Romania, Greece and Albania still contain strong strains of the ancient peoples who dominated the area until the 800s. A diversity of languages and cultures has created vengeful warfare.

The Turks seldom attempted to assimilate local populations during their long tenure, which began in the 1400s. Thus the Slavs gave the Balkan region its cultural identity. For five centuries the area had Turkish government, European culture and a tendency to look toward Russia, the Slavic big brother, as a savior.

The unrest in the Balkans led to the start of World War I in 1914. But that wasn't the end of it, nor the beginning. The Balkans had been a primary battleground between European and Turkish armies for over five hundred years. As the Turkish Empire went into decline, different ethnic groups in the Balkans organized themselves into nationalities and rebelled. In the early 1900s these rebellions succeeded on a large scale. The Turks were just about driven out of Europe. The new Balkan nations then fell upon each other and began a series of conflicts that led to World War I.

Things settled down, sort of, between 1918 and 1939. There were no major wars. Just minor disturbances, some civil disorders and revolutionary activity. The major national entities that came out of all this violence were Bulgaria, Romania, Albania and Greece, which were fairly homogeneous and stable nations. The big problem was the checkerboard of lesser states that comprised the artificial entity known as Yugoslavia. Serbia and Croatia are the principal components of Yugoslavia, with several smaller provinces thrown in just to make matters hopeless. Not only did the provinces of Yugoslavia have a number of ancient internal antagonisms, they also had serious territorial disputes with their neighbors. On top of the ethnic disagreements, there were deadly divisions on whether Yugoslavia should be a kingdom or a republic. Before things could come completely apart, a German army entered Yugoslavia. After five years of serious economic and population losses, Yugoslavia emerged as a Communist dictatorship, under the firm and unifying leadership of Josip Tito. If Tito hadn't existed, he would have had to be invented for Yugoslavia to exist. The ethnic problems remained, and still do. However, Russia has become a serious threat to Yugoslav independence and this has played a large role in keeping the various minorities from tearing each other, and Yugoslavia, apart.

Yugoslavia has all the potential for a vicious civil war. The neighboring states have incentives to intervene. Russia has shown persistent interest, over the last forty years, in taking greater control over Yugoslavia's internal affairs. When enough Yugoslavs forget the past horrors of internal disorder and lose their restraint, the natural instabilities of the nation will do the rest.

Britain and Spain—1815 to the present

Both sides have been extremely diplomatic, and Britain has always carried a bigger stick.

In 1713 the Spanish Empire was carved up. Britain was recognized as the owner of Gibraltar, a small patch of territory that stood on one side of the straits between the Atlantic and the Mediterranean. For a hundred years there were intermittent military attempts by Spain to get Gibraltar back. Britain held on. After 1815, there were no more military attempts, although much ink and rhetoric were spilled over the issue. Part of the reason for such a pacific attitude on the part of Spain was Britain's military superiority. Particularly at sea, Britain had the armed might to hold on to Gibraltar. There is an even more compelling explanation for the lack of bloodshed over an issue (a territorial dispute) that has caused warfare elsewhere—the economic ties between the nations. Spain will most likely eventually get Gibraltar back, without a war.

Syria and Turkey—1920 to the present

The Turks hold the moral high ground, as well as a significantly mightier army.

Some territories retained by Turkey in the breakup of the Turk Empire, are still in dispute. The most contested one is Alexandretta, in southeast Turkey on the Mediterranean coast. The population voted to stay with Turkey, but Syria maintains its claim. Given the warlike attitude of the Syrians, they might be tempted to take on the Turks if conditions seemed suitable. Peace has prevailed because Turkey is so much stronger militarily.

Kurdistan—1920 to the present

The Kurds are not united, their opponents are stronger. Civil disorder persists.

Several million Kurds spread over Turkey, Iraq and Iran would prefer to rule themselves. Possessing a relatively primitive tribal structure, they have so far been unable to pull it off. With outside assistance from, say, Russia, they might succeed. This situation is mentioned only because Russia has considerable incentives to support such a "war of national liberation." The main purpose would not be to foster Kurdish nationalism, but to weaken Turkey, Iran and Iraq. Whenever Russia finds it useful to have all three of these nations on the ropes at the same time, it will be sorely tempted to get behind the Kurds. The Kurds have been more encouraged since the collapse of the Turkish Empire in 1920, not only by the departure of the feared Turks, but because of the willingness of the nations containing Kurdish populations to support the rebellion of Kurds in neighboring nations.

Baluchistan—1948 to the present

Baluchi opponents are stronger, and many Baluchis have been distracted by employment opportunities in the Persian Gulf.

Several million Baluchis are spread over Pakistan, Afghanistan and Iran. Despite their primitive tribal government, they have managed to obtain some autonomy in the past. Russia and India have incentives to support a "war of national liberation." The main purpose would not be to foster Baluchi nationalism, but to weaken Pakistan, Afghanistan and Iran. Russia's current involvement in Afghanistan, and antagonism with Pakistan and Iran, might bring the Baluchis support in the near future. India is primarily interested in seeing Pakistan go to pieces. Ever since Britain left India, resulting in the separate nations of India and Pakistan, the Baluchis have been deprived of much hope for independence. They have been more patient than the Kurds, but have the same desire for independence.

Iran and Afghanistan—1945 to the present

Afghanistan got close to Russia for protection and Iran self-destructed several times. The potential is still there.

These two nations have been at war periodically for several thousand years. Their lack of activity in this century can be attributed to superpower intervention. Both nations have fallen under the influence, and sometimes outright control, of superpower nations. While this has prevented wars between the two nations, it has led to the Russian occupation of Afghanistan. Iran threw off American influence in 1979 and promptly found itself at war with its neighbor Iraq. As long as Russian troops occupy Afghanistan, it is unlikely that there will be any fighting between Iran and Afghanistan. Again, the ability of the superpowers to keep the peace among their clients is demonstrated, even if it does involve attacking one of the clients.

Egypt and Sudan—1945 to the present

Egypt was distracted by Israel, leaving it unable to pursue traditional imperial ambitions to the south.

This is another rivalry going back thousands of years. Egypt has been kept out of Sudan of late because of pressing domestic problems. Whenever things calm down internally, Egypt thinks of expanding to the south. Sometimes this has been a necessity, as when Sudanese soldiers or bandits raid Egypt. Severe internal problems within Sudan have made this less likely in the past century. The history of violence between these two nations goes back a long way and is unlikely to completely disappear.

Could These Wars Have Been Stopped?

"What If?" games are illuminating.

Situations that develop over decades or centuries are not going to be eliminated overnight. However, when you break the situation down to its smallest parts, you do find many opportunities to calm things down. It's the attention to detail that prevents wars. Through revealing those details, we will demonstrate how past wars could have been avoided, or at least delayed. Peace, given a chance, will outlast war. But first you have to defuse those crises that spark wars. If too many things heat up at once, you have a war.

WORLD WAR I IN EUROPE

Many of history's worst conflicts came very close to *not* happening. For example, World War I might have been avoided if Germany had not taken two French provinces in 1871. There might still have been a series of bloody revolutions and civil wars as the Turkish and Austro-Hungarian empires broke up, but there was no reason for France, Britain and Germany to fight a major war over the demise of these empires. These nations had already been involved in several smaller, and equally futile, wars with each other over the same issues. There was ample opportunity to avoid a major bloodbath.

Consider the specific tensions that brought about World War I.

First. Germany had defeated France in 1871 and taken two provinces along the Rhine River. Being defeated was one thing, losing real estate was unforgivable. War with Germany was a constant theme in French politics. Still, France had excellent grounds for avoiding war with its powerful neighbors. France had been defeated by Germany twice in the previous hundred years and faced German armed forces that were stronger than ever.

Second. Germany, now united for the first time in eleven hundred years, grew into an economic and military superpower. The large German fleet began to alarm the British, who traditionally had stayed aloof from continental European rivalries. No two nations in Europe could match Germany militarily. German power made everyone nervous. But the tensions need not have started a war, for the monarchs of Britain, Germany and Russia were related, Germany and Britain had many trade and commercial relationships and Germany's booming economy was only possible because of substantial trade with other European nations. Germany had the most to lose by going to war.

Third. The Austro-Hungarian Empire was coming apart. Germany was willing to use military force to try to keep it together. Germany proved this by going to Austria's aid when Russia declared war on it. Had Germany instead counseled Austria to just sell the revolution-wracked Balkans to the Russians, the probability of World War I would have been reduced.

Fourth. The Turkish Empire was breaking up and the European powers were shopping around for the pieces, particularly in the Balkans. Since the 1400s, Europe had had to accept Turkish domination of the Balkans, the eastern Mediterranean and most of the North African coast. But, as all empires are prone to do, the Turkish hegemony went into decline. The Turks lost their empire to three deadly enemies: revolution, misrule and the Russians. They fought wars with many other powers, including the Austro-Hungarians and the Iranians. But internal revolution cost them the largest number of losses, and Russia was the second most frequent cause of lost territory. The other European powers were reluctant to see Russia take too much of the Turkish lands, particularly Istanbul. This would allow Russia free access to the Mediterranean, which would give the European naval powers another unwanted competitor. By and large, European nations wanted the Turks out of Europe and out of the empire business. This is what eventually happened, speeded up a bit by World War I. But in the early 1900s there was a very heated situation in the Balkans, where

Turkish, Austro-Hungarian, Italian and Russian influences mixed in with the aspirations of the local inhabitants. The locals wanted independence, while the other powers wanted a piece of the action.

During the first twelve years of this century Turkey lost nearly all of its European territories to rebellion or war. These disturbances created one more excuse for the major powers to go to war with each other. Without the squabbles over who should have what part of the Turkish Empire, Russia and Austria would have been much less likely to trigger the war.

Fifth. Russia's czarist government thought foreign adventures would divert attention from its serious internal problems. The chance of war would have diminished had Russia realized that foreign adventures were the last thing it needed. A weak government does not survive the stress of war. Russia's participation, and defeat, in the Russo-Japanese War (1904–5) had nearly brought down the government. Revolts in 1905 were particularly dangerous. By 1914 things had calmed down enough to give Russians the illusion that their current form of government could survive a war. The result was Russia enduring over thirty years of nearly constant warfare and internal violence.

Sixth. By 1914, a series of interlocking mutual defense treaties had been created. The nature of the major armies and their plans for entering war made the declaration of war an irreversible decision. Once the armies were ordered to mobilize, a slow-motion avalanche began. The participants could only watch in horror as all they owned was crushed by carefully preplanned troop movements and war plans.

These diplomatic time bombs were largely the work of France as part of her campaign to recover lost provinces from Germany and avenge the 1871 humiliation. In order for World War I to occur as it did, some unusual alliances had to be forged. Except for France, none of the European powers was particularly interested in getting into a major war with any of its peers. None of these mutual-aid treaties was made with the idea that they would likely be used. Certainly these treaties would have been avoided had all participants known that their interlocking nature would involve all of the major powers in any war.

The armed forces of the major powers had prepared detailed war plans. Few payed attention to what would happen when these rigid, complex and largely unstoppable schemes were put into action. A key component was nearly automatic execution if one or more neighbors even appeared to be executing their own war plans. These mobilization systems were the primary "strategic weapons" of the era. Once the plans were put into motion, millions of reservists were called up from civilian life, armed, organized and sent forward along with the regular forces into battle. Any deviation or attempt to halt the process would throw the forces into chaos. When the Kaiser had misgivings about what he was getting Germany into he instructed his generals to halt the mobilization. When he was informed that that was impossible without putting Germany at a grave disadvantage, he began to realize the enormity of the situation. Unfortunately, few people in power during 1914 realized what a hair trigger their armed forces had.

Seventh. The European military leaders did not understand how much the advances in technology during the 1800s had changed warfare, although several conflicts gave ample warning. In the forty years since the Franco-Prussian War of 1870 alone, enormous and significant changes had occurred. Warfare was now more drawn out and destructive. Two developments made this possible.

In the first place, the enormous wealth generated by the industrialization of the 1800s gave governments the resources to create vast reserve armies. These armies consisted largely of civilians that had previously been conscripted for two years of service and then released. Their training was kept current and their equipment maintained. When war was declared, the reserves were called to active duty according to carefully formulated mobilization plans. As a result, armies of millions of adequately trained, equipped and led troops were available on a few weeks' notice.

The second major development was the invention of the machine gun and rapid-fire artillery. These weapons were radical not just because of their increased firepower, but because a small force could now successfully hold a length of battle frontage against enemy attack. A hundred men with a dozen machine guns could effectively cover a kilometer of front. A million men with ten thousand machine guns were nearly invincible. For the first time in European history, two armies would face each other from nearly impregnable positions stretching from the Alps to the English Channel. Stalemate. Millions would die trying to break this unforeseen deadlock. No one imagined it could be this bad. It was another case of ignorance being a primary cause of a war.

In 1909 a Polish banker had published a book explaining with uncanny precision how modern technology would make warfare a great slaughter and much more costly. Few soldiers believed him. Had enough commanders appreciated these implications, and passed their findings on to the politicians, there might have been a bit more restraint. There is always that moment, as the final decision to declare war is being made, when one more reason can be found to hold back. A more accurate view of what was really going to happen would have given everyone pause, and perhaps peace.

Eighth. The desire to fight. Much of the pre-1914 military activity was driven by desire for combat. The French "elan of war" concept pushed the idea that the offensive was glorious, and that the French were too noble to retreat or fight defensive wars. The Germans wanted to capture glory for Deutschland by beating the French and Russians. As perverse as these attitudes sound, they crop up frequently in history.

Eight contributing causes to the start of World War I. Had any one been absent, the war might not have occurred, or it might have been delayed or less destructive, or it might not have led to the even more destructive World War II. As we know from everyday life, most human events, particularly the complex ones involving many people, do not have a single cause. There are multiple reasons for events, each having a different source and texture. There is rarely a single cause for a war. More often there is a web of causes. The participants become ensnared in a disaster of many sources, and of their own construction. If you can eliminate or weaken one or more of the reasons for fighting, the complex of causes will collapse like a house of cards. Remember, the trend is generally toward peace, not war.

A frequent flaw in attempts to make peace has been focusing on a single potential cause and a desire for short-term results. More success is gained by addressing the wide range of causes and by thinking in the long term. World War II and its aftereffect wars in Korea, Vietnam and the Middle East have taught this lesson.

WORLD WAR II IN EUROPE

The traditional theory still holds up: Early opposition to German aggression would have prevented the war or at least greatly diminished Germany's initial military success.

The European portion of World War II was a direct result of Germany's defeat and dismemberment at the end of World War I. The Germans rebuilt their armed forces in direct violation of the 1918 Versailles peace treaty. German land grabs in the 1930s were initially encouraged by the reluctance of Western powers to confront such aggression. Through forceful diplomacy and military means, Germany proceeded to conquer most of the Western European nations piecemeal between 1938 and 1940. Anxious to avoid a two-front war while so engaged, Germany signed a peace treaty with Russia in 1939. After this phase, the Germans became overconfident and took on more than they could handle, invading Russia in 1941. Germany eventually lost the war, as German generals had initially predicted. Could this war have been avoided? Yes, but it looks easier in hindsight than it would have at the time.

There were some attempts to stop the Germans, but all of them failed, for good reasons. Germany's neighbors were so afraid of another war that they continually avoided armed resistance. Verbal protests had little effect on the Germans.

Fifty years later, it seems incomprehensible that the European democracies did not stop the Germans from grabbing other countries when they could have. The 1918 peace treaty severely limited Germany's armed forces, which gave the other European powers more than adequate military superiority. The problem was that, particularly in the democracies, the memories of the slaughter of World War I stayed the hand of politicians contemplating any military action that could again lead to general warfare.

Suppose France or Britain had sent troops to oppose Germany's initial aggressions. Would they have changed the popular appeal of these aggressions within Germany? Quite likely, as most Germans were not keen on another war, and many were opposed to the Nazis. Germany had plenty of economic and social problems at home, and military adventures were not going to help.

Actually the German General Staff advised holding off on aggressive action until 1945, when rearmament would be complete. Only Hitler wanted to go full speed ahead. This restraint would have created some curious situations. For one thing, Russia was continuing to arm itself at a fearful rate. Stalin had killed off much of Russia's military leadership in a bloody purge in the late 1930s. By 1945, new leadership would have been in place. France would have been no better off by 1945, but Britain would have completed a rearmament plan.

The most curious result of German restraint would have been the shifting of attention to the Pacific. Japan was already committed to war in China. Britain, France, Holland, Russia and the United States were leaning hard on Japan. In the absence of a war in Europe it's possible that this pressure could have forced Japan to withdraw from China.

Back in Europe, a more patient Hitler might have been deposed. Assassination plots against Hitler took place before 1939. Such plots would have continued, and might even have succeeded, after 1939, had Europe not plunged into war. As the German buildup continued, and the General Staff felt more confident, one of two things might have happened. Hitler might have been ousted, or he might have purged the German officer corps. Either way, Germany would have been less likely to go to war successfully.

The 1918 treaty, as it was implemented, would have caused further unrest no matter what anyone did. Just as the French never forgave the Germans for taking Alsace-Lorraine in 1871, so the Germans burned over the territories lost and penalties inflicted in 1918. World War I was a bad war and a worse peace. The best that could have been done after 1918 was to minimize the damage. This was not done, and the war that began in 1914 was finally resolved in a holocaust between 1939 and 1945. Although the verdict of 1945 was more final than that of 1918, all issues were not taken care of. We may yet see another chapter in the 1914–45 war.

All the blame for the growth of World War II from World War I wasn't on the German side. For example, compare how the United States reacted to the devastation of World War II—after 1945, the United States forgave most war debts and poured in financial assistance to rebuild a shattered Europe—with its actions after World War I: following 1918, the United States tried to collect huge war debts from its allies while they in turn extracted huge sums from a devastated Germany. These German reparations included a vast amount of railroad equipment, for example, which destroyed Germany's ability to recover economically. Russia also lay in ruins, ruled by a bloody-minded Communist regime. The United States refused to back France in forming any sort of long-term peacekeeping policy, a major reason why France declined to confront German rearmament and aggression. America was isolationist, so the European democracies could not depend on her for any assistance in restraining Germany. Sometimes you have to get involved, a lesson the United States didn't learn until World War II.

WORLD WAR II IN THE PACIFIC

Less complacency among Americans and European democracies would have lessened the damage, and possibly prevented the war. Never underestimate a cornered aggressor.

The Pacific arena of World War II was less preventable than the European. In the 1930s, Japan was dominated by a militaristic government, as it had been for over seven hundred years. Adoption of Western technology and ideas sixty years earlier had not changed its basic nature. In 1894, less than thirty years after abandoning its two-hundred-fifty-year policy of isolationism, Japan invaded China. This was a first for Japan, which had always feared invasions *from* China. But China was in decline and had been picked over by European powers for nearly a hundred years. Japan's modern army, modeled after Germany's, easily defeated China and obtained territorial and economic concessions.

Ten years later Japan went to war with, and defeated, Russia. Unlike the other European nations, Russia was not just seeking economic advantages in China but was actually annexing portions of the country. They ran into Japan and came out second best. The importance of its defeat is usually underestimated. Had Russia prevailed over Japan in 1905, Manchuria and Korea would have become part of Russia's far eastern territories. Had World War I still happened, Japan would have still tried to grab Russia's far eastern territories after Russia left World War I and lurched into civil war (1918–20). Japan might then have had more success in taking Manchuria and Korea than it actually did in grabbing eastern Siberia. But then, the popular enthusiasm for communism might have kept Manchuria and Korea part of the new Russian Communist empire. Another possibility might have been even shabbier Russian performance in World War I because of the need for garrisons in Manchuria and Korea. Whatever the case, a Russian victory over Japan in 1904 would have changed the wars in that part of the world for half a century or more.

Japan's involvement in China waned until the 1930s. Meanwhile the Japanese military used the excuse of economic and diplomatic problems to tighten its control over the government. Japan then started a program to build a "Greater East Asian Co-Prosperity Sphere," with Japan as the dominant economic power in East Asia. The plan was a threat to European and American economic interests. Where the Japanese could not make headway economically or diplomatically, they resorted to arms; after all, the government was being run by generals and admirals, not businessmen. (Only after 1945 did Japan discover that economic conflict was a safer and more profitable form of warfare.)

As with the Germans from 1939–41, early Japanese victories encouraged the military to think bigger. Again like the Germans, the Japanese overreached. But while the Germans had parity, or even superiority, in combat power through much of World War II, Japan was always inferior except for a few months early in the war. America's vastly superior economic and military power soon made itself felt. Errors caused by optimism put the Japanese on the defensive within a year of their initial surprise attacks.

Most Japanese commanders had a blind faith in their country's capabilities, unusual for professional military establishments. Japan had never been defeated in its more than thousand-year history, and Westerners, largely unaware of this, did not realize that this faith had nothing to do with reality. This was a fatal misunderstanding.

There was an inevitability about the fighting in the Pacific. The Japanese military government was deeply committed to the conquest of China and the local lands held by European powers. The success of its ally Germany in the European fighting encouraged the Japanese. It is unlikely that anything short of military force would have removed them from China. And only overwhelming military force could have given civilian politicians in Japan a chance at regaining power.

Without Nazi Germany to keep the European nations occupied, Japan would have had to back down. The reasons were twofold. The Allies were unlikely to allow Japan to continue its aggressive behavior. They controlled the oil Japan needed and provided the bulk of Japan's export markets and sources of modern technology. Militarily, the Allies had an enormous advantage, especially after they were no longer fighting Germany in Europe. Had there been no war in the Pacific, there might have been civil disorder and war within Japan, but it would have cost much less than World War II.

THE KOREAN CONFLICT

The three major wars after World War II resulted directly from it. The "aftereffect" wars, Korea, Vietnam and the Arab-Israeli conflicts, were all preventable to various degrees.

The presence of American troops, or an unequivocal statement of United States support, would have made the Korean conflict much less likely. Korea was a classic case of misinterpretation and overconfidence. The war between 1950 and 1953 could have easily been avoided.

In 1945 Korea was partitioned, with a Russian-dominated Communist government in the north and an American-supported non-Communist government in the south. This came about because of Russia's entry into the Pacific war a week before Japan surrendered. United States forces made no particular rush to occupy Korea. The Russians did, gaining control of the northern half of the country. They installed a Communist government and began sending agents south to agitate for unification of the country under a Communist regime. During the late 1940s, the United States was demobilizing and attempting to get back to its normal position of indifference toward foreign affairs. North Korea saw American withdrawal from South Korea as an opportunity to speed up the unification of Korea. With Russian support, the North Korean Army invaded South Korea in 1950. The Communists had misjudged American attitudes, for the United States immediately came to South Korea's aid. Even the entry of Communist China into the conflict a few months later did not lessen American resolve. The outcome of the war was to return the situation to where it was before the war.

The United States was a passive diplomatic player before the Korean War, and did not recognize its position as protector of South Korea. America underestimated the aggressiveness and goals of the Communist nations. Worse yet, through ignorance and neglect, the United States excluded Korea from its "sphere of interest" when such things were discussed with Russia before World War II ended. In effect, the United States invited the Russians, Chinese and Koreans to take their pick. America had power, but not the understanding of how to use it best.

The Communists were guilty of aggression, but the United States was guilty of not seeing the danger and taking steps to avert it. Had United States forces swept through all of Korea in 1945, or had the United States maintained a token force in South Korea, the war would have been avoided.

THE VIETNAM WAR

If France and the United States had stayed out of the Vietnamese civil war, the fighting would have been substantially reduced.

The underlying cause of most wars since 1945 has been the breakup of the European colonial empires. These empires were the result of European military and commercial superiority plus a dash of national pride. The colonies ranged from tribal societies with no concept of nationhood to states with more ancient pedigrees than the European countries that conquered them. The whole colonial business was doomed from the start. The European powers made mighty efforts to impose European culture on colonial peoples, but created only a thin veneer of locals indoctrinated and trained in European culture and administration. Moreover, these European-influenced locals usually had much contempt for the West. Backed by the military and commercial power of the colonial powers, the local European clones attempted to make their power permanent. However, throughout the 1800s and early 1900s there was an endless series of revolutions and civil disorders as the local cultures continually rejected these alien influences.

After 1945, two conditions led to the rapid abandonment of the colonies. The principal cause was that the empires were too expensive. Their original justification, the official one, that is, was to provide markets for European manufacturers and sources of raw materials. This was never successfully realized. The expense of maintaining colonial governments and overseas army and naval forces was more than European governments ravaged by World War II could afford.

The second force tearing down the empires was the experience of many of the colonial peoples during the chaos of the war. In the Pacific, Japan seized most European colonies and, although they made noises about local autonomy, basically replaced European occupation forces with Japanese troops. The colonies saw several interesting things happen. Previously invincible European troops were defeated by a non-European army. Then it was found that partisan warfare against the Japanese forces was succeeding. Moreover, the former colonial masters often supported the partisans. The Americans, in particular, made no secret of their belief that the colonial era was over. After all, the United States had already granted independence to the Philippines before the Japanese invaded. So when the Japanese surrendered in 1945, the colonial peoples of the Pacific asserted their independence. Soon, however, some of the European nations attempted to reclaim their wayward colonies. In most cases, the colonies resisted and soon achieved their freedom. Vietnam, for a number of reasons, was a much more drawn out and painful experience for all concerned.

Vietnam had been a French colony for a hundred years when, in 1940, the Japanese announced that they were, as allies of the Germans who had just overrun France, taking charge. The changeover was relatively bloodless, the local French officials following the lead of their superiors back home and collaborating with the conquerors.

There had been some resistance to the French before the Japanese came, mostly organized by the tiny Vietnamese Communist Party. Once Britain and the United States entered the war against Japan in 1941, they provided aid to anyone who would actively resist the Japanese. Thus began America's long relationship with Vietnamese Communists.

While the Vietnamese Communists were taking their cues from Moscow, they were primarily Vietnamese patriots. They looked to Russia only because it was the only major power actively supporting anticolonial activity.

The American agents who went into Vietnam during World War II to assist the resistance got along well with the Vietnamese Communists. The Vietnamese actually preferred American aid over Russian, not just because American aid was more abundant and of higher quality, but also because the United States had a magical reputation as the land where people could be free. President Roosevelt was known to be against colonialism and was planning to bar the French from reentering Vietnam after the war. The Vietnamese also knew that the United States had made and kept pledges to liberate its own colony, the Philippines.

When the Japanese surrendered in late 1945, the prospects for cordial relations between Vietnam and the United States looked bright. But Roosevelt had died earlier in the year and with him went America's willingness to block the French from returning to Vietnam to reclaim their rebellious colony. This was one of the most expensive diplomatic errors in American political history. The French came ashore in Vietnam with guns blazing. The resistance that began against the Japanese simply switched targets and continued until, in 1954, the French decided to get out. The French were not completely beaten. They just saw no more point in the endless fighting and ruinous losses. But substantial segments of the Vietnamese population either did not get along with the Communists or feared for their lives because they had aided the French attempt to reclaim Vietnam. Thus Vietnam was partitioned, with a Communist north and non-Communist, nominally democratic, south. South Vietnam was less democratic than it was divided, while North Vietnam was unified with a harsh Communist discipline. While South Vietnam was trying to deal with its many factions, the North was plotting to reunify the country on its own terms. Enter the Americans.

The United States, still fighting in Korea, had refused to give the French active military aid during the early 1950s, although they had paid for most of their military expenses. By the early 1960s, the United States was less war weary and much was being made of a Communist threat in Vietnam. But Vietnam had become essentially a civil war, one of many in

Vietnamese history. What was unusual was Vietnam obtaining aid from China, normally its mortal enemy. This shows how powerful a force nationalism is.

The North Vietnamese transferred hatred for the French to the Americans. Not all Vietnamese believed the Americans had the same imperialist motives as the French. But as American military involvement increased, it was easy to dislike the source of all the death and destruction.

The northerners never quit, the southerners never united and the United States finally got tired of a frustrating situation and left. Vietnam was unified by the northerners and soon thereafter was fighting Chinese troops on the border. At the same time, Vietnamese armies invaded most of its neighbors. Things were back to normal, as they had been for over a thousand years. The United States and France should never have been there in the first place.

ARAB-ISRAELI WARS

Once Israel was created, a series of Arab-Israeli wars was inevitable.

One of the more curious side effects of World War II was the creation of the state of Israel. Palestine had been the site of ancient Israel, a nation that had ceased to exist over two thousand years earlier. During the late 1800s, Jews again began to migrate to Palestine, which was then part of the Ottoman Empire. If you behaved and paid your taxes, the Turks left you alone. After 1918, the British replaced the Turks and agreed that it would be a good thing to establish a Jewish state. Largely because of the German persecution and near extermination of European Jews during World War II, Jewish agitation for the reestablishment of a Jewish state in Palestine engendered much sympathy in Europe and the United States. There was less sympathy among the Arabs in the region. When Israel declared its independence in 1948, it had to fight the first of many wars with Arab neighbors.

The Arabs had been agitating for their own independence ever since the Turks were driven out in 1918. The European nations that had replaced the Turks as local overlords were inclined to grant independence. By early 1946, nearly all the Arab states in the Middle East were independent. This gave European powers less influence in restraining Arab-Israeli warfare.

European involvement in Middle Eastern politics was a thankless task. The only reason Europeans bothered at all was because of the oil. The

British tried to handle the Arab-Israeli situation in its early stages and were unsuccessful. It was not an easy or simple situation. Many of the Jewish migrants were highly educated Europeans. The trauma of the Nazi exterminations increased their already high level of determination to make Israel viable, at whatever cost. The local Arabs were no match for them technically, diplomatically, emotionally or militarily. The European powers, again because of the memory of the Nazi atrocities against the Jews, were reluctant to come down hard on the Israelis. This in spite of the fact that the Europeans needed the Arabs, and their oil, more than they needed the Israelis.

The Middle East is not an area known for its use of reason and restraint to resolve disputes. Vendetta and imaginative violence are the norm. In the thirty-five years since Israel's founding, five major and several minor wars have been fought. Could any of them have been avoided? Probably not.

Despite most Arabs maintaining that the Palestinian Question is the primary issue in the region, traditional rivalries still absorb most Arab diplomatic and military energies. Most post-1945 wars in the Middle East have not involved Israel. Arabs fighting Arabs (or Iranians, Kurds, Turks or other non-Arabs) is more common. The Israelis are unique because they have not been defeated by the Arabs and they don't have any oil. Moreover, the Israelis, because many of them are migrants from Europe, are seen as an alien presence. Israel aggravates its neighbors on many levels, not just because they displaced the Palestinian Arabs to revive a long-defunct nation.

The Arab world is a web of intrigue that is impenetrable to most Americans and even many Europeans. Any external efforts to prevent the wars between Arabs and Israelis would most likely just introduce another cause of conflict. Keep in mind that the empires that successfully ruled the area in the past used a big stick and deep pockets to maintain the peace. If a massive show of military force did not calm things down, then a generous application of cash would often do the trick. The last, and most expensive, thing you would want to do is actually apply military force.

Comparing the bloody history of the region to the relatively low casualty count of the Arab-Israeli wars, the Israeli presence has proved beneficial. The Arabs have grown increasingly reluctant to take on the Israeli armed forces. This is understandable, as the Israelis always win. Ironically, the Israelis have replaced the dreaded Turks as the peacemakers of the region. Like the Turks, Israel keeps the peace through retribution and reputation.

Blind Alleys: How *Not* to Prevent a War

Just like people, nations have bad habits. Some of these bad habits can short-circuit efforts to avoid a war. The history of war and peace shows that many nations have the same fatal flaws in their diplomacy. Here are three common follies.

WAITING FOR THINGS TO HAPPEN

Diplomatic matters tend to catch a leader's full attention only when they go terribly wrong. This is a mistake, it is wrong in any endeavor. The more you prepare for emergencies, the better you can cope with them when they occur. In foreign affairs, emergencies are inevitable. No matter how carefully you drive a car, you cannot account for some maniac on the road.

If time *is* spent keeping an eye on foreign affairs, there is a tendency to not spend much effort on preventive measures—if it ain't broke, don't fix it. New initiatives in the domestic area are dangerous enough, dealing with a lot of inscrutable foreigners is even more forbidding. Leaders have an enormous number of issues pleading for their attention. Alas, this often results in excessive reluctance to cope with diplomatic issues.

Leaders are often slow to question, quick to answer. A slowness to question overseas situations in the first place sets up these unfortunate situations. Then once the diplomatic disaster happens, they are expected to take care of things promptly. The quick answers are often ill informed and damaging.

Taking preventive action requires money, skilled people and the attention of national leaders. All are in short supply. It takes exceptional discipline for a national leadership to overcome old habits and make the effort. Nations that do this avoid wars, those that persist in waiting for things to happen pay a high price on the battlefield.

DEPENDING ON DIPLOMATIC INTERVENTION

There is little enough one can do to influence the internal politics of a foreign nation. It is important that whatever moves are made in that direction do not make matters worse instead. Wars usually begin in a muddle of avoidable misunderstandings and inflammatory actions. Misdirected diplomacy is the most common form of counterproductive peacemaking.

It is difficult, and costly, to maintain a staff of experts on a wide variety of foreign nations. Particularly in the United States, where studying offshore cultures is not very popular, many of the experts are second-rate compared to their counterparts in other nations. One reason is that in the United States people in government move in and out of positions so often that few stay in one job long enough. The United States has intense economic and/or diplomatic relations with many countries, and there is never enough talent to go around.

The superpowers have a unique problem with their many large intelligence-gathering bureaucracies. The groups often put out contradictory analyses, leaving the leaders to figure out which agency is more accurate. Also, bureaucracies often choose the safe evaluation, even if it is obviously inferior to that from the minority voice. Frequently, a knowledgeable individual will be more perceptive and accurate than a department full of less able analysts. It is said that the CIA has the best information in the world, but the worst analysis—a matter of good input and bad output.

Often the dissension in intelligence does not come to light until it is too late. After the Vietnam War was almost over, the United States found that some of its intelligence agencies and diplomats had been consistently more accurate in their appraisals than others. The same thing happened regarding Iran and Afghanistan in the 1970s. The United States is not the only victim of this malady. Russia misunderstood what was going on in Afghanistan, and was thrown out of Egypt in 1972 for similar reasons.

Effective diplomacy is a two-way street. Yet envoys have found it easier to figure out what is going on in a foreign land than to explain these strange events to the folks back home. A major task of diplomats is to keep the leaders of their own and foreign nations accurately informed of each other's situations. It is a difficult task, particularly in democracies where the leaders change regularly. However, even under the best of conditions, getting the often rapid flow of complex information from foreign nations to the right person at the right time is difficult. Where the diplomatic process usually falls down most dangerously is in getting a useful appraisal of conditions in the foreign land back to your own leadership in a timely fashion.

Third world nations and the United States have the most trouble choosing effective diplomats. Third world nations generally do not have the human or technical resources to do a good job of diplomacy, even though they have far fewer foreign nations to keep track of than superpowers do. This puts more pressure on the major powers to keep the lines of communication from becoming too cluttered with myth and misinformation.

The United States has always had a problem with foreign cultures. Isolated from regular contact, Americans tend to see foreigners as impenetrable exotics or simply as Americans who talk funny. While American diplomats may be improving, the elected officials back home still reflect an isolationist electorate.

A particular disadvantage of Americans is that, while many foreigners read English and peruse American newspapers, far fewer people in the United States can read foreign papers. Even in Russia, many people listen to American radio broadcasts and compare them to their local versions of the same news. It is a revealing exercise to read foreign newspapers and see the local response to your nation's diplomatic activities. It is often surprising how much your nation's well-thought-out foreign policies are misunderstood over there.

Diplomacy and intervention in the affairs of foreign nations can have some impact in preventing wars. Unfortunately, most nations that attempt foreign diplomatic adventures generally stir up more violence than they prevent. The American experience in Vietnam and the European attempts to hang on to their colonies are recent examples. Activist diplomacy is not successful unless you are well informed and prepared for whatever measures are required. Few nations are this well equipped to deal with distant populations and their governments. Good diplomacy is best able to provide accurate and timely warnings. Understanding and defending against foreign aggressions is easier than jumping into a murky situation and attacking.

OVERREACTING TO THE MYTH OF
RUSSIAN WORLD DOMINATION

One surefire blind alley is to make great efforts to halt apparent Russian attempts at world domination. Russia is not interested in conquering the world. Misinterpreting and overreacting to Russian actions could lead to a war no one wants.

Russia has its hands full keeping Russia under control; the last thing it wants is many more tempestuous foreigners under its control.

The Russian leadership does not seriously strive toward this official goal of spreading communism throughout the planet, but they do attempt to create disorder wherever possible. From a Russian perspective, order is strength and disorder is weakness. Any action that creates disorder for the other world powers makes these nations weaker, and makes Russia stronger and safer from aggression.

Russia is uncompromising on national security. Meddling in Russian internal affairs puts the Russians in a very stubborn and nasty mood. Nearly as bad is interference with Russian-dominated nations on Russia's borders. Eastern Europe is the most sensitive area, as these nations are seen as a buffer against Western military aggression and, perhaps more importantly, unwelcome Western ideas.

Russian diplomatic efforts have met with mixed success. Their cynicism toward treaties and foreign policy has made other nations wary. Typical Russian diplomacy:

- Assassination of uncooperative heads of state. That's how they got involved in Afghanistan.
- Switching sides in disputes with other Russian clients. Example: When Ethiopia expressed an interest, Russia dropped Ethiopia's enemy Somalia as an ally and backed the larger nation, Ethiopia.
- A tightfisted attitude toward foreign aid. Example: Libya owes Russia over four billion dollars for arms, as of 1986. While the United States does not expect such debts to be repaid, Russia does.
- Support of more pro-Russian factions within its own client states. Example: A savage civil war in Yemen was the result of Russia backing a

more pro-Russian faction against the already pro-Russian Yemen government.

This heavy-handed style of diplomacy recalls German practices in World Wars I and II. The Germans installed puppet governments in conquered nations and backed them up with ruthless German advisers and troops. Whenever possible, local forces were used to do the dirty work. Many of the fiercest Nazi SS troops were not German at all, but locally recruited. The Germans played on ethnic animosities and condoned atrocities of one group against another so long as it served German needs.

Russia's feeling is that where a light touch may be suitable, a heavy hand is a guarantee of success. As students of history, Russian leaders have seen that their most ruthless and bloody-minded leaders were the most successful. Ivan the Terrible (or "the Dread," depending on your translation) is more admired than other notable, but less vicious, figures in Russian history. Josef Stalin, responsible for more dead Russians than any other individual (twenty million), is admired by a new generation of Russians. Stalin is seen as a strong leader, one who did what had to be done against internal and external enemies. Consider national heroes of other nations: Abraham Lincoln (freed the slaves, preserved national unity) is a hero in the United States, Napoleon (new legal system and "glory") in France, Gandhi (peaceful liberation) in India and Confucius (code of social conduct and respect for learning) in China. You can tell a lot about a country by asking its inhabitants who their historical heroes are, and why.

Russia's goals in world diplomacy are unsavory, their methods repugnant. But Russia is not willing to risk war unless it has what it considers a guarantee of success. Against a nation with nuclear weapons, success is not possible. The primary danger of Russian attitudes is that they will be misinterpreted and lead to a war no one wants.

THE ARMS RACE TRAP

One of the most expensive and doomed ways to try to prevent war is a good old-fashioned arms race. "Peace through strength" is the usual refrain. The cause is fear of military inferiority and an abundance of wealth to protect. (If you haven't got the money to buy weapons, you concentrate on diplomacy and making the most of whatever armed forces you can afford.)

The experience of the last hundred years, ever since the creation of large industrial economies, is that arms races tend to lead to war. Despite our experience, we have yet to break out of this deadly cycle.

These arms-buying exercises generally lead to bankrupt economies, nasty wars or both. The arms race approach fails for two reasons.

First, it's easier to pile up arms than to keep talking. National leaders are attuned to local matters. Putting across larger arms budgets seems safer than dealing with foreigners.

Second, an arms race creates too many weapons that don't work as intended, but give the owners the illusion they will.

Consider the last few arms races. The first one of this century began when the United States began building a new type of battleship, one that was bigger, better protected, faster and more heavily armed. The British quickly realized that their status as the preeminent world naval power was in danger. So the British began building a similar ship. They were in such a hurry that they finished theirs before the American ship. The result was the battleship *Dreadnought,* which became the generic name for a new class of ships. Germany saw an opportunity to catch up with Britain in a naval arms race. So Germany began building Dreadnought-class ships. Construction of these ships went on for forty years, although most of the one hundred seventy built worldwide were finished in time for World War I. Their total cost was over $160 billion (1987 dollars). The battleships fought in very few battles. Most of the decisive naval action in World War I was conducted with mines and submarines.

In the category of "too many weapons that don't work as intended," consider the twenty thousand armored vehicles Russia built in preparation for World War II. It was the world's largest tank force. About fifteen thousand tanks were combat ready when Germany invaded in 1941. Less than six months later, nearly all were lost. Russia lost over ten thousand aircraft in the same manner. Russia had a quality problem, not so much with the weapons as with troop training, organization and leadership. On paper, the Russians were far more formidable.

In the late 1960s, American aircraft entered combat over North Vietnam. It had been a dozen years since the United States fought an air war. In the early 1950s over Korea, American aircraft had destroyed over ten enemy aircraft for each they lost. Over Vietnam, the ratio was only 2:1. It was quickly realized that the expensive, new, high-performance aircraft were not being used efficiently. Changes in tactics and training promptly raised the ratio to over 5:1. This was acceptably close to the Korean experience, because ground-based antiaircraft missiles and cannon were much more heavily used in Vietnam.

New, expensive weapons are constantly being developed today. Generally, the buyers are uncertain whether they will perform as expected. Whenever an untried new weapon is used in combat, and works as advertised, the price goes up.

Weapons don't always work as advertised, and remedies are frequently not successful. Russian weapons have had a long series of failures. This is a curious repetition of their experience with tanks in the opening stages of World War II. Eventually they got it right. It appears that one of the two foremost participants in the current arms race is having a difficult time obtaining a reasonable return on investment. U.S. weapons have the same problems, but are used more often so that flaws can be found and fixed.

Russian weapons, whether used by them or a foreign customer, tend to function much worse than expected. This shabby track record might be expected to contribute to world peace by making all concerned more reluctant to depend on unreliable weapons. But no, both Russians and their potential adversaries tend to excuse the shabby weapons' performance. Arms makers and buyers tend to be eternal optimists. More seems better, whether it works or not.

An arms race consumes enormous quantities of national wealth, produces armed forces of questionable value and induces leaders to shoot instead of talk.

13

Two Military Traditions

The question always is: "Which past war is the next one going to imitate?" History is often ignored, though, because the new incarnations of the past have minor variations, and it's simply too much of a chore to connect a current event with the appropriate historical predecessor. The suitable historical connections can be more easily made if you look not at individual conflicts but at how nations at war have behaved. *Nations tend to fight the same way over and over.*

The less developed nations tend to fight disorganized, spasmodic wars that often do not end but continue for years as an endemic condition. Industrialized nations cannot afford this state of perpetual disorder. Their populations require a functioning industrial society to survive at all. Industrial nations possessing abundant natural resources can mobilize enormous armed forces. Such nations fight highly mechanized, intensely violent and relatively short wars.

As examples of national styles, we present the United States and Russia. They have very different styles, and the differences greatly increase the potential for conflict. If you look at their military histories, you will see why these different styles evolved, and how true it is that nations tend to fight the same way over and over.

THE UNITED STATES

America has an extensive history of warfare for a country with such a short existence. With two exceptions, all these wars were fought on someone else's territory. The patterns are instructive.

America's three-hundred-year military history may be divided into four periods:

Survival, 1600–1815
Expansion, 1815–1916
World Wars, 1917–45
Keeping the Peace, 1946 to the present

The first period started 176 years before there even was a United States. In that time the population that was to become the United States participated in wars at Great Britain's behest to establish British primacy in North America and to protect the thirteen colonies from local and European threats. These wars culminated in the American Revolution, in which the colonists demonstrated that they were even capable of overwhelming their colonial masters. The victory was won with crucial support from France, which showed that the Americans were also able to negotiate the tricky currents of international diplomacy.

European conflicts often had local counterparts in the new world: Queen Anne's War (1702–13) was the North American version of the War of the Spanish Succession in Europe, King George's War (1740–48) was the War of the Austrian Succession in Europe, the French and Indian War (1754–63) was likewise the Seven Years' War, while the War of 1812 was an extension of the Napoleonic Wars.

When the Revolutionary War ended, most of North America was unexplored and undeveloped. The United States began to swallow up the best territories. This sometimes involved war, although usually diligent and relentless migration got the job done. In the middle of a hundred years of expansion there was a civil war that settled disputes between regions of the United States and affirmed the supreme power of the central government. In the late 1800s, most of the fighting was with the Native Americans on the Great Plains. The last phase of expansion was a short war with Spain in 1898, which led to the liberation of the last major European colonies in the Americas and the acquisition of significant foreign colonies by the United States.

The wars fought between the aboriginal Americans—Indians—and the European invaders were minor militarily, but played a major role in shaping the military attitudes of America. The Indians had inhabited North America for thousands of year, but were several thousand years behind Europeans in technological and political development. However, the biggest disadvantage for the Indians was their lack of resistance to European diseases. Because the Americas were physically isolated from the rest of the world for so many thousands of years, and because the populations of Europe and Asia were much larger, Europeans were exposed to, and developed a resistance to, a far wider range of diseases than the Indians. Once the Indians were exposed to European diseases, most of them died. It appears that over 80 percent of the (fifty million plus) original Indian population was killed off by such familiar European diseases as measles and smallpox. The survivors developed immunity, just as the Europeans had many centuries before. A much smaller number were killed by warfare and slavery.

So the Europeans usually had superiority in numbers as well as more efficient organization and weapons. In the East, the Indians were a threat to the peace, but rarely to the existence, of the European settlements.

When the Europeans became Americans, fighting with the Indians continued. The Indians in the middle of the continent were different from those on the East Coast. First, many out West had already been exposed to the European diseases. Nearly two hundred years passed between their first encounters with a few Europeans and their confrontation with many. The Plains Indians had time to rebuild their disease-ravaged populations. Second, the Plains Indians acquired horses from the earliest Europeans they encountered and quickly learned how to use them. This increased their standard of living, as well as their mobility. The Plains Indians were freed up to spend more time on their favorite leisure activity, warfare. This made them very effective warriors, although they rarely demonstrated soldierly discipline. Lastly, the Plains Indians knew what had happened to the Indians back East. They were not about to let the Europeans roll right over them.

The American army that finally subdued the Indians was the closest the United States ever came to an effective peacetime professional army until 1945. It was a very small force, never more than 100,000 troops, but was made remarkably effective by constant service on the frontier. Led by men who had fought in the Civil War, this army enabled the United States to enter the twentieth century with an effective military tradition. America needed all the military tradition it could get, for it was not a military-minded nation.

All of these survival and expansion wars were fought by a pacifist nation. Most United States citizens wanted nothing to do with the military and, except for a short period during the Civil War, the army was small and volunteer. In 1917, this changed.

The forty years of worldwide warfare that began in the early 1900s was at first avoided by the United States. The first major war, between Japan and Russia in 1904, was mediated by the United States because most world powers considered it a major power with no significant political or military ambitions beyond its own borders. But the major European fighting which began in 1914 made America's enormous economic and potential military power too important to ignore.

Before the end of 1914, the major warring powers were flocking to the United States to either purchase arms, or prevent their enemies from doing so. Quickly it was perceived that America's military power could also be engaged in the bloodbath that was overtaking Europe. By 1917 American armed forces were fighting on the side of Britain and France against Germany. When World War I ended, the United States attempted once more to withdraw from world military affairs. When the fighting picked up again in the 1930s, the United States resisted active involvement until attacked by Japan in late 1941. When this fighting ended in 1945, the United States again attempted to withdraw into its own internal affairs. But the world situation, and America, had changed.

By the late 1940s, after forty years of fighting, the world balance of power had shifted dramatically. Where before there had been a number of world-class powers, by 1945 there was only one, the United States. Soon Russia rebuilt its economy and armed forces and became a threat to its neighbors. Meanwhile, the contraction of the economies and military power of the former European world powers led to unrest in their colonies. To make matters worse, Russia supported this unrest in the name of socialist revolution and to acquire far-flung allies.

The only nation that could oppose Russia was the United States. Initially, the United States was still reluctant to get involved in world politics. This changed dramatically when Russia sponsored an invasion of American-supported South Korea. The United States found itself at war once more.

The United States was ill prepared for a worldwide peacekeeping role.

Unlike the European powers, the United States had little experience in international diplomacy. This ignorance was exploited by Russia and many smaller nations. The nation with the most abundant resources to maintain world peace had little desire, or experience, to do so.

America found itself involved in a series of nasty, costly and often unsuccessful military and diplomatic situations. Korea, Lebanon (1950s and 1980s, respectively), Cuba, Central America, the Dominican Republic, Vietnam, Iran and others severely tested American resources. Most of the former European world powers were only too glad to abandon their foreign affairs problems to America.

When fighting a war in its new role, United States forces relied on their economic advantages and buried their opponents under a mountain of munitions and equipment. But many of the potential military situations the United States found itself in after 1945 did not lend themselves to the sledgehammer approach. America's lack of foreign affairs experience could not be compensated for by raw military power.

While American diplomats, military leaders and politicians have learned from their experiences since 1945, they have had a difficult time keeping up with an ever-changing world situation. But even more experienced nations have the same problems in constantly adapting to new conditions. Overall, the "experience gap" is closing. More diplomats can speak the language of the nations they serve in. Support staffs are more knowledgeable about how foreign cultures operate. Most important, Americans in international corporations have learned how to deal with foreigners on many different levels.

Meanwhile, America has three major advantages in international relations that increase in value as it becomes a more adroit participant in world affairs:

- America has the world's greatest capability to invade other continents.
- The American economy has outposts throughout the world. This gives Americans economic influence in more countries than most other nations. Also, these outposts act as unofficial eyes and ears throughout the world. The people that serve overseas provide a pool of experience that can be drawn upon in peacetime and during a war. They are familiar with how other governments work and how their people think.
- The combined economies, military forces and diplomatic resources of America's major allies are far larger than Russia's.

Today the American military is a volunteer force, as it has been through most of its history. But there are nearly ten times as many in uniform now, in proportion to the population, than at any other peacetime period. With 1.5 percent of the population in the military, the armed forces have become a major economic and social organization. There is one major problem with a volunteer army, poor leadership. America has never been too keen on the military. The most capable people are not attracted to military careers. Many able individuals who do join leave in disgust at the ineptitude they find. Those who persevere to senior rank are spread thin and spend too much of their time dealing with their less capable associates.

This dearth of good leadership is recognized in several ways. Within the military there is a tacit recognition that we tend to depend on technological superiority and massive firepower where other nations would use highly skilled troops to achieve the same results at the same cost in troop losses. The senior leadership, which does tend to have a higher proportion of talented officers, constantly institutes reforms to overcome leadership deficiencies. They take measures like increasing standards for troops and officers, and keeping people in the same unit longer. But progress is slow.

Although there has never been any question that the government controls the military, since 1945 the legislature and executive branches have increasingly gotten involved in the actual management of military affairs. This problem first became an issue during Vietnam when platoon commanders would find themselves being supervised from the White House. It persists today.

The American tradition is to keep the military on a short leash during peacetime, and fill it up with capable civilians when a major war comes along. This works only if you have months or years to mobilize and train these civilians. Nuclear powers use their conventional forces for rapidly developing small wars. In these actions you cannot afford too many mistakes, as the situation could rapidly escalate to a nuclear holocaust.

The world sees the United States as a major military power, but unpredictable. The problem, as America's allies and potential enemies see it, is America's lack of experience and military tradition. Russia suffers no such problem, having been recognized for centuries as a brutal and expansionist power. Not nice people, but at least you know how they will act.

American forces in World War II were, at best, adequate and often much less. An abundance of weapons and equipment, and stalwart citizen soldiers, had to make up for poor leadership. After 1945, the abundance of matériel dried up and the citizen soldiers went home. Most of the combat-experienced troops from World War II retired in the early 1960s, just before the Vietnam War, where they were sorely missed. The American army that went into Vietnam was largely ignorant of what war was really like. With few combat-experienced leaders, a troop-rotation system that prevented anyone from gaining any experience and not much military tradition to begin with, Vietnam took a decidedly unfavorable course. Finally, the United States declared that it had won and left the scene. That's what lack of a military tradition can do.

Military experience and tradition are no trivial matters. They are "force multipliers," something that will enhance the human and material components of military power. These components have always been America's strong suit, particularly in this century. Lots of weapons and equipment, much of it very innovative and effective. But the mighty military machine has an unrealistically high opinion of its own capabilities. This frightens our allies, as well as our enemies. Our allies see the United States as rash, unpredictable and unreliable. Russia takes much the same view.

America's history of isolationism makes its allies uneasy about just how reliable she would be in a crisis. During its first one hundred twenty years as a nation, the United States was largely ignored by the other world powers. But by the beginning of this century, it was obvious to all that there was a new world power. Starting in 1898, the United States fought successful, although often reluctant, wars against Spain, the Philippines, Germany, Italy and Japan. After 1945 the United States gradually dropped its reluctance and went eagerly into global politics as the mightiest economic and military power in the world.

At first, this was welcomed by most nations. America's fiscal generosity was needed in many war-ravaged regions. Soon, however, the U.S. State Department demonstrated little skill in its dealings with the many different cultures encountered around the globe. The image of the Ugly American began to form as the United States sent forth well-meaning but inexperienced emissaries to preach a seemingly heartfelt but often inappropriate gospel of American-style freedom and democracy. Thus began the world's uneasy relationship with Pax Americana.

That the United States has the largest arsenal of nuclear weapons was therefore doubly worrisome. This, combined with the world's largest economy, largest fleet and most successful aircraft and electronics industry, made the United States a military power that could not be ignored. Yet, in the end, what worries other nations most is that the United States does not seem to really know how to use all this military power effectively. Ameri-

ca's traditions indicate that it does not really want to use its awesome
military forces. The world nervously hopes this is so.

RUSSIA

Russia was founded as a military power. Before there were Slavs called
Russians, there were Slavic tribes living on the open plains of Eurasia, just
north of present-day Ukraine. With no natural barriers, the Slavs lived on
a heavily traveled highway for nomadic tribes going east or west looking
for plunder. About 2,700 years ago the traffic picked up and the Slavs had
to either adapt or perish. They adapted by arming, organizing and, when
they could, getting out of the way. In 600 B.C. the Scythians came out of
the East and ravaged southern Russia until, four hundred years later, the
Sarmatians roared out of the East and replaced them. The Slavs kept their
heads down and their swords sharpened. Then, in 200 A.D., the Goths (a
wandering Germanic people) came from the West and drove the Asiatic
nomads from power. Two hundred and fifty years later came the Huns
from the East. The Goths disappeared, the Slavs kept a low profile. The
local gene pool was getting complicated.

By 450 A.D., the nomads had lost control, leaving the battle-hardened
nucleus of the modern Russian people. For a hundred years the Slavs
expanded their power. But around 560 A.D. still another group of Asian
nomads appeared, the Avars. The Slavs recovered quickly, even holding off
still another Asian horde, the Jewish Khazars.

Then, starting in 800 A.D., the Vikings came down from the North. The
two cultures merged to produce Russians and Ukranians. Along about
980, everyone became Christian. Until the 1200s, Russian power waxed
and waned. Then came one of those events that changes nationalities forever. From the East came the Mongols. All the Slavs, except for those
northwest of Moscow, were conquered. At the same time, Germans were
again advancing from the West. For two hundred years, the remnant Russian state fought for its existence. By 1500, the Germans and Mongols had
been defeated, and the country called Russia was a reality. Because the
Moscow Slavs had resisted the Mongols, the leadership of Russia shifted
from Kiev in the Ukraine to Moscow.

In addition, the Russians had acquired some of Western Europe's social,
political and technological advantages by the 1500s. Russia changed from
a survivor of nomad depredations to a major power in world politics.

Russia was (and is) surrounded by present or potential enemies. From 1500 to 1786 (the first year our survey covers), there were Turks to the south, Swedes to the north, Poles and Lithuanians to the west and nomads to the east.

The wars that have kept the army so busy since 1787 were of three types.

- In the West, the army either fought European invaders or, usually by invitation, participated in wars between European powers.
- To the south there was an endless series of wars with the Turks.
- To the east there was an equally endless struggle against the oriental peoples. Even though the Russian Empire extended to the Pacific, it did so at the expense of good relations with the peoples who were encountered or conquered along the way.

Wars with Europeans, and by extension Americans, frighten the Russians most, for emotional and pragmatic reasons. Russia considers itself part of the European cultural community and is miffed when the Europeans do not wholeheartedly concur. Europe has been the source of most new technology in Russia. A feeling of inferiority makes Russia more nervous about its prospects in dealing with Europeans. Also, invasions by European powers have been a regular feature of Russian history for seven hundred years. In the last two hundred years, there have been five. Thus, despite the seemingly peaceful relations between Russia and Europe, Russia still considers the primary threat to be on its western border.

Until 1918, the Turkish Empire was a constant threat to Russia's southern borders. One reason for centuries of warfare was Russia's desire to conquer Istanbul and gain access to a warm water port. This aim has long been opposed by the Turks, and also by most Europeans and other neighbors of Russia.

Russia's relationships with its neighbors in the East have been dominated by fear. The neighbors are afraid about what territory Russia will grab next, and Russia is afraid of reprisals. Russia's eastern territories are sparsely settled and adjacent to nations that have larger populations and long lists of grievances. The principal threat is China. During the 1800s, Russia grabbed large tracts of traditionally Chinese territory. Despite Russia's aid to the Chinese Communists during the Chinese civil wars of the 1930s and '40s, there was never any serious talk of returning these lands. The falling out between Russia and China during the 1960s had a lot to do with this underlying quarrel. Another sore point was that Russia wanted

to be the leader in the Marxist-Leninist revolution. The Chinese feel subservient to no one. Also, Russia dragged its feet on giving China nuclear
weapons. Russia has a lesser set of territorial problems with Japan as well
as decidedly frosty relationships with South Korea and Taiwan.

To make matters worse, the Asiatic peoples Russia absorbed during the
1800s were not completely assimilated. These largely Moslem populations
are rapidly increasing and still maintain their cultural identity. Russia does
not completely trust them, and this distrust was reinforced when Asiatic
soldiers proved unreliable in Afghanistan.

To meet the threat from the West, Russia stations its most powerful
combat forces facing Western Europe. Because Russia has widely proclaimed a doctrine of defending by attacking first, this concentration of
troops makes the West nervous. Historically, Russia has not performed
efficiently in the opening stages of a war. However, because you can't
depend on all concerned to pay close attention to history's lessons, Russia's Western European border remains dangerous.

Elsewhere on its borders, Russia is less reluctant to take up arms. Russia is heavily armed and slightly paranoid, so it has a constant temptation
to use this mighty army if there appears to be little possibility of retribution. This brought about Afghanistan, and almost precipitated large-scale
conflict with China in the 1970s. The Chinese adventure was aborted by
the fear that it would become uncontrollable.

Suppression of upheavals in Eastern Europe is another matter. Anything that could motivate European nations to unite and advance east
frightens Russia like nothing else. Occupying several Eastern European
nations and controlling their foreign policy and, to a large extent, their
internal affairs gives Russia a degree of security in the West that they have
never had before. Alas, as Russia well remembers, European vassals tend
to be fickle. For over a hundred years Finland, Poland and the Baltic states
were Russian territory. As soon as the Russian government fell into chaos
after 1917, all of these areas declared independence, along with most other
non-Russian parts of Russia. With German connivance they got the Baltic
states back in 1940, and sort of recovered Poland. But Finland seems to be
lost for good. When Poland slipped into disorder in the late 1970s, Russian
leaders saw an old pattern reappearing. Only energetic measures by the
Polish government, a military coup in fact, stopped the Russian Army
from marching that familiar road into Poland. Poland may yet suffer the
unwelcome presence of invading Russians. The Russian hold on Eastern

Europe is tenuous. These nations look west, not east. So Russia prefers to face west behind a phalanx of tanks and missiles.

Despite the prominence of the military in Russian history, Russia is not a military dictatorship, and never has been. The government has always controlled the military by keeping it out of the government. Also, the leadership has always managed to keep it physically away from the center of the national government. Part of this isolation is a natural result of Russia's widespread defense needs. The wars on its frontiers were many hundreds, and sometimes thousands, of miles from the population and economic centers. Every unit of the Soviet Army contains a political officer, representing the Communist Party, who is responsible for the doctrinal purity of officers and troops. This officer can overrule decisions by the military commander. Officers are encouraged to apply for membership in the Communist Party; high rank is impossible without it. This adds still another layer of control.

The secret police (KGB) also serve to stifle any potential military takeover. For several hundred years the Russian secret police have controlled the population and the military. Every unit has secret police spies. Except for senior members of military intelligence, which also spies on the armed forces, any member of the military may be arrested without cause by the secret police. The secret police also have several divisions of combat troops and a small navy (the coast guard). With all these resources, the secret police can deal with just about any form of military insurrection. The Russian military is strong, but its power within Russia is severely constrained.

External enemies were not the only opponents the Russian Army faced. The army was also crucial in keeping the population in line. For over four hundred years, Russia has had substantial non-Russian populations under its control. The government would station soldiers in areas where they did not speak the same language. This made a joint effort against the government by soldiers and locals unlikely. The most loyal troops were stationed around the capital. The system worked well enough until 1917. When the Communist Party took over the government, it essentially continued the centuries-old system of handling the military. The armed forces were treated very well, but were kept isolated and away from the centers of real power.

Russia's military today is unchanged in its basic traditions and outlook. This in itself brings problems. More than in the past, the military is dependent on high technology and untried weapons. The record in this area has not been good, as any instance of modern Russian weapons use will attest. A more ancient problem is the rapid decline in efficiency the military suffers the longer it goes without fighting a war. The Russian military press is full of articles on these two topics. Afghanistan helps somewhat, but it involves a small portion of the forces and is not the kind of war the army is trained and equipped to fight.

Russia does attract the most capable people to the military, so there is no lack of awareness and attention to the problems they have. There is, however, no long-term solution. The Russian armed forces are a mighty organization that would stagger into a major war with unpredictable results. The Russian leadership is aware of this, perhaps more so than most foreigners. Russia wants peace, but a characteristically Russian form of peace.

Peace, to a Russian, means being stronger than any collection of neighbors. Peace, to a Russian, means sending your armies against any adjacent state that shows signs of threatening Russia's security. Peace, then, has a different meaning to Russians than it does to, say, Americans.

How, then, does one achieve a state of peace with Russia? First, you must appreciate the Russian concept of peace. Next, you must realize that Russians are far more concerned with what happens on their own borders than they are about anything else. If you want to preoccupy the Russians and keep them out of mischief in the rest of the world, you must keep them busy at home.

Imagine that you were in charge of defending Russia. First, you have to defend the longest land border in the world. Next, you have to accept that you have, for all practical purposes, no reliable allies. Those nominal allies that you do have in Eastern Europe are people who heartily dislike Russians. Given a choice, these allies would prefer to fight against you rather than with you. For most of Eastern Europe's history they have been doing just that. Therefore, to defend Russia, you must be ready to fight your own allies.

To make matters worse, just about every nation on your border has a grudge against you. All of your neighbors look upon you as a threat to their existence.

Your troubles are not over. About half of the soldiers in your army are not ethnic Russians, but the descendants of once-conquered people who were invited to join the Russian Empire at gunpoint.

Let's throw in a few other historical characteristics that define Russian society and military performance. Russia has always been technologically inferior to many of its primary opponents (Western Europe, the United States and Japan). Russia seems incapable of eliminating this technology gap. In terms of military history, this has forced Russia to rely on quantity instead of quality. Russian soldiers are not terribly efficient in the opening stages of a war. Russia has generally won its major wars by absorbing massive and devastating invasions. While wearing the invader down, Russian soldiers gain valuable experience and eventually triumph. At least most of the time.

The prescription for peace with Russia is to support Russia's neighbors, which preoccupy most of Russian efforts in foreign affairs. Russia is less likely to disturb the global peace if Russia's borders are teeming with strong, independent countries.

Changing Russia's bellicose attitude toward the world is a less likely prospect. Peace is a relative concept and to obtain it you often have to achieve it on your opponent's terms.

Part 3

Predicting the Future

There's no magic involved in foretelling the future, just a bag of tricks and techniques. The methods are easily understood and quickly applied. The following chapters are to be used with the data base.

Major Warning Signs

Want to spot a war in the making? Here are the major warning signs.

One nation feels it is strong enough to conquer another.

This causes a sixth of all wars. There does not have to be an actual imbalance, it's the perception that counts. A nation that is the aggressor in a war will lose most of the time. However, of all the aggressors, nations going to war primarily because of a sense of superiority are often correct and are more often victorious. Such nations are not always the immediate attacker. Often they simply goad their opponents into attacking. Going to war largely because victory seems assured is usually the approach of a major power. Colonial wars are often this type. The crazy quilt of super-power alliances since 1945 has caused this approach to decline in frequency.

It is important to know the antagonist's own evaluation of the relative military strength. Most aggressors in wars have very low opinions of their victim's military capabilities. They are often wrong, and most lose.

To determine what a nation really thinks of its potential opponent's armed forces, look for comments made before the situation became very tense. Recent examples of wars initiated largely due to underestimating the enemy's ability to fight include the Falklands War, Iran-Iraq and Afghanistan.

Don't forget that new element, superpower patronage. Many nations cannot make war without permission.

Nations have a habit of grabbing whatever they think they can get away with. The trick is to establish when one nation has crossed the line from desire to imagined success.

Significant grievances between the two antagonists.

Watch for new grievances added to complaints of longer standing. Using one of our favorite examples, Iran and Iraq have an ancient dispute over who should control a waterway on their border. Iran also considers all the land bordering the Persian Gulf to be part of its ancient empire. This claim assumed a new urgency with the discovery of oil in the region.

Only diplomats of exemplary competence are able to detect when the leaders of a nation are going to attempt something violent. You can't read minds, but you can carefully follow the major trends of a nation's past and try to find the numerous harmonics of current events.

Again, few wars are surprises if you know the history of the participants.

The aggressor population is provoked.

Grievances encouraged by government propaganda, historical memory or a sensationalist local press can create a warlike atmosphere. The combination of old and new disputes, inflamed by deliberate government policy or the media's search for news, has often led to war.

The classic example in the United States was the Spanish-American War in the 1890s. Americans had long been upset at the Spanish treatment of Cuban and Puerto Rican revolutionaries. The accidental explosion of the United States battleship *Maine* in Havana harbor gave United States newspapers a big story. The American population was riled up, the United States government was pushed to make demands on the Spanish and a very popular war ensued. In this case the aggressor won—a rare exception that has contributed to America's false sense of how the world really works.

Beware that an enraged population may not always be noticed from a distance, or even close up. Remember Iran in 1979.

Inability or unwillingness of the potential aggressor to negotiate a settlement.

When you see resistance to negotiation by the stronger antagonist, there is very likely to be a war. If the situation is very heated, and there is no possibility for negotiation, either there will be a war, or those who refused to negotiate will face a domestic crisis. If the government of the stronger power is unstable, it may simply be forced into a war. A more stable government may be able to weather the crisis, but often with a change in leadership. In these situations, it is possible for a government to talk itself into a war that is not winnable. Examples? Again, our favorite recent wars all fit this mold. Iran had demanded the head of Iraq's president (literally), so it is difficult for Iran to talk settlement. The Russians have made a commitment to "pacifying" Afghanistan.

Activity that seeks to inflame the situation.

In this century, improvements in transportation and communication, as well as a vast increase in wealth, have made active interference in faraway nations a common practice. This is particularly true of the two superpowers. Even though the superpowers cannot risk making war on each other directly, they circumvent this taboo by making war on each other's allies and client states. In the nuclear age, such troublemaking could create a major war no one wants.

Historical willingness of one side or the other to settle disputes through military action.

Britain has always favored diplomacy. Russia has favored invasion. Geography has something to do with this. Britain is an island nation dependent on trade, and it has a strong navy. Russia is surrounded by enemies who can walk right in and it lives in constant, and justified, fear of internal disorder. But part of a country's mind-set is simply national character. Japan and the United States are also insular nations dependent on sea trade, and they have vastly different patterns of settling disputes. Until 1945, Japan relied on aggressive military action: Since then it has discovered the efficiency of economic power. The United States has traditionally been neutralistic and pacifist, even today. The Reagan administration's unauthorized diplomacy through the National Security Council (1982–86) is an example of what happens when you don't play according to the generally accepted rules of conduct. Actively supporting both sides in a war and carrying on a covert war against another nation in the face of congressional opposition is a sharp break with the American inclination to leave problems alone or talk them to death.

Significant internal unrest within the potential defender.

It's common for a potential attacker to overestimate the extent to which internal unrest has debilitated the military power of a potential victim. Iran and Iraq in 1980, Afghanistan in 1979 and Lebanon in 1982 are excellent recent examples. Just because the neighbors are preoccupied, don't think they won't notice you sneaking in. A neighbor in civil disorder may actually be quite dangerous. Its leaders may often look to external warfare to stabilize things on the home front. A neighbor's disorder may put you on the receiving end of an invasion.

WHO IS BREAKING THE RULES?

There are rules a nation should follow to avoid wars. If these rules are broken, war usually follows, and defeat is usually not too far behind. Look at each potential war situation and apply these rules to see who is headed for combat.

1. Don't get into arguments. Disagreements will always be there. Good diplomacy, patience and taking the long view will prevent escalation of disagreements into noisy and heated disputes.

2. Don't go to war with anyone who can defeat you. This alone would eliminate most of the major wars. To accomplish this would require more candor in appraising your own and potential opponents' combat capabilities. This will be difficult, as military proficiency is usually a political football.

3. It's cheaper to buy off an opponent than fight one. Everyone involved in the war- and peacemaking process should have a sound knowledge of accounting and economics. As the Japanese continue to demonstrate, it's easier to conquer through trade than warfare.

4. Words are cheaper than bullets. If all else fails, stay away from your weapons and keep talking. Modern guerrilla warfare, largely developed and practiced by Communist groups, uses this technique quite effectively. They use bullets, too, but far more words.

5. Remember that dictators speak mainly for themselves. The key problem is persuading the dictators that this is the case. In the 1980s it has become more common for dictators to be removed from power through the persuasion of a powerful ally. This is an apt application of number 4 (above).

6. Stay out of domestic disputes. An outsider, no matter how well intentioned, only makes matters worse. Any police officer can confirm this. The history of intervention in revolutions or civil wars confirms this.

7. Defenders win more wars than attackers. Every nation embarking on an offensive war should take note. This ties in with number 2 (above).

8. A lot of little wars are preferable to a single big one. This is about the only justification for going to war, but is more often than not abused. Sometimes a war is justified, such as when a civil terror is going on within another nation. Just be very careful.

Future Wars

Having seen how wars start and stop, it's time to apply this knowledge to potential wars. Each entry starts with signs that would show the situation is too close to combat. Each entry then gives you a briefing on the sources and nature of the conflict. Data on each potential war is given in the Future Wars Chart at the end of the book.

THE BIG ONE (UNITED STATES/RUSSIA)

- High tension level, most likely over a disturbance in Eastern Europe.
- Russia mobilizes its army. This is a massive undertaking, affecting millions of people all over the country. It would be difficult to hide this from foreigners, much less American intelligence organizations.
- A worsening Russian internal situation, especially one caused by falling production of a resource like oil. This presents Russia with opportunities to go after a neighbor's resources, such as oil in the Persian Gulf. National emergency, you know.

This is the most dangerous of potential wars, and perhaps the most unlikely. The United States and Russia do not possess many of the traits typical of potential combatants. Neither country can easily invade the other's territory. Although the United States has a formidable capability to move air, naval and ground units anywhere in the world, Russia possesses the world's most powerful land forces. American forces can reach Russia, but not in sufficient strength to make a dent in the vast Russian defenses. The Russian armies cannot walk on water, thus making the United States safe from invasion. The only decisive weapon each has against the other is nuclear. This option offers negligible benefits, as there is little opportunity to achieve a victory without suffering catastrophic losses.

Both superpowers have been reduced to long-range sparring through other nations. This is less dangerous and more dangerous at the same time. Obviously, anything that prevents American and Russian military forces from coming into contact with each other is helpful. However, conducting conflicts through third parties increases the potential for misunderstanding and error.

For example, consider Cuba and Turkey. We have had a fairly intimate relationship with Cuba for nearly a hundred years, yet Cuba has become a close ally of Russia. How well, you may ask, does Russia understand Cuba? Consider Turkey, sharing a border, and hundreds of years of disputes, with Russia. Turkey is a firm ally of the United States. But does the United States understand Turkey any better than Russia understands Cuba? Imagine the opportunities for errors in judgment and perception when the United States, Turkey and Russia are entangled in a dispute. Or when the United States, Russia and Cuba get wrapped up in one of their regular disagreements.

Russia feels more threatened by meddling in its neighborhood as it is surrounded by an imposing array of American allies. The Western European nations, Turkey, China and Japan together can muster more economic and military power than Russia can contend with all at once. Misunderstanding Russia's bloody history, the United States simply takes its bad relations with its neighbors as bad manners and attempts to thwart them at every turn. This makes Russia even more wary and warlike.

Russia and the United States have very different ethical standards in international affairs. Russia takes an "ends justify the means" approach. The United States is more frequently idealistic. You could also say that the United States is a status quo power, meaning that it is basically happy with the world as it is. The Russians, because of their Communist revolutionary doctrine, are revisionists because they want to change the world.

Such philosophical differences, when not fully appreciated by one or more of the parties involved, often lead to war. The restraints imposed by nuclear weapons are a benefit in this case, as the United States is relatively new, and sometimes erratic, at the diplomacy game. Russia, while having a long history of diplomatic endeavor, has never been so relatively strong nor possessed of such a militant ideology. Ideology makes the leading world powers diametrically opposed to each other. This is rare in history, and when it has occurred has led to catastrophic wars. The Taiping Rebellion and the Napoleonic wars are examples of what happens when ideology gets mixed up with massive military power.

Operating beneath the nuclear umbrella of their allies, minor powers carry on under the assumption that superpower restraint will prevent things from getting completely out of hand. Their adventurism is most likely to get the superpowers fighting one another. Maintaining the peace between the superpowers depends largely on watching what is occurring on the fringes of superpower relations.

EASTERN EUROPE

- Local agitation for anything that threatens Russian control of the area.
- Russia moves to impose unpopular economic and political measures.

Eastern Europe has long been a battleground for other nations while being subjugated to the political will of larger neighbors. In the past, large portions of the region were components of other nations. Poland was carved up between Germany, Austria and Russia from the late 1700s to 1919 as well as from 1939–45. Hungary and Czechoslovakia were components of the Austro-Hungarian Empire until 1918. Bulgaria and Romania were part of the Ottoman (Turkish) Empire until the early part of this century.

Although these states are nominally independent today, their foreign policies and most of their domestic affairs are dictated from Moscow. These nations have not lost their desire for independence, which has been the cause of wars and revolutions for several hundred years. Eastern Europeans have learned to bide their time in the face of overwhelming external power. In this case, Russia is the overwhelming power and is well aware of the rambunctious history of the region. It is only a matter of time before the lid blows off. Since 1953, there have been four major upheavals and numerous lesser ones. The good news is that Russia has no intention of allowing any of these nations to obtain nuclear weapons.

Certain trends going on in Eastern Europe and Russia make any long-term peace prospects in Eastern Europe unlikely. Although Russia has tried strenuously to mold Eastern European societies after its own, they are becoming more like Western Europe. They have a higher standard of living than Russia, which rankles the Russians. East European populations are also upset because they are not as well off as Western Europeans. East Germans watch West German TV. It's hard to watch your brothers living such a better life. There is only so much Russians can do to counteract the bad influence of Western European cultures and lifestyles. Limited immigration eliminates troublemakers and economic burdens, like the elderly. Education with a heavy dose of propaganda has had some effect. The new generation of East Germans is, however, still German. This continues to bother the Russians.

Although the Russians were able to round up a number of dedicated local Communists in the 1940s to staff their East European satellite states, even those cadres were not able to generate sustained enthusiasm for Communist forms of government. Eastern Europe had traditionally looked west. This orientation is an ongoing cause of unrest, and a great concern to the Russians.

Russia tried the strong-arm approach to keeping Eastern European nations in line, and it was not successful. Lately, they have tried using the carrot instead of the stick, allowing Eastern European nations to pursue more liberal, more capitalist and more democratic policies. Russia looks the other way as long as the correct dogma is uttered in public. An unpleasant side effect is the restiveness created in the Russian population as they see their socialist allies living better under a less orthodox form of communism.

The Russians are students of history. They know that their liberal policies in East Europe will bring short-term benefits and long-term dangers. Eastern European social practices and political practices steadily drift further away from the Russian model. People begin to think about how wonderful it would be to live in a nation that was not subservient to a foreign power. The younger folk don't know how rough the Russian Army can be. Desire for change and little memory of how costly this change can be creates instability.

A great fear among the Russians is that an uprising might occur in two or more Eastern European nations at the same time. Another fear is that any unrest might spread. The greatest fear is that one or more nations in Western Europe, or even the United States, might get involved.

Russia has been historically afraid of disorder, internally as well as among its neighbors. It is prone to intervening in its neighbors' affairs to restore order. Sometimes it does this by invitation, sometimes not. Russia's goal is to protect the mother country from invasion. This is something of a minor religion and it has historically reacted very strongly to real or imagined threats to its national integrity.

Not all of the potential unrest in Eastern Europe is directed at the Russians. These nations have a large number of unresolved grievances among themselves. Most resulted from their liberation from former masters after 1918. Another round of rearranging took place in 1945. Consider the following list of disputes:

Germany and Poland. In 1945 Russia gave Poland large chunks of East Germany. The German population was expelled or killed. The Germans haven't forgotten, particularly those who fled the "old territories" and now live in West Germany. The bitterness fades as the years go by, but the memories always remain.

Poland and Russia. While Russia was giving Poland parts of East Germany, it was taking large tracts of eastern Poland for itself. Many Poles are still waiting to be reunited with their fellow countrymen.

Poland and Czechoslovakia. There are some differences of opinion on exactly where the borders should be. Either nation would make adjustments if the risk were not too great.

Czechoslovakia and Russia. After 1945 Russia grabbed a chunk of eastern Czechoslovakia "for security purposes." The Czechs would like it back. Please.

Czechoslovakia and Hungary. Similar to the Poland-Czechoslovakia border differences.

Hungary and Romania. A very nasty dispute over a significant amount of territory. Russia has kept the noise level down, but the unfriendly feelings remain.

Romania and Russia. A large chunk of eastern Romania has changed hands several times in this century. Russia now has it, and plans to keep it. Romania would grab it back if it thought it could get away with it.

Bulgaria, Yugoslavia and Greece. Everyone is in a dither over just who should rule Macedonia. In addition, the Macedonians would rather do it themselves.

Another problem that could contribute to unrest in the East is Germany's desire for reunification. After 1945 a large portion of Germany found itself under indirect Russian rule. In addition, 600,000 German prisoners of war in World War II disappeared in the hands of the Russians. Most were starved to death in camps after the war.

The German concept of national unity has been strong throughout its history. This dream was constantly thwarted by petty jealousies and outside interference. There were also geographic problems, as Germany occupies a central position in Europe. Surrounded by stronger national states, Germany has served as the battleground for others. The Germans are aware that they could be someone else's battleground again. They believe that only a strong, united Germany will prevent this.

Working against unification is unusually strong regionalism. For this reason Austria continues to exist as an independent German ethnic state. Russia has wisely played upon regional identification in the portion of Germany they control. It has provided a counterbalance for the intensely anti-Russian and pro-reunification attitudes among the East Germans.

Russia takes additional precautions to ensure that their Germans do not become overly restive. They allow controlled immigration to get rid of malcontents. They also station a substantial army in East Germany. The nineteen combat divisions Russia maintains in East Germany are the strongest concentration of Russian ground forces in the world (Russia does have more troops strung out along the Chinese border). Finally, Russia sends many of its best political and police "advisers" to East Germany. Their task is to ensure that nothing unpleasant happens between the two Germanies.

WESTERN EUROPE

- Heightened tension between Greece and Turkey.

There is a peace in Western Europe unlike any experienced there in over a thousand years. There remain very few issues that could spark a war. The principal threat of war in Western Europe is voluntary or involuntary participation in a war instigated by unrest in Eastern Europe.

The only other threat of major war is the one so many have been preparing for since 1945: a Russian invasion of Western Europe. In hindsight, it is obvious that Russian military force has rarely been strong enough to have any hope of succeeding in an attack into Western Europe.

However, in the last ten years Russia has significantly increased the quality, and to a lesser extent the quantity, of its combat forces in Eastern Europe. This is variously interpreted as an attempt to achieve an offensive capability or as simply a response to improvements in NATO forces. The primary danger is an expensive arms race that would weaken the economies of the competing nations. Weak economies are prone to internal disorder, the most common cause of wars.

Much of the disorder that already exists in Western Europe springs from economic problems. Radical terrorist groups can trace their origins to unemployment and general lack of opportunities for educated youth, in addition to ethnic and ideological issues. Russia has supported the radicals, but even so, they have been unable to generate dangerous instability. But things could go from bad to worse to war.

The Irish Republican Army, Basque nationalists, Yugoslav separatists and sundry terrorists aside, there is one area in which a real old-fashioned war is brewing. In the Aegean Sea that separates Greece and Turkey, a dispute goes back over three thousand years. It was only during the early 1800s that Greece was liberated from several centuries of Turkish domination. Each nation feels intrinsically superior to the other. The islands in the Aegean, as well as the larger island of Cyprus to the south, have long been claimed by Greece and Turkey. Both nations have more to fear from Russian ambitions in the area than from each other, and the islands themselves are of no particular value. There may be oil there, maybe not. Either way, Greeks and Turks would be at each other's throats. These nominal allies are poised for war. Ironically it is the smaller power, Greece, that holds the islands and makes the most warlike noises. Turkey has made several attempts to build nuclear weapons. Ancient animosities endure.

MIDDLE EAST

- Increased economic problems in the more populous nations lacking oil.
- More violent demonstrations by fundamentalist groups.
- Changes in government which produce more radical governments.
- Israel getting weaker militarily, even if only in perception.

The earliest recorded war occurred in the Middle East. There hasn't been much peace since that ancient scrap between the Hittites (from Turkey) and Egyptians in the vicinity of modern Palestine. The only periods of relative quiet have occurred when much of the region was occupied by one or more imperial powers. The last empire to enforce peace was the Turkish. The empire was broken up in 1918. Various European powers kept things quiet until 1945 and then withdrew. There has been constant strife in the area ever since. Short of bringing back the Ottoman Empire, or some other external power strong enough to enforce a peace, there is little prospect of settling things down. Unfortunately, no one seems eager to establish hegemony over the area at the moment, or to see anyone else do so.

Many of the major powers pursue their own goals in the area, and attempt to thwart those of their real or perceived opponents. Nations that are more dependent on Middle Eastern oil tend to oppose those that have other sources. This sometimes puts oil producers Britain, the United States and Russia on the same side of the fence and opposing nonproducers like Japan and Western Europe.

Britain, Italy and France have been in and out of the Middle East for over eight hundred years. They have developed economic and, more importantly in this part of the world, personal ties. The recent players, Japan and the United States, often lack their depth of perception.

Russia and the United States use the Middle East as an arena for their foreign policy conflicts. Local nations take advantage of the situation and switch sides as often as suits their current needs.

Israel is often proclaimed the chief cause of unrest in the area. Yet in a larger perspective Israel is just another contentious Middle Eastern nation. Actually Israel is a stabilizing influence, because Israel is too strong for any local nation to attack and because it has consistent alliances. Most other nations have switched between the United States, Russia and neutrality at least once.

Middle Eastern nations have long memories. Ancient glories and territorial claims are the basis for current national objectives. Syria lays claim to Lebanon as a long-lost province. Israel seeks to reestablish the 2,500-year-old borders of the ancient Jewish kingdom. Iran and Iraq battle over historically vague frontiers and Egypt wants Libya to become a province again. There are more of these claims than in most other parts of the world and they are taken more seriously, often unto death.

The Middle East today is often compared to the Balkans before 1914.

Unrest in the Balkans was one of the chief causes of the forty years of fighting that climaxed in 1945. The Balkans had been in turmoil long before 1914, are relatively quiet today, yet still harbor animosities that could develop into widespread violence.

Why have the Balkans settled down and the Middle East has not? The reasons suggest things that can be done to calm down the Middle East.

The abundance of oil in the area has been a curse as well as a blessing. Wealth produced rapid change. This will cause unrest in any society; moreover Orthodox Islam and Judaism are particularly opposed to many aspects of social change. So social unrest was made worse by religious repression. Fluctuations in the price of oil and worldwide demand have added further instability. Oil money has caused wide gaps in income levels. When people's expectations are not met, when people become frustrated, they often turn ugly. Orthodox religious leaders then fan the flames higher. The revolution and subsequent unrest in Iran are but one example of the dark side of new wealth in a historically poor region.

The only solution to the wealth "problem" is to slow down wealth's rate of growth in the area. This is unlikely to happen by design, but the oil will eventually run out. Unfortunately, this will *also* cause a period of distress, as there will be squabbling over the division of the smaller pool of wealth. The only interim solution is for the wealthy nations to control their use of the wealth. Some have tried to do this, with limited success. It takes an exceptionally strong government to hold back once the population senses there is a better life to be had.

The rest of the world could help by showing some restraint in selling the oil states things they don't need and in the long term cannot afford. Of course, this is easier said than done.

The oil producers are getting better at spending their wealth on long-term economic projects instead of short-term luxuries. But damage has been done, and not all the players have fully learned how to handle the situation. When oil prices dropped drastically in the early 1980s, oil producers got a preview of what happens when the oil runs out. This was a painful lesson, but a very useful one.

Overshadowing all this are the attempts of some oil-rich nations to obtain nuclear technology and weapons. Fortunately, a growing sense of prudence is cutting back their arms purchasing in general.

Oil is not the only cause of unrest in the Middle East. Although Israel has defeated all of its enemies on the battlefield, it is losing the war on the home front. Israeli society is split several ways. There is the European/

non-European Jew problem. There is a division between religious and non-religious Jews. There is an Arab population that will soon outnumber the Jews. The cost of maintaining one of the strongest military forces in the world has bankrupted the Israeli economy, which functions only through billions of dollars in American aid. This constant strain has caused more migration, particularly to the United States. Israel is a tenuous entity.

The Palestinian Arabs dispossessed by the creation of Israel are still scattered all over the Middle East. Their presence has caused several wars and disturbances. There have been other population movements. Most of the Jewish residents of Arab countries have migrated to Israel. They have in common only their religion. This has caused a significant amount of division within Israel. There have been several other population movements, including workers from the non-oil-producing nations to those with oil. These population movements, added to the unrest generated by the oil wealth, have made the pot boil a bit faster.

There is one final cause of Middle East unrest—recent colonial heritage. For several hundred years, most of the Middle East did not consist of independent states. The Turkish Empire ruled it for nearly five hundred years. Then European nations moved into the non-Turkish portions of the empire. Indeed, they had been moving in even before the empire was pulled completely apart in 1918. This colonial period lasted until the late 1940s, when the European nations began to withdraw from the Middle East. They left behind some nations that had not ruled themselves for several hundred years, if ever. The European nations rearranged borders that were immediately disputed and left in charge rulers who were not in touch with their own people. Disputes involving Iraq, Syria, Jordan and Lebanon can be traced to lines hastily drawn on maps. These new nations were left in disarray when they needed all the stability they could get.

Arguable borders, ancient animosities and massive new wealth cause the Middle Eastern peoples to exist in a perpetual state of agitation. Because of the region's oil wealth, Middle Eastern problems are now global problems.

ISRAEL VS. ARABS

- Settlement of conflicts between Arab nations.
- An Arab nation obtains nuclear weapons.
- Fundamentalist regimes take over more nations, including Israel.
- Successful Syrian takeover of Lebanon.

Arabs saw the creation of Israel in 1948 as Europeans destroying an Arab state (Palestine) to create a new nation (Israel) for European refugees (European Jews). Anti-Jewish feelings increased throughout the Arab world, and most Jews in Arab nations emigrated to Israel. At the same time, much of the Arab population of Palestine moved to other Arab countries, many of which lacked the economic strength to absorb them. Lebanon eventually lapsed into chronic civil war, abetted by Syria. Syria, of course, is Israel's primary Arab adversary, and if it took over Lebanon, it would be on Israel's border. Jordan's heavily Palestinian province (the West Bank) was annexed by Israel in 1967. Syria and Egypt were drawn into a series of unsuccessful wars with Israel.

The Palestinian refugees organized themselves into a paramilitary terrorist group, the Palestinian Liberation Organization. Israel became one of the ten strongest military powers in the world. The other Arab states armed themselves as heavily as they could. The presence of enormous oil wealth in the region made an extensive rearmament program possible.

Five major wars have been fought between Arabs and Israel (1948, 1957, 1967, 1973, 1982). The Arabs lost all of them. Egypt finally made peace, and Jordan reached a series of unofficial understandings. Of the Arab states bordering Israel, only Syria has persisted in warlike declarations and intentions.

That's the good news. The bad news is that Israel has bankrupted itself to maintain its military might. A third of the Israeli work force is employed by the civil service. The economy is kept afloat only by billions of dollars donated by the United States government each year.

It gets worse. Because the Jewish portion of the population is growing much more slowly than the Arab segment, Israel is becoming a Jewish state with a non-Jewish majority. In response, Israeli extremist groups are calling for forcible expulsion of non-Jewish groups (mainly Arabs) from Israel.

Civil war is becoming more likely than invasion—the wealthier European Jews squaring off against the more numerous African and Asian Jews. Even more volatile is the split between religious and nonreligious Jews. These two conflicts have already created riots, murders and even the destruction of synagogues by Jews. Added to this violence is the continued armed resistance of the Arab population to Jewish rule. We can expect to see the government use potential external threats to defuse internal unrest.

ARABS VS. IRANIANS

- Reigniting of traditional Iranian attempts to control the Persian Gulf area.
- Iran, Syria or Turkey tries to partition Iraq.

The Persians have been calling themselves Iranians for the last fifty years, but nothing else has changed. The antagonism between Arabs and Persians is the most ancient in the region.

For three thousand years, no conqueror has been able to control the Persians for any length of time. The Greeks under Alexander the Great came and went over two thousand years ago. The newly Moslem Arabs came by and just as quickly left twelve hundred years ago, but converted the Persians to Islam. The religion promptly mutated into a heretical form which further estranged them from their Arab neighbors. Several waves of Turkish invaders came from the East, killing a third of the population and moving on. In this century, Russia and Britain moved in, then left. In between these major events there was a series of smaller wars.

Iranians are well aware of their ability to survive a conqueror. They look with disdain on their Arab and Afghan neighbors, for social, ethic and religious reasons.

There has always been a possibility that Iran would grab the land of its Arab neighbors for economic reasons even when a pro-Western Shah ruled Iran. Arabs control most of the oil, and Iran has most of the people and the healthiest nonoil economy.

The imperial government of Iran was replaced by a religious one in 1979. This has set Iran against all of its neighbors. It also precipitated a persistent war with Iraq. The people of Iraq are the descendants of the ancient Assyrians, who were fighting Persians over three thousand years ago. Some things never change.

Another unchanging aspect of the region is the use of major powers from outside the area as allies against the Iranians. Eighteen hundred years ago the local Semitic peoples called in the Romans; today the Arabs still call upon the stronger foreign powers for assistance against the Iranians.

Neither Iran nor Iraq is likely to get nuclear weapons in the immediate future. Israel has launched one air strike against Iraqi nuclear research facilities and appears willing to do so again. Iran is in no shape to do nuclear research. By the turn of the century, who knows?

The 1980 Iran-Iraq war will not be the last of a long series of wars against Arabs. As long as Iran exists, and especially as long as there is enormous oil wealth in Arab states, Iran will feel the urge to grab. It has a consistent, three-thousand-year history of aggression; it is unlikely to do otherwise. You can expect to see growing armed resistance to Iranian aggression by Arabs and their allies.

ARABS VS. ARABS

■ Settlement of wars in the two Yemens, and continued Russian influence there would threaten Saudi Arabia and Persian Gulf states.
■ A militarily weak Israel would encourage neighboring Arab states to settle scores with each other.

The appearance of Israel in 1948, and the subsequent Arab-Israeli wars, left the impression that most conflicts in the region were between Arabs and Israelis. Actually there have been far more wars between Arab states since 1948. Were Israel not present, there would have been many more.

All of these unfought Arab versus Arab wars would have been a natural consequence of the breakup of the Turkish Empire in 1918. For several hundred years, the Turks had controlled, to varying degrees, all the Arab states. The North African Arab states were the first to break away in the 1800s. The Turks held on to present-day Syria, Israel (Palestine), Lebanon, Iraq and the Arabian peninsula right to the end.

With the Turks suddenly gone, there was a free-for-all on who would rule what. Initially, Saudi Arabian sheiks attempted to assume power. Saudi Arabia had never really been conquered by the Turks (there wasn't much worth conquering in the desert), so Saudi warriors had led what resistance there was to the Turks. Britain and France had other ideas as they replaced the Turkish garrisons with their own troops. The European powers drew the national boundaries and chose local dignitaries to assume power.

By 1948, all but Palestine had been handed over to local governments. Even before the wars over Palestine/Israel began, numerous disputes between Arab states were brewing. Syria had designs on Lebanon, Palestine, Jordan and part of Turkey. Iraq saw itself as the rightful ruler of the Arabian peninsula and parts of Iran. Jordan perceived Palestine as part of its territory. Egypt had claims against all of its neighbors. To this day, the nations in the Arabian peninsula have maps with borders labeled "unde-fined." Iraq and Syria thought each should be ruling the other. Mixed in with the counterclaims were several serious religious and political disputes. All of this was in place before the oil money became a major factor.

Old disputes and new wealth are a volatile combination. When the Turks ruled the area, they used a heavy hand. Their indigenous successors have used the same bloody-minded approach, but with much less success.

The most likely up and coming wars in the middle East:

Egypt and Libya. Libya has oil wealth and a tiny population, plus a provocative leader and radical government. Egypt is just waiting for the right political conditions so that it can invade without being condemned by other Arab states. If Libya should settle down, war could be averted.

Syria and Iraq. Each feels that it should be ruling both nations. Over several thousand years, there has never been much peace between these two.

Syria and Lebanon. Syria feels that Lebanon is a lost province. When-ever the shooting dies down inside Lebanon, Syria stands ready to move in and grab whatever is left.

Iraq and Kuwait. Iraq feels that Kuwait is a lost province.

Saudi Arabia and Iraq. Saudi Arabia likes things just the way they are and would go to war to keep them that way. Iraq sees itself as the true ruler of the Arabian peninsula. This feeling never manifested itself when the peninsula was populated by poverty-stricken Bedouin nomads. How-ever, now there's a lot of oil that needs looking after.

Yemen. Traditionally, the southern portion of the Arabian peninsula held most of the peninsula's population. Yemen is rent by civil war, but is not averse to fighting anyone nearby who has something worth fighting over.

In addition there are sundry domestic disturbances. Some are based on tribal loyalties, some on religious differences. There are five major kinds of Islam in the area. Each considers the other's religious beliefs misguided or heretical. In addition there are three kinds of Catholics, plus several differ-ent persuasions of other Christians and Jews. Each group, particularly the Jews and Moslems, has ultraorthodox hardliners who would prefer a reli-gious government. The Iranians got their wish. Several other nations base their civil law on scriptures and Israel is moving in that direction. This is a very contentious part of the world.

One bright spot is that none of these nations is close to obtaining nu-clear weapons.

ARABS VS. AFRICANS

- Endemic unrest in nations with African and Arab populations continues to provide ample cause for wars.
- Continued potential for strife between African and Arab nations that have dense populations on their common borders.

The relationship between the Arabs and their African neighbors has never been cordial. The Arabs have generally had an edge in technology and political organization. This has given Arabs economic and military advantages which they have been quick to exploit.

In the east, Ethiopia has always maintained its independence. By and large, however, the Arabs have encroached on the Africans, not the other way around.

Libya has been more or less at war with Chad throughout the 1970s and '80s. Several other African states with Arab populations find themselves in perpetual civil disorder. The animosities between Arabs and Africans do not make for civil tranquility.

Sudan has a mix of Arabs in the north and Black Africans in the south. The Africans have traditionally gotten the worst of it. In the last ten years the Blacks have been in a perpetual state of rebellion. The Arabs have responded with the usual savagery. The deaths have numbered in the hundreds of thousands, refugees in the millions. Accurate record keeping has been a low priority, but indications are that the situation is grim and growing worse.

This pattern can be expected to continue throughout the area. The wars will be informal but quite deadly. Civilian losses will continue to be considerable, not from direct military action but from starvation and disease caused when populations are pushed around.

Nuclear weapons are not a factor in these conflicts.

FAR EAST—VIETNAM

- Loss of Russian patronage by Vietnam or a warming up of relations between China and Russia means trouble between China and Vietnam.

■ Further decline in Vietnamese economy fuels more internal rebellion.

■ Improved Vietnamese economy encourages more involvement in Cambodia and Laos, possibly a move against Thailand.

Thailand, Cambodia, Vietnam and China have been fighting for supremacy in Indochina for over five hundred years. Currently, Vietnam is in the lead. The Chinese have allied themselves with the Cambodians against Vietnam while Thailand waits on the sidelines. Rebellions continue in Laos, Thailand, Cambodia and Vietnam. Don't expect peace to break out anytime soon.

China has nuclear weapons, and no one else in the area seems likely to obtain them anytime soon. Vietnam has forestalled China's nuclear, and conventional, superiority by allying itself with Russia.

INDONESIA

■ Continued economic decline raises potential for bloody revolution.

■ Reversal of economic decline increases grabs at neighboring territory.

Through most of its history, Indonesia was a collection of separate states spread over several large islands. It took several hundred years of Dutch colonial activity to unify them. After 1945, Indonesia became independent and the value of its oil began to rise. With oil wealth came ambition. With ambition came attempts to forcibly realign the ethnic composition of several of its larger islands. The populations involved have frequently resisted violently. The Indonesian government responded with even greater violence. All this mayhem has not attracted much attention in the West, despite the six-figure death toll and the use of air power and other modern weapons against nearly defenseless victims. Expect to see more civil disorder and rebellion within Indonesia. No nuclear weapons in the offing, all the killing is done the old-fashioned way.

KOREA

■ North Korea instigates a violent border incident.

Because of the bizarre Communist government in North Korea, a constant threat of war has existed since 1953. In that year war started by North Korea in 1950 was interrupted by a negotiated cease-fire. That war has never officially ended. Substantial combat forces have been maintained on both sides of the cease-fire line ever since.

North Korea is ruled (as of 1987) by Kim Il Sung, who was installed by the Russians after World War II. During the early 1980s, Kim began attempting to turn his powers over to his son. Although the government is nominally Communist, it is a hereditary military dictatorship. The Kim family takes good care of the armed forces, and the armed forces keep the population in line. South Korea, with a slightly more democratic, capitalistic approach, has a per capita income twice that of North Korea. In addition, the South has twice as many people, giving it a national income four times that of the North.

South Korea also has a military-dominated government, although the opposition is active and even has a chance of installing a more democratic government.

But for now, both Koreas are ruled by military dictatorships. Each Korea maintains a large military establishment for the primary purpose of preventing the other Korea from taking it over. North Korea occasionally sends in terrorist teams or assassinates South Korean officials in other nations. The United States restrains South Korea from retaliation, through the presence of American troops and extensive economic ties. Russia likewise restrains North Korea, but has no troops there, although substantial forces are available near the border they share. Russia has less control over North Korea, and a new war could be triggered if North Korea instigates a violent enough border incident.

No nuclear weapons, although South Korea is rapidly developing the capability to produce them.

THE AMERICAS

■ Social and economic problems create endless revolutions.

■ Long-standing animosity toward the United States makes American involvement a cause as often as a cure for strife.

You can't go to war in the Western Hemisphere without the acquiescence of the United States. In a pattern common with leading military powers, its area of predominance is considered off-limits to foreign nations, ideologies and disputes.

Latin American armed forces have much more experience fighting their own citizens than other soldiers. The United States has largely taken a hands-off attitude toward this internal violence, unless, of course, there was involvement by nations outside the Western Hemisphere, especially Russia. This double standard has caused contention in American politics. Aside from United States partisans of both left- and right-wing revolutionaries, there is an undercurrent of demand for fair play and consistent treatment of unrest.

Cuba has shown that a Latin American nation can be transformed into a Russian-style Communist state. This did not bring prosperity to Cuba, but it did alleviate extreme poverty. Cuba has survived the wrath of the United States *and* has gotten Russia to pay the bills for a Communist Cuban economy that doesn't work. Very macho.

Most Latin American disorders spring from social, economic and political inequality. It is difficult to solve these problems through internal revolution. The most ruthless and best organized revolutionaries tend to be the last group you want running the government. Most of the population, particularly in the poorer nations, is not interested in the tumultuous process of revolution. The groups in power are even less accommodating to revolutionary social change.

The United States has recognized the basic social problems in Latin America and has realized that they must be addressed to prevent unrest. Frustration in coping with tangled social problems might, as it has in the past, cause us to send in the Marines. Such actions, in turn, would cause unrest on the American political scene as well as south of the border.

Many Latin American nations are sliding further into social distress. Some will be tempted to try some form of socialism, a situation that would be distasteful to an American government. The United States will intervene with greater amounts of military and diplomatic force, or the offending nations will back down. The latter is more likely in Central America, where none of the nations is strong enough to withstand American strength.

Russian foreign policy is more pragmatic and does not have to worry about any resulting dissent back home. Keeping the Latin American pot boiling costs Russia little, and causes the United States a great deal of political and economic grief.

Nuclear weapons are not a current threat, although Argentina and Brazil are capable of producing them.

RUSSIA AND CHINA

- Internal disorder in Russia would tempt China to reclaim lost territories.
- Revival of radicalism in China could trigger an attempt at recovering lost territories.
- Rapid growth of the Chinese economy and continued stagnation in Russia would create pressure within Russia to attack China before it became too strong.

This might not trigger World War III, but it would certainly be the messiest conflict in history, with Russia prepared to use chemical and nuclear weapons.

Russia has a history of taking territory and not giving it back. Most of Russia's far eastern regions, including all of its ports and naval bases on the Pacific, were seized from China in the 1800s. Also, Outer Mongolia was removed from China's control and made a vassal state of Russia. From the Russian perspective, territories in eastern China, sparsely populated by non-Chinese Orientals, are likely targets for acquisition.

The Chinese civilian population near the border outnumbers the Russians by over 10 to 1. About a third of Chinese ground forces are stationed here, making both sides roughly equal in number of soldiers. However, the Russian units depend on a single rail line to the west for their supplies. Were the Chinese to make a real go of it, the Russians would have a difficult time resisting, were it not for nuclear weapons. Short-, medium- and long-range missiles are aimed at most of China. Although the Chinese have built up a nuclear arsenal, there is no doubt who would come out a distant second in a nuclear exchange.

At this point, only the Chinese are likely to force the issue. The Chinese take the long view and are inclined to pick away at Russia's world position. When Russia falls into a state of internal disorder, or is otherwise more inclined to negotiate, the lost lands would be reclaimed. As long as over a million heavily armed troops stare at each other across the border, there is always the possibility of things getting worse.

SOUTH AFRICA

- Increased white emigration encourages blacks, demoralizes whites, increases the chance of large-scale insurrection.
- Suppression of rebellions in states bordering South Africa increases support for an uprising in South Africa.

Throughout history, whenever a minority rules one or more larger groups, eventually the majority gets the upper hand. Never before, however, has the minority had nuclear weapons.

That is the situation in South Africa. A minority of Dutch and British descent rules a majority of indigenous Africans and people of mixed race. The ruling minority has superior firepower, even without the nuclear weapons. It also has superior technical, economic and organizational skills. This is unusual in the history of minority rule situations; usually the minority has achieved control through military power alone.

Many other African nations have minority rule. The South African situation is different because of the racial divisions. Somehow, political and economic domination is more palatable if the exploiters look like the exploited. The racial angle is carried further in the world press. It is assumed that whites should know better than to engage in such unsavory behavior.

Many white South Africans compound the problem by agreeing with much of what their overseas critics say. In other parts of Africa, minority despots simply cry racism when foreigners confront them with their abominable behavior. But these local potentates are even more severe to their critics than the white South Africans are. In annual casualties from civil disorder in African nations, South Africa barely makes the top ten.

Only a minority of white South Africans cling to the permanent separation of the races and legalized dominance of the whites. What nearly all whites fear is a black-dominated government that might allow society to crumble into the chaos and tyranny found in so many other black-ruled African nations. Added to the bleak political prospects is the tendency of most newly independent black nations to wreck their economies with ill-conceived attempts at socialism. Again, there is hope; the most economically successful African nations are not socialist and the socialist nations are finally noticing this and changing.

Unlike the rest of Africa, where despair and stagnation are the rule, South Africa has a robust economy that few of its citizens want to see sacrificed in the name of political change. Many of the whites, who have the most to lose, realize that the longer they resist political accommodations with the nonwhites, the greater the risk of a catastrophic conflict.

Even if majority rule were achieved, avoiding civil war will not be easy. The nonwhite community has several ethnic and political factions which cannot agree with each other on how to achieve a new political order. This is a familiar pattern in newly minted nations, particularly in Africa.

Like most other African nations, the nonwhite South Africans still have a tribal outlook, even in cities. Throughout Africa, many prospective leaders have tended to play upon tribal loyalties to establish dictatorships. They then trash the economy and kill large numbers of citizens, either directly for holding dissident ideas or indirectly through increasingly wretched living conditions. This is the nightmare the white minority of South Africa fears. One of the few exceptions to this pattern lies just north of South Africa. Zimbabwe (Rhodesia) was formerly ruled by a white minority. After much civil strife and international pressure, political accommodation was reached. But the black resistance promptly split along tribal lines, with the larger group seizing power and persecuting the smaller tribes. However, the black leadership protected the minority whites. Most of the whites who stayed (about half) were farmers. Zimbabwe continues to feed itself, and enjoys economic prosperity rarely seen in Africa. However, this prosperity is dependent on South African trade and transport. Zimbabwe is largely an agricultural nation, while South Africa possesses a large industrial economy.

Today, if the South African economy is to survive, the economic reward system will have to change. There are not enough whites to fill all the skilled jobs. More black managers, professionals and technicians will make political democracy difficult to put off. Many whites, and nonwhite middle-class South Africans, are uncertain whether these changes would be to their benefit. What is becoming increasingly obvious is that no change at all will certainly harm everyone.

A likely outcome will be increased unrest, followed by increased exodus of the white population and the middle classes of the other ethnic groups. This would make it increasingly difficult to muster trained manpower to maintain order. Such a "white flight" would also demoralize the substantial portion of the nonwhite population that has backed the minority government. It might well result in a settlement in favor of majority rule.

There is another, more violent possibility. In the past, the white minority has turned on the black majority with a savage display of force. As many other nations have demonstrated, a minority can govern an insubordinate majority by ruthlessly applying armed force. A few massacres here and there usually quiet things down. The Boers and Zulus have one thing in common: Both have achieved their warrior reputations by prodigious slaughter of their opponents. Suppression has happened in South Africa in the past, and may very well happen again.

A future war in South Africa would likely be one of slaughters, not battles. The South African government has arranged the location and layout of black townships to make it easy for the military to attack them. In addition to military losses, the townships are at the mercy of white-controlled food and medicine distribution systems. If unrest persisted, there would be massive losses from starvation and disease. To implement this slaughter the whites would have to destroy much of what they have. This might be difficult for the English-speaking whites, but the Boers have done it before and appear capable of doing it again. There is much incentive for compromise and accommodation, for the alternative is, as the chief of the Zulus constantly reminds everyone, "a great slaughter."

BLACK AFRICA

- Continued economic decline fosters perpetual unrest. More economic distress moves these nations closer to war.
- Improvement of economies without political equity makes possible larger-scale revolts and coups. This pattern will continue.

The nations lying between the Sahara and South Africa are the residue of tribal Africa. The area is disease-ridden jungle or dry plains. Much of it has only been populated in the last fifteen hundred years. Most of South

Africa was largely unpopulated until four hundred years ago. By and large, the area did not develop economic, administrative and technical mechanisms at the same rate as Europe, North Africa and Asia. Although iron was being worked as early as 200 B.C., only a few feudal kingdoms developed.

The persistent tribal nature of Africa left it vulnerable to the depredations of better armed and organized Arabs and Europeans. No outside groups advanced beyond the coasts, however, until they had developed some protection against the imposing array of diseases central Africa possesses to this day. Even the considerable slave trade was conducted from coastal forts or ships off shore. Here, local kings and chiefs would sell their criminals and war prisoners to European, American and Arab slave traders.

After less than two hundred years of serious colonial activity, the Europeans left, because most colonies were economic liabilities. The Europeans had introduced just enough medical and administrative skills to touch off a population explosion. The primitive African agricultural and technical skills could not support a large population, and the colonial administrations did not see these matters as worthy of much attention. The educational and administrative superstructure left behind by the colonial powers was just enough to make local rulers feel that they could control the essentially tribal political organizations. In fact, European weapons maintained whatever degree of nationhood that existed. Most of the population was too busy getting by to bother with whoever was proclaiming himself president or emperor for life.

Misrule, and popular and tribal resentment of it, created a state of constant violence. Even in Ethiopia, which has endured as a nation for over two thousand years, population growth and lack of skills to cope with it have created chaos.

The superpowers support governments or insurgents as it fits their purpose. This is a safe place for the superpowers to get violent with each other, or rather each other's unfortunate proxies. Africa, particularly South Africa, contains some raw materials vital to Western industry. For Russia, seeing these raw materials disappear would simply give them some monopoly markets. Aside from this, there is little of vital interest to either the United States or Russia in Africa.

16

Data Base

This data base describes all of the wars referred to in the book. This is a reference section which backs up our conclusions and gives you a good opportunity to make your own case for differing views.

There are three main charts: Two Hundred Years of War, Wars That Never Happened and Future Wars. Preceding them are keys defining each term and brief descriptions of the conflicts in the first chart (Wars That Never Happened are described in chapter 10, Future Wars in 15). The conflict descriptions include starting date, which will help you locate wars in their chronological order in the chart.

Not all the information we compiled on the last two centuries of war could be printed out here, as it would have made a book all by itself. But we have provided descriptions of all the information in the original data base in the key. The items shown in the main historical data base chart are in boldface. As examples of the total scope of the data base, ten wars (five historical and five future) are given in their entirety.

The next chapter will extract some of the important trends we've spotted in these numbers, and will get you started at finding patterns on your own. (In some cases numbers have been rounded off and, if they are percentaged, will not add to 100 percent.)

TERMS

(Before each item there is a short acronym, such as DEND (Decision to END war), that makes it easier for the computer, and sometimes people, to refer to the data.)

War Identification Section

These items provide the basic information about the war.

War: Name of war. In many cases the name of the country in which the war was fought or the name of the nation most involved.

Side: Name of the side involved in the war. Usually this is a nation. In that case we use its current name. For example, Persia is called Iran, Abyssinia is called Ethiopia, Java and environs are called Indonesia. We use Russia, not the Soviet Union, because Russia is the Russian Empire, as it always has been. When the participant is not a nation, we use generic terms like Rebels and Insurgents, or a more specific name.

REGION of fighting.

1. Africa. All of Africa south of the Arab or Moslem nations in the north.
2. East Asia. All of Asia east of India to the Pacific rim.
3. Russia. Wars involving Russia or fought in Russia or on the Russian border.
4. Europe. All of Europe up to the Russian and Turkish border.
5. India Vicinity. Pakistan, India, Nepal, Ceylon, etc.
6. Middle East-North Africa east to Afghanistan.
7. Americas. North, Central and South America.

Began: Year in which the war began. Sometimes it differs from the official starting date. We used the date at which hostilities or large-scale unrest began. For Future Wars and Wars That Did Not Happen we used the date on which a war became likely.

End: Year in which the war ended. This may differ from the official ending date. Many large wars rage on even after several participants have declared them over. The Taiping Rebellion was a classic case; it ended several times before it finally ended. Also, several wars were waged spasmodically. We have made judgment calls on extended wars. If unrest and civil disorder remained between the active "wars," then we combined them into one conflict. This is particularly true in Africa during the 1800s, when colonial powers were often constantly at war with restless tribes. Tribes such as the Ashanti and Zulus rose up regularly against the British. There was actually one continual war interrupted only by temporary exhaustion on the part of the rebels.

Pop: Population of nation at start of war. Many people think this is a measure of the military power of a nation. We include it here to demonstrate that it is often misleading in millions.

SCALE: Level of conflict:

0—Terrorist activity handled largely by police forces.
1—Terrorist activity requiring paramilitary action. Also low-level guerrilla wars.
2—Terrorist activity involving nearly all armed forces. Also medium-level guerrilla war involving regular armed forces.
3—High-intensity guerrilla war and high level of terrorist activity.
4—Sustained guerrilla or low-level conventional war.
5—State of war, continuous operations using primarily conventional forces.
6—Low-scale, conventional war (Falklands, Lebanon).
7—Medium-size, local conventional war (Iran/Iraq).
8—Multitheater conventional war (Chinese, United States Civil Wars).
9—Worldwide war (Napoleonic, World War I, World War II).

DUR: Duration of the war (in years or fractions of a year).

War Resources Section

These items measured what the participants had available to fight a war.

GOV: Type of government. To see if certain types of governments are more prone to warlike behavior than others, we categorized each war's participants by type of government.

AM—Absolute Monarchy
CD—Civilian Dictatorship
CM—Constitutional Monarchy
DM—Democracy
IN—Insurgency
MD—Military Dictatorship
RD—Religious Dictatorship

SD—Socialist Dictatorship
TR—Tribal

GSTAB: Government stability. 9 = most stable, 1 = most unstable. This value suggests the likelihood a nation will get involved in a war or be able to continue it.

SUPT: Major power support. A powerful ally supplying noncombat support. Degree of support indicated by a number from 1–9. A 1 indicates no appreciable support while a 9 indicates maximum support short of sending in combat units. This type of support is not always a matter of public record. But it is often the cause of a war, as the patron nation encourages its client to do its dirty work. A classic case is Angola, where Russia arms and encourages one side while America does likewise for the opposition.

PWRSTAT: Power status. Ranking of a nation's military power at the time the war began. 1–3 indicates a militarily insignificant power, 4–6 is a minor power and 7–9 a major power. These values are derived by the analog method. That is, take all nations at the time of the war and rank them in order of perceived military power. The top third are 7–9, etc. We use this value to look for any relationships between superior military power and tendencies toward war.

LADV: Long-term advantages in waging war. A 1–9 scale (1 = worst, 9 = best). This indicates resources that enable the nation to increase its combat capability considerably the longer the war goes on. This estimate was used to look for propensity to go to war.

SADV: Short-term advantages in waging war. A 1–9 scale (1 = worst, 9 = best). Initial advantage. A combination of military, geographical, political and other factors which make one side more powerful than the other in the opening stages of a war.

CMBT: Combat forces (number of troops) in thousands. We found that the raw number of troops usually has more to do with a war getting started than with predicting who will win.

QUAL: Armed forces quality (.1 to 1 = best quality). This is an estimate based on past performance of that nation's armed forces and the actual performance in the war in question. This value often is quite different from what a nation's leaders thought it was before they got themselves involved in a war.

PWR: Combat power. We multiplied CMBT by QUAL to show actual combat ability. This has to be considered when calculating how well each side estimates the other's combat ability. (In the charts, the figures for PWR were divided by 10.)

War Causes Section

The elements that brought the participants to a warlike mood.

POPINV: Popular enthusiasm. To what degree was the majority of the population in favor of the war? On a 1–9 scale where 1 = opposition, 5 = resignation, 9 = enthusiasm. This may help to push a nation over the brink to war.

PI: Perception of inferiority. A value from 1–9 indicating that side's perception of the other side's military inferiority. A 5 indicates perceived parity, 9 is absolute superiority and 1 absolute inferiority of the other side. This is a likely to be a crucial variable in predicting whether a nation will attack.

SG: Grievances. A value from 1–9 indicating intensity of grievances toward the other side. 1 is lowest, 9 is most intense. This is primarily a matter of public opinion, either among the ruling class or in a democracy among a larger group. Popular pressure to set things right can easily create a warlike atmosphere.

NO: Negotiation. A value from 0–9 indicating degree to which the side is willing to negotiate grievances. 0 indicates absolute willingness while 9 indicates absolute unwillingness. A low value here, combined with a high Grievance value (above) will demonstrate a high probability of war.

AC: Activity to inflame. A value from 0–9 indicating activity by that side to inflame opinion on grievances. A 0 indicates no activity, 9 indicates maximum activity to inflame. This indicates the intention of the government to dampen or heighten tensions. As this value goes, negotiation willingness (above) should also. If not, then deviousness is the order of the day.

HI: Historical patterns. A value from 1–9 indicating historical patterns in settling grievances. A 1 indicates a strong pattern of nonviolent settlement while 9 indicates a strong pattern of using force to settle grievances. This is a good indicator of how the nation will ultimately deal with the situation. Russia has a high value.

DU: Perceived unrest. A value from 1–9 indicating *perceived* instability of the other side's government and population. A 1 indicates perception of low unrest and instability in the other nation, a 9 indicates assumption of near total anarchy and breakdown of civil order in the other nation. This critical factor is independent of actual conditions in the other nation. A perception of chaos on the other side is an invitation to attack. Iraq going after Iran in 1980 is a classic case.

Risk: Danger level. A combination of the above values indicating probability of war breaking out. The higher the value, the higher the probability a war will occur.

Type: Type of war. We categorized wars into the following groups:

C—Civil terror
R—Social revolution
S—Secessionist movement
T—Territorial conflict

ISTAB: Instability. What types of decisions caused instability between combatants that led to war. There might have been a combination. For the purposes of analysis we had to choose the leading cause.

FA—Fear of being attacked
ID—Internal disorder
LG—Long-standing grievances
SS—Sense of military superiority

INIT: Loss of control. What types of decisions precipitated the start of war. There might have been a combination; for the purposes of analysis we had to choose the leading cause.

AM—Attack enemy in compliance with treaty obligation
AT—Attack enemy deliberately to force decision
DF—Attacked by enemy
TE—Tension between states or antagonists leads to action

War Termination Section

These are the items which contributed to the war's ending.

KDESP: Key situation during conduct of war. What attitude during the war set the stage for the war ending.

EX—Exhaustion of states leads to slowing, halting war
MP—Military prowess leads nation to think victory is imminent
NG—Negotiation with enemy
SM—Stalemate leads to stopping war
SU—Surrender
UN—Unresolved conflict

DEND: Key decision that ended the war. What situation precipitated the end of war. We are looking for patterns.

CS—Collapse of society
MD—Military defeat
MS—Military stalemate
MV—Military victory
NC—No combat between nations

Result: What was accomplished because of the war.

DI—Issues that caused war resolved by destroying defeated nation
IR—Issues that caused the war resolved
NR—Issues that caused the war not resolved

War Results Section

After the fighting was over, what was the result?

Losses: Military and civilian. Keep in mind that it is often difficult to separate them. A further complication is that civilian losses are often not noted in histories.

INT: Intensity. Casualties per million population for that nation in the war. Shows how well prepared a nation is to absorb losses.

CONCEN: Concentration of the war. Intensity value (above) divided by duration. A war that causes more losses in a shorter period of time is more likely to lead the participants to consider peace.

INV: Involvement. This is calculated by multiplying duration (DUR) times effort (EFRT) times power status (PWRSTAT) times scale (SCALE). It is a measure of the degree to which the nation was involved in a war.

EFRT: Effort. Relative effort each side made in this war. Britain, for example, made little effort in any colonial war it fought during the nineteenth century. Britain's opponents, however, often made much larger efforts. On a 1–9 scale, 1–3 = use of peacetime forces, 4–6 = partial mobilization of wartime resources, 7–9 = total war, mobilization of maximum resources.

WAR DESCRIPTIONS

The descriptions for the Wars That Never Happened and the Future Wars are found in chapters 10 and 15.

This section gives basic descriptions of the wars. We focus on the participants. In larger wars, there are often a number of independent wars going on at the same time. Not all of the participants are fighting every other participant on the other side. Because we consider a large war a single action, we also consider all of the participants sufficiently linked by self-interest or mutual enemies to consider all to be fighting in the same war. World War II is the best example of such a war.

To find a description of a war in the data base, look for the countries involved or look for the war itself. In this way, you will be able to learn about the war and to see how it fits the pattern for specific countries.

Afghanistan. Between 1798 and 1986, Iran, Britain, the Punjab and now the Russians have tried many times to conquer the tough tribal populations. These are known often as the Afghan Wars. (See 1810, 1816, 1818, 1836, 1838, 1850, 1856, 1863, 1878, 1919 and 1978.)

Algeria. Between 1815 and 1963 European powers vied for control of Algeria. In 1815 the United States landed some troops in response to domestic unrest. In the 1950s France had its own "Vietnam War" in Algeria, eventually withdrawing. (See 1830.)

Amazon War. In the Sudan, the Fulani and Tukulör tribes were dominant, although the Ashanti and Dahomey tribes competed for control. From 1818–58 the Dahomey tribe's Amazon army gained control.

Angola. In 1902 Portugal made Angola a colony. Numerous rebel groups fought the Portuguese to regain control. In 1975 Cuban troops with Russian and East German advisers supported a Marxist insurgency. (See 1961.)

Arabs. The Arabs are a collection of different tribes that only recently united into nations. From 1839 to 1939, the British, Germans and Arabs fought for control of the Middle East. Since World War II and the dissolution of the British Empire, religious schisms and instability have marked Mideast politics. (See 1900 and 1914.)

Ashanti. In the early 1600s the Akan people in West Africa settled in the Volta region. In the 1800s there was a series of wars between the Ashanti tribe and Britain, which the British forces won. In 1806–7 the

Ashantis and Coastals fought in the Gold Coast War. (See 1821, 1873 and 1895.)

Austria. Between 1848–49 Austria went to war to prevent Italian unification. In 1848–49 there were the Austro-Sardinian War, the Austro-Italian War and the Austrian Civil War. In 1866 Austria, Germany and Italy fought the Austro-Prussian War, also known as the Seven Weeks War. This was followed by Italian unification. (See 1787, 1789, 1792, 1803, 1815, 1820, 1839, 1853, 1859, 1885 and 1914.)

Bali War. From 1839 to 1849 Holland fought the Bali in the Bali War, another colonial war.

Balkan War. During 1912–13 the Balkan Wars acted as the rehearsal for World War I. The First Balkan War, in 1912–13, and the Second Balkan War, in 1913, involved Montenegro, Serbia, Greece, Turkey and Bulgaria.

Batetela War. Belgian forces crushed the ferocious Batetela tribe in the Upper Congo between 1897–1900.

Belgian Revolution. In 1830 Dutch forces and civilians revolted against William I (Prince of Orange). Shortly thereafter, Belgium declared independence. Belgium, Holland and France were involved after the Kingdom of the Netherlands was dissolved. (For other Belgian Wars see 1885, 1897 and 1940.)

Bhurtpore. In the Third Maratha War in India British forces intervened in 1825–26 in the city of Bhurtpore in a violent battle.

Bhutan War. The British tried to quell disorder in Bhutan, along the Indian border in 1865. Bhutanese forces defeated the British, but the British counterattacked and defeated the Bhutanese.

Black Hawk War. The Black Hawk War in 1832 was one of many Indian wars. The Sac and Fox tribes in Illinois and Wisconsin, under chief Black Hawk, sought to regain control over their territory. Colonel, later President, Zachary Taylor ended the war at the Battle of the Bad Ax.

Boer Wars. Between 1799 and 1914 the white South Africans fought the Bantu, Xhosa, Zulu and Basuto tribes. The most formidable tribe, the Zulus, fought some of the bloodiest battles. Later, the British became involved in wars with the Boers over trade, winning by starving the Boers out. (See 1799, 1811, 1834, 1838, 1842, 1858, 1862, 1880, 1899 and 1914.)

Bolivar's Wars. In 1811 Venezuela, Simon Bolivar, in cooperation with José de San Martín in Argentina, started a resistance movement against the Spanish. In 1824 Spanish forces were withdrawn, marking the end of Spanish conquest in the New World.

Bornu Rebellion. In 1893 the Sudanese tribes of Bornu and Zobeir were involved in battles with Egypt and Britain, often switching sides. This led to the conquest of the ancient Sultanate of Bornu by Britain. (See 1804.)

Brabant Revolt. The Austrians violated civil rights in the Austrian Netherlands, which resulted in an armed insurrection in 1789–90.

Brazil-Argentina War. From 1825–28, Argentina tried to acquire Uruguay by aiding a rebellion in Banda Oriental (Uruguay), a Brazilian province. (See 1843, 1864, 1893 and 1944.)

Buraimi. In 1952 Saudi forces invaded the Buraimi Oasis territory that was claimed by the Sultan of Muscat and Oman. British-led forces of Muscat and Oman repulsed the invading Saudi forces in 1955.

Burma. Burmese politics is dominated by various ethnic and political groups. The Arakan Revolt in 1811, the Assam War in 1819 and the Burmese Civil War in 1838 were among the many conflicts between ethnic groups, and from 1823 to 1946 Britain was involved. Since 1948 there has been a continuous drug war between Burmese Communist rebels, Chinese Nationalist forces, Laotian royalists and insurgents in the mountains. (See 1852, 1885 and 1956.)

Burundi Civil War. Burundi, a small African nation that borders Zaire, Rwanda and Tanzania, had a civil war in 1970–72.

Cambodia. Vietnam, Thailand and rebel groups have fought in Cambodia for hundreds of years. In 1812 Cambodian rebels, Thailand and Vietnam fought one another. In the 1940s and 1950s France became embroiled in a colonial war. Since the 1960s the Khmer Rouge and rightist groups have fought Vietnam over centuries-old antagonisms. (See 1831, 1841, 1866, 1964, 1970, 1975 and 1978.)

Cameroon. In the late nineteenth century, Germany established colonies in Africa, including Cameroon. In 1905–7 Germany fought tribes in Cameroon but eventually lost. After minor French incursions in 1956–59, the Cameroon civil war continued from 1962 to 1971.

Central America. In the 1830s and 1840s rebel groups fought in Central America. In the twentieth century U.S. troops were sent to Central America to quell insurrections and revolutions from the turn of the century to the present. In the 1980s, Nicaragua, Honduras and El Salvador are fighting internally and one another.

Chaco War. Fought from 1928–35 between Paraguay and Bolivia. Bolivia wanted access to the sea, but Paraguay won what it wanted, control over the Chaco region. Losses were extremely heavy.

Chad. Bordered by Libya, Sudan, the Central African Republic, Niger, Cameroon and Nigeria, Chad is a primitive, poor nation. When the French defeated Islamic fiefdoms from 1899 to 1900, Chad became part of French Equatorial Africa. There was more fighting between French, Chadian and Arab forces in 1965–71, and a coup in 1975.

Chile. In the nineteenth century Spain fought in Chile, one of the last outposts of Spanish control in South America. Spain eventually was pushed out of Chile. (See 1836, 1865 and 1879.)

China. The world's most enduring civilization (5,000 years old), China has been involved in countless wars through a succession of dynasties. From 1796 through the 1800s, Asian and European powers fought the Chinese over access to Chinese markets. In the Kashgari War (1825–31) China fought Turkomen. In 1839, Britain fought the Opium War, and France sent troops to China. The Taiping Rebellion raged from 1850–81. The Japanese fought the Chinese in the 1894–95 Sino-Japanese War, and there was the Boxer Rebellion in 1899. In the 1930s Japan invaded Manchuria. From 1911 to 1948 there was a Chinese civil war between the Communist forces of Mao Tse-tung and the Nationalist forces of Chiang Kai-shek. Other incidents in the 1950s, the Korean War and fighting between Chinese and Tibetan forces, and the Cultural Revolution in the 1960s and 1970s add to China's turbulent past. There was a minor border skirmish in 1969 between Chinese and Russian forces. The invasion of Vietnam by Chinese in 1979 seemed to signal the end of Chinese patience with Vietnam. (See 1847, 1856, 1882, 1884, 1941, 1946, 1948, 1950, 1956, 1959, 1961, 1962 and 1966.)

Colombia. In addition to a civil war in 1860–61, since 1948 Colombia has been involved in an insurgency by loosely affiliated groups. (See 1863, 1903 and 1958.)

Congo War. Before the Congo was renamed Zaire after independence in 1960, it was an unstable region of tribal fighting. This fighting led to the collapse of the Tshombe regime, and by 1967 the insurgency was crushed and the rebels escaped into Angola. (See 1949.)

Convict Rebellion. The Irish Convict Rebellion. In 1804 in a New South Wales penal colony, Irish political prisoners, arrested in the Irish revolution of 1798, rebelled. The government ruthlessly suppressed the rebellion.

Crete Revolution. Between 1866 and 1868 an insurrection on the Turkish-ruled island of Crete was instigated by Greek inhabitants and by

Greece. Lasting two years, the Cretan Insurrection ended after bloody fighting.

Crimean War. The Crimean War was one of the major European wars of the nineteenth century. It involved Britain, France, Russia and Turkey. Russia wanted entry into the Mediterranean, France did not want Russia to become more powerful and Britain sought to maintain the balance of power. (See 1853.)

Cuba. After decades of unrest in Cuba, Spanish control of Cuba was challenged in the insurrection of 1868–78, known as the Ten Years War. In 1895–98 popular discontent with the Spanish colonial government led to the Cuban Insurrection that Spain crushed. (See 1912, 1956, 1974, 1975 and 1981.)

Cyprus. Clashes in Cyprus revolved around historical antagonisms between Greek and Turkish inhabitants that were exacerbated by a joint Turkish-Cypriot declaration of a federal state. After a conflict with Britain and Greece from 1952–59, a United Nations peacekeeping force enforced a cease-fire between Greek and Turkish troops in 1964. There were additional clashes in 1974.

Czechoslovakia. In 1968 Russian forces invaded Czechoslovakia to crush an uprising. (See 1919.)

Dahomey. The Dahomey were an aggressive tribe in West Africa near the Sudan and the Volta River. In 1889 the First Dahomey-French War led to the creation of a French protectorate. In the Second Dahomey-French War in 1892, France defeated the Dahomey and annexed the area. Uprisings continued from 1893–99. (See 1818 and 1963.)

Dhofar. The Dhofar Province has been the site of low-level conflict between Oman and South Yemen since the early 1960s. South Yemen provides arms and supplies to Dhofar rebels. Guerrilla battles on a larger scale began in the late 1960s and early 1970s. The Dhofari insurgents suffered a defeat in 1974 by forces from Oman, Iran and Britain.

Druse Rebellion. The Druse are an Islamic sect in the Shuf Mountains in Lebanon. In 1925 the Druse Rebellion challenged French control of Lebanon, and in 1926 the rebellion swept through Damascus. In 1927 the rebellion collapsed in the face of French firepower. (See 1953.)

East Germany. In June 1953 riots by anticommunist supporters in East Germany and East Berlin were crushed by the Soviet Army.

Ecuador. Long-standing border dispute with Colombia. (See 1827 and 1863.)

Egypt. In 1786 Turkish forces crushed a revolt in Egypt, which was controlled by the Ottoman Empire. Between 1805–11, Britain and Turkey fought various rebel groups. In 1839 Austria, Britain and Turkey fought the Egyptian War, and Arabs and Egyptians fought the Red Sea War beginning in 1865. In 1871–75 Egypt and Sudan fought the Sudan War, which was really the second phase of the Red Sea War, and the Upper Nile War was in 1874–79 between Egypt and rebels. British forces occupied Egypt from 1881–82. Many of the wars in Egypt resulted from attempts by the Ottoman Empire to retain control over territory in North Africa. (See 1820, 1832, 1875, 1948, 1956, 1961, 1967 and 1973.)

El Salvador. Since the 1970s Marxist-Leninist insurgency has fomented instability and violence in El Salvador. Supported by the Soviets, Cubans and Nicaraguans, the insurgents have fought U.S. government-backed forces. (See 1979.)

Ethiopia. Known also as Abyssinia, Ethiopia fought against the Kwara tribe in 1841. In the Anglo-Abyssinian War from 1867–68 a British expedition defeated Ethiopian forces. Egypt and Ethiopia fought the Abyssinian War from 1875 to 1879. In 1868–72 and 1889–99 there were civil wars that unified the disparate tribes, and also the Shoa War with the Shoa tribe. Italian forces fought Ethiopian forces from 1895–96, and in 1935 Italy invaded Ethiopia. In 1961, the emperor was overthrown, and from 1974 to now the Eritrean War and insurgencies in Ethiopia have been thwarted by government forces supported by Cuban troops, plus East German and Soviet advisers. (See 1854, 1881, 1889, 1895, 1899, 1941, 1964 and 1974.)

Falklands. After Argentinian forces invaded the Falkland Islands in 1982, Britain responded with naval and ground forces. In six weeks Argentinian forces surrendered or were destroyed by superior British forces.

Formosa War. In April to October 1874, Japan sent forces to Formosa to retaliate for the murder of sailors on the Ryukyu Islands, which Japan claimed as sovereign territory.

Franco-Prussian War. After the Prussian political leader Bismarck established a loose confederation of German states under the control of Prussia, he attempted to install a German prince as king of Spain. Napoleon III of France was thus threatened by Germans on two fronts. France declared war and German forces defeated the French, forcing France to cede Alsace-Lorraine to Germany. (See 1870.)

Franco-Spanish War. A revolt in 1821 in Spain led to French intervention in 1823. The revolution ended in 1823 with the destruction of the rebels and the freeing of King Ferdinand IV.

French Conquest. After an uprising in the French Congo in 1905, French forces established control over the Congo.

French Revolution. The French Revolution from 1792–1802 eventually resulted in the destruction of the old monarchic order in Europe. While the revolution was fought first as an internal war, France under Napoleon fought against Russia, Spain, Austria, Britain and Germany.

Fulani Wars. The Fulani tribe in Nigeria in 1790 fomented discontent against the ruling Hausa tribe and almost overthrew the Hausa Empire. From 1804–10 the Fulani succeeded in overthrowing the Hausa Empire. (See 1897.)

German Revolt. Unrest in Germany from 1847–48 was part of the general revolutionary discontent in Europe.

Great Indian Mutiny. From 1857–58 the British suppressed rebellious native forces with extreme harshness.

Greece. From 1821–32 the Greek War of Independence involved France, Britain, Egypt, Russia, and Turkey. In the revolution of 1862 King Otto was replaced by a Danish prince. The Greeks fought a Communist insurgency from 1944–49. After early British support, U.S. and United Nations forces helped end the insurgency in 1949. (See 1866, 1897, 1912, 1913, 1917, 1919, 1940, 1952 and 1963.)

Guatemala. Since 1960 a small Communist insurgency has been a continuing source of instability. (See 1960.)

Guinea-Bissau. Since the 1960s, a continuing insurgency in Portuguese Guinea is one of those small but always potentially disruptive rebellions. (See 1962.)

Gun War. From 1880–81 the Basuto tribe rebelled but was suppressed by British forces. The causes of the Gun War originated in the Basuto Wars of the Orange Free State from 1858–68, when Britain annexed what is today South Africa.

Gurkha War. From 1814–16 the British Indian Army sent an expeditionary force into Nepal to stop raids by Gurkhas into northern India. In intense fighting British forces encountered stiff resistance from the Gurkhas, but eventually subdued them.

Haiti. France attempted to control Haiti but was repulsed by Haitian forces in a savage guerrilla war from 1791–1803. Until 1822 massacres of whites and attempts by Britain and Spain to regain control dominated Haitian politics. (See 1844 and 1912.)

Honduras Wars. In 1907 Honduras was conquered by Nicaragua. From 1909–11 there was a civil war in Honduras, ending in stalemate. The insurgency in Honduras since 1980, sponsored in part by Nicaragua, is consistent with the historic animosity between the nations. (See 1912.)

Hottentot Uprising. In 1903–8 German forces suppressed an uprising by the Hottentot tribe in German Southwest Africa.

Hungary. Between 1919 and 1920 Czech, Romanian and Hungarian forces clashed in the Hungarian War, an aftermath of World War I. In 1956 Russian forces invaded Hungary to crush a popular revolt that sought to create Western-style democracy. (See 1941.)

Ifni. In 1957 Spanish forces defeated Moroccan irregular troops after the Moroccans seized the colony of Ifni. Spain agreed to cede Ifni to Morocco in 1958.

India. India was plagued by wars among ethnic and religious groups. Between 1789 and 1854 Indian groups (the Mysore, Sikhs and Maratha) and British forces fought wars, attempts by the British to bring the restive and warlike groups and tribes under central government. The British colonial government lasted until Indian independence after World War II. In 1962–63 India and China clashed in the Sino-Indian War. (See 1799, 1857, 1947, 1953 and 1971.)

Indian Wars. Wars between Indian tribes in the American Midwest and Southwest between 1850 and 1891 led to the destruction of the tribes and to U.S. control over the country. The Indians were ferocious warriors, and bloody battles and guerrilla warfare became common.

Indonesia. Created from several Dutch colonies, what is now Indonesia had first been Portuguese. It experienced numerous conflicts between colonial powers and unstable minorities. There was the Bantam Conquest in 1808, the Great Java War from 1825–30 and the Achinese War with Holland in 1900–8. Since the 1960s, the South Moluccan insurgency has threatened the Indonesian government. The insurgencies in the West Irians and Timors continue today. (See 1849, 1926, 1945, 1950, 1963, 1965, 1969 and 1975.)

Iran. Before Persia became Iran in 1935, it fought the Russians and Georgians, Afghans, Britain and rebel groups. Iran revolted against Britain in 1905. Iran has a long tradition of animosity toward Iraq, which it has occupied three times since 1500. The Gulf War that began in 1980 is only the latest conflict between Iran and Iraq, which revolves around who shall rule the Arab and Kurdish populations on both sides of the border. (See 1795, 1798, 1804, 1816, 1821, 1825, 1836, 1856, 1925, 1939, 1945, 1969, 1973 and 1979.)

Iraq Revolution. An insurrection in 1920, led by Arab nationalists, that Britain suppressed. Later the British met Arab demands for greater autonomy. (See 1939, 1967, 1969, 1973, 1979 and 1980.)

Ireland. The 1795 rebellion was one of many against British rule. A 1916–21 rebellion against Britain, and establishment of the Irish republic, led to a continuing terror campaign by the Irish Republican Army, a splinter group that opposed British rule of Northern Ireland. The war continues on a low level of terrorism.

Israel. From the war in 1948 with Syria, Jordan, Palestine and Egypt, to the wars in 1956, 1967 and 1973, Israel has had a violent history. In 1982 the Israeli Defense Force invaded Lebanon to destroy PLO forces that used Lebanon as a sanctuary for attacks against Israeli settlements. (See 1945.)

Italy. The Italian Wars include all those conflicts that Italy was involved in between 1815 and 1859. In 1820 and 1848 Italy was seized with revolutionary zeal for the ideals of unification and democracy. Italy fought its War of Independence from 1848–49 and the Roman Republic War in 1848–49, and in 1859 the Italian War of unification was fought. (See 1820, 1859, 1866, 1867, 1895, 1899, 1911, 1915, 1935, 1940 and 1947.)

Japan. From 1863–68 internal strife led to the expulsion of Westerners from Japan. This movement by the Choshu and and Satsuma clans involved intrigue, murder and civil war. In 1877 the samurai warrior class led the Satsuma Rebellion against the government in Tokyo. (See 1874, 1882, 1894, 1904, 1911, 1914, 1931, 1938 and 1941.)

Jordan. From 1970–71 King Hussein of Jordan expelled the Palestine Liberation Organization (PLO) during the Black September War. The PLO then moved into Lebanon where it was entrenched until the Israeli invasion of Lebanon in 1982. (See 1948, 1967 and 1973.)

Kaffir War. From 1846–78 Britain was involved in the Kaffir Wars in South Africa against the Boers and the Kaffirs or Xhosa tribes, who were virtually annihilated—actually starved—by the British. The final conflict was the Ninth Kaffir War from 1877–78 that led to British annexation of Kaffraria. (See 1846.)

Kashmir Dispute. When the state of Kashmir joined India in 1947 the Moslem population—which wanted to join Pakistan—rebelled. Indian troops crushed the rebellion, which led to involvement by Pakistani troops in Kashmir to help the Moslem fighters.

Kedah War. In 1821 the Siamese (Burmese) government launched an invasion of Kedah, which was a Malayan sultanate in which Britain had an interest.

Korea. In the late 1800s instability in Korea led to invasions by Japan and China, and intervention by Russia. In 1950, Russian-backed North Korea invaded American-supported South Korea. (See 1882.)

Khivan War. Russia fought against the Khivan tribe from 1839–47.

Kurdish Revolt. An independent mountain people in the border region between Iraq, Turkey and Iran, the Kurds sought to eliminate the influence of the British and the Arabs. In 1925–32 the Kurdish revolt was suppressed. (See 1979.)

La Violencia. La Violencia is the name of the Colombian civil war. In 1948 an uprising in Bogotá was suppressed by the government. A series of military coups began in 1953.

Laos. King Chao Anou of Laos (then Vientiane) sought to free himself from the control of Siam (now Burma). After building a formidable army, he invaded Siam in 1826, whereupon the Siamese invaded Laos. The war ended in 1829 with the defeat of the king and the scattering of his troops. (See 1953.)

Lebanon. Lebanon's history is marked by nearly continuous warfare. In 1958 U.S. Marines and army troops were deployed to protect Lebanon from an invasion by Syria. Since 1969, Lebanon has been a battlefield for numerous religious and ethnic groups. (See 1973 and 1975.)

López War. Also known as the War of the Triple Alliance (1864–70). The López War started after Paraguay attacked Argentina, Uruguay and Brazil. This was an exceedingly costly mistake with horrific losses on all sides.

Madagascar. The island of Madagascar played a role in English-French antagonisms in the Napoleonic Wars. There was a revolt in 1863 before France established a claim to the island, and a nationalist uprising from 1947–48 that France suppressed. Madagascar gained independence in 1960. (See 1883 and 1894.)

Malakand War. From 1896–97 there was a civil war in Chitral, India, that a British expedition suppressed.

Malaysia. From 1947–60 Britain, Australia and New Zealand fought a Communist insurgency in Malaysia. The British conducted a superb counterinsurgency campaign against the rebels. Eventually Malaysia became a constitutional monarchy. In the late 1960s the Communist insurgency revived. (See 1963 and 1968.)

Mandinga War. In West Africa in 1885 France fought the Mandinga Wars against the Ivory Coast tribes. Although France established a protectorate in 1889, the second and third Mandinga Wars were fought in 1894 and 1898.

Maori War. In New Zealand from 1843–48 the First Maori War involved British settlers and native Maoris in a guerrilla war. The Second Maori War from 1860–70 was an uprising by Maori tribes against British settlers.

Matabele Revolt. In 1893 Matabele tribes attempted to conquer the Mashonas tribe, but were unsuccessful due to British intervention. In 1896 there was another uprising by the Matabele, which the British suppressed.

Mau Mau War. The Mau Mau, a secret group in Kenya, fought an extremely violent and bloody revolt. Britain sent forces to suppress the uprising but the guerrilla war spread throughout Kenya. In 1956 the revolt was crushed.

Maumee War. The Maumee Indians in the United States launched several attacks in 1790 against settlements in the Ohio River Valley. In 1794 U.S. troops finally destroyed the Maumee Indian force.

Mauretania. From 1908–9 the French conquered Mauretania during the French colonial wars in Africa.

Mexico. After revolts against Spain in the nineteenth century, Mexico became involved in several wars with the United States. The War of Texan Independence (1835–36) started when Texan settlers rebelled against the Mexican government. The U.S.-Mexican War (1846–48) originated over the issue of the annexation of Texas to the United States. There was a civil war in Mexico from 1857–77. During the U.S. Civil War Spain, Britain and France sent forces to Mexico which resulted in an Austrian noble being made king. Native rule was returned in 1867. A Mexican civil war that started in 1911 continued sporadically until 1929. (See 1829, 1838 and 1862.)

Mombasa. British forces occupied Mombasa from 1824–28 after a dispute with the Imam of Muscat and Oman.

Morocco. During the dissolution of the Spanish Empire, there was a revolt against the Moors in Morocco from 1859–60. In 1953 there was an uprising in Morocco, and in 1955 France granted it independence. (See 1908, 1957, 1963, 1971 and 1975.)

Mozambique. A conflict between Mozambique rebels and Portuguese forces in the 1960s and 1970s turned into a Communist insurgency that continues today. (See 1962, 1975 and 1980.)

Namibia. South-West Africa was given to South Africa after World War I as a protectorate. Known today as Namibia, it is dominated by a Marxist group called SWAPO (South West Africa People's Organization) that makes war with the South African occupation forces.

Napoleonic Wars. From 1803 to 1815 France, under Napoleon I, fought Austria, Spain, Britain, Germany and Russia. A military strategist and superb tactician, Napoleon ultimately was defeated by too many powerful enemies.

Natal War. The Natal War from 1842–43 was one of the early conflicts between Britain and the Boers (See Boer Wars).

Naval Rebellion. From 1893–95 Brazilian naval and ground forces suppressed a revolt.

Nepal. In 1953 India sent troops to crush a Communist revolt in Nepal. (See 1814 and 1961.)

Nicaragua. After the overthrow of the Somoza regime in 1979 the Sandinistas formed a junta, which established a Marxist-Leninist state with support from Cuba, the Soviet Union and east European states. (See 1907, 1912, 1980 and 1981.)

Niger. From 1961 to 1974 the Niger Civil War was suppressed by the government.

Nigeria. Britain and the Nigerian Hausa and Ibo tribes fought several wars in the first decade of the twentieth century. In the late 1960s, Nigeria fought a civil war with its province of Biafra. (See 1903, 1965 and 1967.)

Ogaden. Since the 1960s an insurgency in Ogaden has been sponsored by Somalia and lately by Ethiopia and Cuba. Ogaden was defeated in a war with Somalia from 1977–78.

Pakistan. After Pakistani troops crossed into Kashmir to help Moslem rebels, Indian forces crushed the rebellion and defeated the Pakistani forces. UN mediation ended this conflict. There was another war between Pakistan and India in 1971. (See 1947 and 1972.)

PLO (Palestine Liberation Organization). Founded to oppose the usurpation of Arab lands by the State of Israel in 1948, the PLO is a terrorist organization committed to destroying Israel. Its leader, Yasir Arafat, suffered a major tactical defeat after he was forced to evacuate from Lebanon in 1982 under Egyptian protection. The chart analyzes the continuing struggles between the Arafat-led part of the PLO and its Syrian-backed sections.

Panama Revolution. After U.S. attempts to buy land for the Panama Canal were rejected by Colombia, the U.S. Navy supported a revolution in

Panama in 1903. After the United States recognized Panamanian independence, Panama signed an agreement that granted the Canal Zone to the United States.

Papal States. In 1867 during the Austro-Prussian War, Garibaldi, an Italian soldier, tried to invade the Papal States. Attempts to overthrow the Italian government resulted in the return of French forces to Italy.

Papineau's Rebellion. In 1869, a Canadian uprising started because of grievances that French Canadians were not accorded their due by the British Crown. This uprising, which occurred in Lower Canada in Quebec Province, was suppressed by British forces. (See 1885, 1914 and 1939.)

Peru. In 1827–29 Peru waged wars with Bolivia and Ecuador. In 1841 Peru invaded Bolivia, but was defeated. Peru in 1864–66 was involved in a war with Spain that was mediated by the U.S. in 1871. (See 1836, 1879 and 1980.)

Peruvian-Bolivian Confederation. After Bolivia and Peru declared a confederation in 1836, Chile declared war and defeated Bolivia in 1839 to dissolve it.

Philippines. In the Spanish-American War, (1898) Spanish and American forces clashed in the Philippines. Since 1946 the Huk Rebellion and revolts by the Moros have provided a nearly continuous Communist insurgency in the Philippines. (See 1896, 1946, 1964 and 1972.)

Poland. Poland was invaded in 1792 by Russia and Prussia. In 1863 the Second Polish Revolution spread into Lithuania and White Russia, and was suppressed ruthlessly. In World War II Poland was decimated by the Germans and Russians. From 1956–57 Russia quelled a Polish rebellion. In 1970 high prices and short supplies of meat and other foodstuffs caused riots. And in 1980 Solidarity was suppressed by the Polish government under threats of Russian invasion. (See 1794, 1919 and 1939.)

Portugal. In 1820 Portugal fought its civil war. The Miguelite War, which was a revolt in the Azores from 1828–34, was started by supporters of the Queen of Portugal. These forces were defeated by troops from England, France and Brazil. (See 1834, 1902, 1907, 1916, 1961 and 1962.)

Riel Rebellion. The Riel Rebellions in Canada from 1869–70 and in 1885 occurred in Manitoba. Started by Louis Riel after the Hudson Bay Company gave the area to the Dominion of Canada, the rebellions were crushed by Canadian forces.

Riff Wars. In 1893 Spanish forces fought Berber tribesmen in the Riff Mountains along the coast of Spanish Morocco. The tribesmen were repulsed by a Spanish force. From 1912–26 Riff Berber tribesmen were defeated by Spanish and French forces.

Rosas War. In 1843 domestic discord in Argentina and Uruguay led to intervention by England, France and Brazil. Juan Manuel de Rosas, the President of Argentina, tried to conquer Uruguay but was defeated by English, French and Brazilian forces.

Russia. From 1787 through World War II and to the present, Russia has been involved in numerous wars: the Napoleonic Wars in the early 1800s, as well as wars with Afghanistan (1978), Austria (1848), Britain (1853), Czechoslovakia (1968), East Germany (1953), France (1853), Hungary (1956), Iran (1804, 1825, 1905, 1945), Japan (1904), Khiva (1839), Merv (1884), Poland (1792, 1863, 1919, 1956), Sardinia (1853), Sweden (1788, 1808–9), Turkey (1787, 1806, 1821, 1828, 1853, 1877), Turkoman and Turkestan (Syr Darya War in 1850). There was the 1917 Russian Revolution and Civil War, and the Stalinist Terror in (1927–40) that killed twenty million. (See 1794, 1803, 1808, 1850, 1895, 1914, 1919, 1927, 1938, 1939, 1941, 1945, 1968, 1975 and 1980.)

Rwanda Civil War. Belgium suppressed a civil war between the Tutsi and Hutu tribes in West Africa from 1959–61. Another civil war in the 1960s resulted in severe losses.

South Africa. Before South Africa became independent after World War II, the Afrikaners (Boers, of Dutch descent) fought a constant series of wars with local blacks, the British and each other (1838–1914). South Africa faces a continuing rebellion by blacks against apartheid as violence slowly escalates to the point where civil war may erupt. (See 1939, 1966 and 1975.)

Sahara War. In 1900 French forces conquered the northern Sahara after a protracted desert war that resulted in the establishment of French presence there.

San Martín. In 1814–24 San Martín, the contemporary of Simon Bolivar, led a war against Spain in Argentina, Chile and Peru. Help from English, Irish, German and North American forces doomed Spanish efforts to retain control over South America.

Santo Domingo. In 1844 inhabitants of the colony of Haiti, which was part of the island of Santo Domingo, rebelled successfully against French control.

Schleswig-Holstein War. From 1848–50 Denmark, Germany and Sweden sent troops into Schleswig-Holstein to establish control. After the First Schleswig-Holstein Revolt, Prussia and Austria decided to settle the issue in 1864. German and Austrian forces attacked Danish forces in February. By August Denmark sued for peace, and in October the Treaty of Vienna ended the war.

Seminole Wars. The First Seminole War in 1818 originated in the War of 1812, when Seminole Indians allied with the British. After the Seminoles conducted raids and massacres, General Andrew Jackson led an army to destroy the Seminoles and occupy Florida. The Second Seminole War from 1835–43 resulted from the refusal of Seminole and Creek Indians to leave Florida. A low-level guerrilla war persisted for several years.

Serbo-Bulgarian War. From 1885–86 Serbia, Austria and Bulgaria fought the Serbo-Bulgarian War. Serbia invaded Bulgaria, but was defeated by Bulgarian forces. The Treaty of Bucharest ended the war.

Sierra Leone. A series of coups, revolutions and civil disorder in this West African area. (See 1967.)

Slave Wars. Between 1885 and 1898 Arab slave traders in the Upper Congo in West Africa revolted because they were threatened by growing European involvement in the slave trade. The uprising was suppressed by Belgian and British troops.

Somalia. Conflict from 1899–1920 between British and Italian forces and various tribes in Ethiopia and Somalia was consistent with the historic antagonisms in that region. Between 1964 and 1965 Somalia was involved in hostilities with Kenya and Ethiopia.

Spain. Spain has fought countless wars, beginning with the Napoleonic Wars. Britain and France, as well as the Carlists (and other rebel groups), fought in Spain in 1834. The United States fought Spain in the Spanish-American War at the end of the nineteenth century. The Spanish Civil War from 1936–1939 was particularly bloody. (See 1792, 1803, 1807, 1810, 1811, 1814, 1821, 1828, 1829, 1834, 1837, 1840, 1854, 1859, 1864, 1865, 1868, 1893, 1895, 1896, 1898, 1912, and 1957.)

Sri Lanka. In 1795 British forces defeated Dutch forces in Ceylon (now Sri Lanka). It became a British crown colony in 1798. Between 1956 and 1961 there were Tamil uprisings that began again in the 1970s and continue today.

Sudan. After Britain and France left the Sudan, the army launched a coup in 1955. In the 1960s and 1970s Sudan was plagued by a series of rebellions of ethnic and tribal groups. Today, Christians and animists are in open conflict, supplied by Libya and Ethiopia. (See 1820, 1871, 1881, 1969 and 1983.)

Syria. Since the 1950s Syria has seen numerous revolts and coups. There have been border skirmishes with Israel, and since 1975 Syria has fought in Lebanon and the Bekaa Valley. (See 1948, 1953, 1957, 1961, 1967, 1970, 1973 and 1975.)

Tecumseh War. In 1811 Tecumseh, chief of the Shawnee Indians, tried to establish a confederation of Indian tribes to remove white settlers from Indian lands. American forces routed Indian forces at the Battle of Tippecanoe.

Thailand. Fought a series of wars throughout the 1800s. Since World War II, Thailand has been affected by insurgencies, which the government has largely quelled. Thailand, however, still has problems with numerous heavily armed drug dealers in remote parts of the country. (See 1812, 1821, 1826, 1831, 1841, 1939, 1949, 1964 and 1965.)

Tirah War. Afridi tribesmen, operating on the Afghan frontier, seized the Khyber Pass and made a general nuisance of themselves in 1897. The British responded and heavy losses ensued.

Trieste Incident. In 1947 Yugoslavia threatened Italian-occupied Trieste, but an incident was avoided by the deployment of U.S. troops. This incident caused considerable tension, but there were only a few casualties.

Tripoli War. In 1801 the United States sent a punitive expedition to Tripoli after it raised the tribute that Western powers paid to them to protect commerce. A two-year U.S. blockade was ineffective.

Tuareg War. In West Africa in 1893 France conducted operations against the Tuareg tribe on the Niger River.

Tukulör War. In 1810 the Moslem Tukulör kingdom conquered the Bambara and Massina tribes near the Senegal and Niger rivers. From 1854–64 France fought the Tukulörs, and from 1864–90 dynastic battles marked the Tukulör Civil Wars.

Tunis War. The Occupation of Tunis in 1881 by France was an important step in French efforts to develop an empire in Africa.

Tunisia. After discontent with French rule, France granted independence to Tunisia. Occasional border clashes and punitive French responses to Tunisian attacks against French outposts ended in 1962 when French forces were evacuated. (See 1957.)

Tupamaros. From 1967 to 1973 the Tupamaro insurgents waged civil terror in Paraguay.

Turkey. From 1787 to 1922 Turkey was involved in a great deal of civil unrest and numerous wars with Russia, Serbia, Montenegro (the Montenegro War in 1852 and the Herzegovina War in 1860), Iran and other states.

Much of the conflict in the nineteenth and twentieth centuries can be traced to the decline of the Ottoman Empire. The Turkish Revolt from 1909–13 and the Armenian Terror from 1915–22 were extremely bloody, and today memories about the latter fuel the hatred between Turks and Armenians. (See 1786, 1804, 1805, 1806, 1815, 1821, 1828, 1832, 1839, 1853, 1866, 1876, 1877, 1897, 1911, 1912, 1913, 1914, 1915, 1925, 1957, 1963, 1974 and 1979.)

U.S. Civil War. Between 1861–1865 the U.S. Civil War between the North and South was fought over freedom for the slaves in the South. An immensely destructive war; hundreds of thousands died.

U.S. Intervention. Between 1912 and 1919 U.S. forces intervened in Haiti, Nicaragua, Honduras and Cuba to maintain order. These interventions involved small numbers of troops and usually encountered minor resistance.

Uganda. From 1885–89 there were religious wars in Uganda between Moslems and Catholics. The Moslems won. In 1897 Ugandan forces mutinied against the British. The Uganda Terror continues today, despite the overthrow of Idi Amin. Revolutionary local and tribal armies still fight for control over vital areas. (See 1971 and 1979.)

Ulster. Since 1969 the Irish Republican Army has battled British forces in Ulster. This civil terror by the IRA has been costly for the British.

Vietnam Wars. Since the 1800s Vietnam has fought colonial powers and regional nations based on long-standing ethnic and national hostilities. The French intervened in Vietnam from 1824–47, fought the first Vietnam War from 1851–95, and again after World War II France attempted to control Vietnam. However, an insurgency by Ho Chi Minh broke the will of the French. The French involvement lasted until 1954, and U.S. involvement until 1975. In the 1980s, Vietnam is fighting in Laos, Cambodia and Thailand. (See 1812, 1841, 1851, 1953, 1978 and 1979.)

Wadai War. During the French colonial wars in Africa, French forces, between 1909 and 1911, conquered the Wadai, a mountainous, arid region in eastern Chad and central Sudan.

Wahehe War. From 1891–93 in German East Africa, German forces suppressed a rebellion by the Wahehe tribe.

Wahhabi War. From 1811–18 Egyptian forces in the Sudan fought the Wahhabi, a Moslem sect that occupied Mecca, Medina and Jidda, and threatened Syria. After seven years of war, Egyptian forces restored order and brought the Red Sea coast under their control.

War of 1812. Encroachments on U.S. neutrality and sovereignty by Britain and France during the Napoleonic Wars engendered increasing anti-British sentiment in the United States. An effective U.S. Navy scored some convincing victories against the one hundred times larger British naval forces.

War of the Pacific. In 1879 Chile went to war because Peru and Bolivia levied high taxes against Chilean companies. As a result Bolivia lost its ocean port of Atacama to Chile. To this day Bolivia still calls for negotiations on the matter, while Chile claims the issue is settled.

Waziristan Revolt. In India in 1919, after attacks by Masud tribesmen, British forces conducted a punitive expedition against the Masud, who were defeated.

West Indies War. French operations in the West Indies during the French Revolution caused strain with the United States. From 1798–1800 this quasi-war with France was marked by several small naval engagements.

World War I—1914–18. Nationalist fervor and latent instability in Europe brought the war that all sides seemed to want so desperately. Total dead in World War I approached ten million.

World War II—1939–45. The territorial ambitions of Hitler and the weakness of Britain and France were the origins of World War II. Casualties approached fifty million dead.

Yemen. Since 1961, North and South Yemen have been places of trouble. In 1961 the Egyptian Army under Nasser fought a ruthless war in Yemen against Yemeni royalist tribesmen. A guerrilla movement, however, forced the Egyptians to withdraw. Supported by Russia and various Eastern European states, South Yemen continues to wage war against Yemen, also known as North Yemen. (See 1963, 1968 and 1972.)

Zaire. Since the Congo War, 1949–67, Zaire has been plagued with unrest. In 1978 Katangan insurgents launched an offensive against the town of Kolwezi in Zaire to weaken Zaire's economy. Driven by intense tribal hatreds, this insurgency has kept Zaire in a political and economic shambles. (See 1965.)

Zanzibar Uprising. After Britain established a protectorate over Zanzibar, an uprising in 1896 was suppressed by a British naval bombardment.

Zimbabwe. Rhodesia became Zimbabwe after the 1971 war for independence. Anti-Rhodesian forces have taken up armed resistance against the government because they are dissatisfied with political developments. Today, insurgents limit their actions to terrorist attacks, but the insurgency may expand if tribal sympathies are exacerbated by the behavior of Zimbabwe's army. (See 1980.)

Zulu Wars. From 1807–87 the Zulu tribe was involved in wars with various tribes and Britain. The reign of Dingiswayo of Zululand started the development of the highly efficient and ferocious Zulu military system. There were civil wars from 1818–19 and in 1856. In 1887 the Zulu leader Dinizulu led a rebellion against Britain that resulted in his defeat. (See 1838, 1878 and 1883.)

TWO HUNDRED YEARS OF WAR

WAR: Name of war, or in some cases the name of the country in which the war was fought or the name of the nation most involved.

SIDE: Name of the side involved in the war. If this is a nation, we use its current name. If it is a rebel group, we use rebel or insurgent.

BEGAN: Year in which the war began.

END: Year in which the war ended.

POP: Population (in millions) of nation at start of war.

CMBT: Combat forces (number of troops) in thousands.

RISK: Danger level. A combination of values indicating probability of war breaking out. The higher the value, the higher the probability a war will occur.

KDESP: Key situation during conduct of war. What attitude during the war set the stage for the war ending.

EX—Exhaustion of states leads to slowing, halting war
MP—Military prowess leads nation to think victory is imminent
NG—Negotiation with enemy
SM—Stalemate leads to stopping war
SU—Surrender
UN—Unresolved conflict

DEND: Key decision that ended the war. What situation precipitated end of war?

CS—Collapse of society
MD—Military defeat
MS—Military stalemate

MV—Military victory

NC—No combat between nations

RESULT: What was accomplished because of the war.

DI—Issues that caused war resolved by destroying defeated nation

IR—Issues that caused the war resolved

NR—Issues that caused the war not resolved

LOSSES: Military and civilian.

INT: Intensity. Casualties per million population for that nation in the war.

WARS THAT NEVER HAPPENED AND FUTURE WARS

Wars That Never Happened and Future Wars have the same format as Two Hundred Years of War. But, of course, wars that never happened and future wars don't have losses, results, key decision points and other items that only a war that actually happened would have.

In the Future Wars and Wars That Never Happened Charts, we provide eight basic fields: WAR, SIDE, BEGAN, POP, COMBT, RISK, TYPE, and ESCP. All are described before the main data base and in more detail on page 180. However, TYPE and ESCP, which are important for future or never-happened wars, are not shown in the main data base.

TYPE: Type of war. For a future war or war that never happened, this is the type of war that could happen or might have happened. For instance, the Sino-Soviet War, which might have happened in the late 1960s, would have been a territorial conflict. In the future wars, a U.S.-Soviet War probably would be a territorial conflict that escalated to nuclear attacks.

ESCALATION: Escalation potential—9 = most likely to escalate, 1 = least likely to escalate. This is a prediction of the war's potential for escalation. We take into account the side's history, political culture and external geopolitical factors (like the importance of oil in the Middle East).

As a general rule, predicting what could happen in a future war or what might have happened in a near-miss war is tricky. Values in the Future Wars and Wars That Never Happened charts are estimates. For some data, the answers are easy. A nation's population or combat forces can be found, even the type of war can be estimated. But who will win or why is harder to predict. There are no right or wrong numbers for wars that have not happened. Do your own political or intelligence forecasting. It's interesting to think about what might happen and why.

TWO HUNDRED YEARS OF WAR

WAR	SIDE	BEGAN	END	POP	CMBT	RISK	KDESP	DEND	RESULT	LOSSES	INT
Egyptian-Turkish War	Egypt	1786	1786	12	100	43	EX	MD	NR	8	0.67
	Turkey	1786	1786	20	350	108	MP	MV	IR	10	0.50
					450					18	
Ottoman War	Austria	1787	1790	20	300	67	MP	MV	IR	20	1.00
	Russia	1787	1792	28	600	162	MP	MV	IR	50	1.79
	Turkey	1787	1792	20	350	90	EX	MD	NR	35	1.75
					1250					105	
Russo-Swedish War	Denmark	1788	1790	1	50	75	MP	MV	IR	15	15.00
	Russia	1788	1790	28	600	225	MP	MV	IR	50	1.79
	Sweden	1788	1790	2.3	80	150	EX	MD	NR	25	10.87
					730					90	
Brabant Revolt	Austria	1789	1790	20	400	36	EX	MD	NR	2	0.10
	Netherlands	1789	1790	2	25	18	MP	MV	IR	2	1.00
					425					4	
Mysore	Britain	1789	1792	14	25	67	MP	MV	IR	3	0.21
	Mysore	1789	1792	0.5	35	123	EX	MD	NR	25	50.00
					60					28	
Fulani War	Fulani	1790	1801	8	100	43	EX	MD	NR	20	2.50
	Hausa	1790	1801	9	100	104	MP	MV	IR	40	4.44
					200					60	
Maumee War	Maumee	1790	1794	0.35	50	93	EX	MD	NR	15	42.86
	U.S.A.	1790	1794	4	4.6	125	MP	MV	IR	2	0.50
					54.6					17	
Haiti Rebellion	France	1791	1822	28	10	63	EX	MD	NR	3	0.11
	Rebels	1791	1822	0.1	3	108	MP	MV	IR	1	10.00
					13					4	
French Revolution	Austria	1792	1802	21	450	130	EX	MD	NR	100	4.76
	Britain	1792	1802	15	200	108	EX	MD	NR	40	2.67
	France	1792	1802	28	750	233	MP	MV	IR	1000	35.71
	Germany	1792	1802	17.5	500	181	EX	MD	NR	200	11.43
	Russia	1792	1802	29	1200	243	EX	MD	NR	500	17.24
	Spain	1792	1802	11.4	100	147	EX	MD	NR	75	6.58
					3200					1915	

TWO HUNDRED YEARS OF WAR

WAR	SIDE	BEGAN	END	POP	CMBT	RISK	KDESP	DEND	RESULT	LOSSES	INT
Boer War	Bantu	1793	1795	1		69	NG	MD	NR	35	35.00
	Boers	1793	1795	0.022	3	156	MP	MV	NR	1	45.45
					83					36	
Polish Rebellion	Poland	1794	1795	9	100	110	EX	MD	NR	30	3.33
	Prussia	1794	1795	1	100	112	MP	MV	NR	30	30.00
	Russia	1794	1795	29	1200	194	MP	MV	NR	40	1.38
					1400					100	
Sri Lanka War	Britain	1795	1796	15	25	120	MP	MV	IR	2	0.13
	Netherlands	1795	1796	2	50	90	EX	MD	NR	2	1.00
	Sri Lanka	1795	1796	4	40	24	MP	MV	IR	15	3.75
					115					19	
Iranian-Georgian War	Georgia	1795	1796	3	100	104	EX	MD	NR	15	5.00
	Iran	1795	1796	5	100	64	MP	MV	NR	10	2.00
					200					25	
Irish Rebellion	Britain	1795	1798	15	25	67	MP	MV	IR	4	0.27
	Ireland	1795	1798	5.25	10	92	EX	MD	NR	3	0.57
					35					7	
White Lotus War	China	1796	1804	320	2000	53	MP	MV	IR	250	0.78
	White Lotus	1796	1804	1	100	108	EX	MD	NR	25	25.00
					2100					275	
Afghan Wars	Afghanistan	1798	1798	3	60	147	EX	MD	NR	15	5.00
	Iran	1798	1798	5	100	108	MP	MV	NR	15	3.00
					160					30	
West Indies	France	1798	1800	29	10	53	SM	MD	NR	2	0.07
	U.S.A.	1798	1800	5	5	50	SM	MV	IR	2	0.40
					15					4	
Boer War	Boers	1799	1801	0.025	3	212	MP	MV	NR	1	40.00
	Xhosa	1799	1801	3	75	113	EX	MD	NR	30	10.00
					78					31	
Mysore	Britain	1799	1799	15	25	120	MP	MV	IR	4	0.27
	Mysore	1799	1799	0.5	35	117	EX	MD	NR	15	30.00
					60					19	

WAR	SIDE	BEGAN	END	POP	CMBT	RISK	KDESP	DEND	RESULT	LOSSES	INT
Punjab War	India	1799	1802	200	500	68	NG	MD	NR	70	0.35
	Sikhs	1799	1802	3	100	104	NG	MV	IR	50	16.67
					600					120	
Tripoli War	Tripoli	1801	1805	0.2	10	135	NG	MD	NR	2	10.00
	U.S.A.	1801	1805	6	25	98	NG	MV	IR	5	0.83
					35					7	
Maratha War	Britain	1802	1805	16	200	100	NG	MV	IR	15	0.94
	Maratha	1802	1805	10	40	113	NG	MD	NR	10	1.00
					240					25	
Napoleonic War	Austria	1803	1815	26	600	123	NG	MV	IR	150	5.77
	Britain	1803	1815	16	250	207	NG	MV	IR	100	6.25
	France	1803	1815	30	1000	227	NG	MD	NR	2000	66.67
	Germany	1803	1815	18	500	227	NG	MV	IR	150	8.33
	Russia	1803	1815	30	1200	272	NG	MV	IR	2000	66.67
	Spain	1803	1815	11.6	100	130	NG	MV	IR	25	2.16
					3650					4425	
Convict Rebellion	Australia	1804	1808	0.01	35	48	MP	MV	IR	5	0.83
	Rebels	1804	1808		2	113	EX	MD	NR	0.5	50.00
					37					5.5	
Fulani Wars	Bornu	1804	1810	10	75	39	EX	MD	NR	25	2.50
	Fulani	1804	1810	10	100	79	MP	MV	NR	25	2.50
	Hausa	1804	1810	10	100	110	EX	MD	NR	35	3.50
					275					85	
Russo-Persian War	Iran	1804	1813	6	100	47	EX	MD	NR	25	4.17
	Russia	1804	1813	30	1200	216	MP	MV	NR	20	0.67
					1300					45	
Serbian Revolt	Serbia	1804	1817	4	25	108	MP	MV	NR	15	3.75
	Turkey	1804	1817	22	400	24	EX	MD	NR	50	2.27
					425					65	
Egyptian Rebellion	Britain	1805	1807	16	25	64	EX	MD	NR	5	0.31
	Egypt	1805	1811	14	100	34	MP	MV	IR	39	2.79
	Rebels	1805	1811	0.3	10	120	EX	MD	NR	3	10.00
	Turkey	1805	1811	22	400	130	EX	MD	NR	9	0.41
					535					56	

TWO HUNDRED YEARS OF WAR

WAR	SIDE	BEGAN	END	POP	CMBT	RISK	KDESP	DEND	RESULT	LOSSES	INT
Gold Coast War	Ashanti	1806	1807	1	50	105	MP	MV	NR	9	9.00
	Coastals	1806	1807	1	80	117	EX	MD	NR	20	20.00
					130					29	
Russo-Turkish War I	Russia	1806	1812	31	1200	122	MP	MV	NR	70	2.26
	Turkey	1806	1812	22	400	194	EX	MD	NR	100	4.55
					1600					170	
Spanish Rebellion	Rebels	1807	1814	1	75	113	NG	MD	NR	25	25.00
	Spain	1807	1814	11.7	100	20	NG	MV	IR	35	2.99
					175					60	
Zulu Expansion	Bantu	1807	1828	1	100	117	NG	MD	NR	30	30.00
	Zulu	1807	1828	2	100	118	MP	MV	NR	55	27.50
					200					85	
Bantam Conquest	Bantam	1808	1808	1	20	112	NG	MD	NR	8	8.00
	Indonesia	1808	1808	65	100	63	MP	MV	NR	8	0.12
					120					16	
Russo-Swedish War II	Russia	1808	1809	32	1200	61	MP	MV	IR	30	0.94
	Sweden	1808	1809	3	80	130	EX	MD	NR	35	11.67
					1280					65	
Indonesian War	Britain	1810	1811	16	25	120	MP	MV	IR	3	0.19
	Netherlands	1810	1811	2.2	50	30	EX	MD	NR	3	1.36
					75					6	
Mexican Rebellion	Rebels	1810	1823	1	60	105	MP	MV	IR	15	15.00
	Spain	1810	1823	12	100	58	EX	MD	NR	8	0.67
					160					23	
Punjab War	Afghanistan	1810	1820	4	60	176	EX	MD	NR	25	6.25
	Punjab	1810	1820	5	100	29	MP	MV	NR	40	8.00
					160					65	
Tukulor War	Bambara	1810	1810	1	10	108	NG	MD	NR	4	4.00
	Senegal	1810	1810	0.6	50	126	NG	MV	IR	6	10.00
					60					10	

WAR	SIDE	BEGAN	END	POP	CMBT	RISK	KDESP	DEND	RESULT	LOSSES	INT
Arakan Revolt	Burma	1811	1815	6.2	36	147	NG	MV	IR	13	2.10
	Rebels	1811	1815	0.5	40	108	EX	MD	NR	5	10.00
					76					18	
Bolivar's Wars	Bolivar	1811	1824	1	50	54	MP	MV	IR	10	10.00
	Spain	1811	1824	12	100	72	EX	MD	NR	10	0.83
					150					20	
Tecumseh War	Shawnees	1811	1811	0.2	10	125	EX	CS	DI	2	10.00
	U.S.A.	1811	1811	9.5	100	60	MP	MV	IR	5	0.53
					110					7	
Wahhabi War	Egypt	1811	1818	14	100	108	MP	MV	NR	15	1.07
	Rebels	1811	1818	0.4	35	108	EX	MD	NR	5	12.50
					135					20	
Xhosa War	Boers	1811	1819	0.06	5	90	MP	MV	NR	1	16.67
	Xhosa	1811	1819	3.5	100	108	EX	MD	NR	25	7.14
					105					26	
Cambodian Rebellion	Cambodia	1812	1812	.2	50	121	MP	MV	NR	19	9.50
	Rebels	1812	1812	0.25	10	105	EX	MD	NR	4	16.00
	Thailand	1812	1812	3	50	120	EX	MD	NR	5	1.67
	Vietnam	1812	1812	4	50	108	EX	MD	NR	9	2.25
					160					37	
War of 1812	Britain	1812	1814	17	50	150	EX	MD	NR	5	0.29
	U.S.A.	1812	1814	9.7	100	120	MP	MV	IR	12	1.24
					150					17	
Gurkha War	Britain	1814	1816	17	25	112	MP	MV	IR	5	0.29
	Nepal	1814	1816	2	25	108	EX	MD	NR	20	10.00
					50					25	
San Martin's War	San Martin	1814	1824	0.2	10	29	MP	MV	IR	2	10.00
	Spain	1814	1824	12	100	173	EX	MD	NR	6	0.50
					110					8	
Algerian War	Algeria	1815	1824	6	50	64	EX	MD	NR	15	2.50
	Britain	1815	1824	17	25	37	MP	MV	IR	6	0.35
	Netherlands	1815	1815	2.4	50	17	MP	MV	NR	2	0.83
	U.S.A.	1815	1815	10.5	5	95	MP	MV	IR	1	0.10
					130					24	

TWO HUNDRED YEARS OF WAR

WAR	SIDE	BEGAN	END	POP	CMBT	RISK	KDESP	DEND	RESULT	LOSSES	INT
Neapolitan War	Austria	1815	1815	28	600	168	MP	MV	NR	10	0.36
	Italy	1815	1815	21	250	30	EX	MD	NR	10	0.48
					850					20	
Serbo-Turkish War	Serbia	1815	1817	4	25	108	EX	MD	NR	10	2.50
	Turkey	1815	1817	23	400	36	MP	MV	IR	20	0.87
					425					30	
Iranian-Afghan War	Afghanistan	1816	1816	4	65	176	NG	MV	IR	8	2.00
	Iran	1816	1816	6.3	100	51	EX	MD	NR	25	3.97
					165					33	
Maratha War	Britain	1817	1818	18	25	41	MP	MV	IR	2	0.11
	Maratha	1817	1818	10	50	125	EX	MD	NR	10	1.00
					75					12	
Afghan Rebellion	Afghanistan	1818	1818	0.6	85	22	MP	MV	NR	22	5.50
	Rebels	1818	1818		50	123	EX	MD	NR	10	16.67
					135					32	
Amazon War	Dahomey	1818	1858	1	50	126	MP	MV	NR	30	30.00
	Tribes	1818	1858	1	100	113	EX	MD	NR	30	30.00
					150					60	
Seminole War	Seminole	1818	1818	0.15	10	101	EX	CS	DI	5	33.33
	U.S.A.	1818	1818	12	100	60	MP	MV	IR	3	0.25
					110					8	
Zulu Wars	Bantu	1818	1828	1.25	100	98	NG	MD	NR	40	32.00
	Zulu	1818	1828	2	100	101	MP	MV	NR	20	10.00
					200					60	
Assam War	Assam	1819	1822	1	50	108	EX	MD	NR	18	18.00
	Burma	1819	1822	6.5	40	120	MP	MV	NR	8	1.23
					90					26	
Italian Revolts	Austria	1820	1849	30	600	84	MP	MV	IR	50	1.67
	Italy	1820	1849	22	250	105	EX	MD	NR	40	1.82
					850					90	

WAR	SIDE	BEGAN	END	POP	CMBT	RISK	KDESP	DEND	RESULT	LOSSES	INT
Portuguese Civil War	Britain	1820	1834	19	50	68	NG	MV	IR	10	0.53
	Portugal	1820	1834	2.9	30	112	NG	MV	IR	5	1.72
	Republicans	1820	1834	1	25	60	NG	MD	NR	15	15.00
					105					30	
Sudan Conquest	Egypt	1820	1839	15	100	125	MP	MV	NR	10	0.67
	Sudan	1820	1839	5.4	25	24	EX	MD	NR	10	1.85
					125					20	
Ashanti War	Ashanti	1821	1826	1	60	130	NG	MD	IR	3	3.00
	Britain	1821	1826	20	40	85	MP	MV	NR	0.1	0.01
					100					3.1	
Franco-Spanish War	France	1823	1823	32	25	180	MP	MV	IR	3	0.09
	Rebels	1823	1823	0.3	10	108	EX	MD	NR	3.5	11.67
	Spain	1821	1823	13.2	100	70	NG	MV	IR	50	3.79
					135					56.5	
Greek Revolt	Britain	1827	1832	19	8	80	NG	MD	NR	0.1	0.01
	Egypt	1825	1832	17	12	130	NG	MD	IR	5	0.29
	France	1827	1832	32	10	108	NG	MD	NR	0.1	0.00
	France	1821	1832	2.4	100	101	NG	MD	NR	50	20.83
	Russia	1827	1832	40	1200	162	NG	MV	IR	10	0.25
	Turkey	1821	1832	23	400	130	NG	MV	IR	15	0.65
					1730					80.2	
Kedah War	Kedah	1821	1821	1	50	130	EX	MD	NR	16	16.00
	Thailand	1821	1821	3	50	108	NG	MV	IR	5	1.67
					100					21	
Turko-Persian War	Iran	1821	1823	6.6	100	88	NG	MD	NR	1	0.15
	Turkey	1821	1823	23	400	135	MP	MV	NR	1	0.04
					500					2	
Anglo-Burmese War	Britain	1823	1826	20	50	72	MP	MV	IR	20	1.00
	Burma	1823	1826	8	40	100	NG	MD	NR	10	1.25
					90					30	
French Intervention	France	1824	1847	32	50	113	MP	MV	IR	10	0.31
	Vietnam	1824	1847	4.5	50	107	NG	MD	NR	10	2.22
					100					20	

TWO HUNDRED YEARS OF WAR

WAR	SIDE	BEGAN	END	POP	CMBT	RISK	KDESP	DEND	RESULT	LOSSES	INT
Mombassa War	Britain	1824	1828	20	25	40	MP	MV	IR	5	0.25
	Muscat	1824	1828	0.2	20	126	EX	MD	NR	5	25.00
					45					10	
Argentine-Brazil War	Argentina	1825	1828	0.65	35	108	NG	MV	IR	2	3.08
	Brazil	1825	1828	5	100	28	EX	MD	NR	5	1.00
					135					7	
Bhurtpore War	Bhurtpore	1825	1826	1	25	65	NG	MD	NR	8	8.00
	Britain	1825	1826	20	25	32	MP	MV	IR	5	0.25
					50					13	
Great Java War	Indonesia	1825	1830	75	100	82	NG	MD	NR	10	0.13
	Netherlands	1825	1830	2.5	50	144	MP	MV	NR	1	0.40
					150					11	
Kashgari War	China	1825	1831	370	2000	144	MP	MV	IR	20	0.05
	Turkomen	1825	1831	1	25	120	NG	MD	NR	5	5.00
					2025					25	
Russo-Persian War	Iran	1825	1828	6.7	100	96	NG	MD	NR	10	1.49
	Russia	1825	1828	43	1200	158	MP	MV	IR	2.5	0.06
					1300					12.5	
Laos War	Laos	1826	1829	1	25	126	EX	MD	NR	24	24.00
	Thailand	1826	1829	3.5	50	101	MP	MV	NR	7	2.00
					75					31	
Peruvian War	Bolivia	1827	1829	1	80	113	MP	MV	IR	25	25.00
	Ecuador	1827	1829	3	5	21	MP	MV	IR	1	0.33
	Peru	1827	1829	1.6	15	90	EX	MD	NR	3	1.88
					100					29	
Miguelite War	Britain	1828	1834	21	10	47	MP	MV	IR	2	0.10
	France	1828	1834	33	20	147	MP	MV	IR	8	0.24
	Portugal	1828	1834	3	30	26	MP	MV	IR	3	1.00
	Rebels	1828	1834	0.5	50	101	SU	MD	NR	5	10.00
	Spain	1828	1834	13.4	100	75	MP	MV	IR	5	0.37
					210					23	
Russo-Turkish War II	Russia	1828	1829	45	1200	270	MP	MV	NR	50	1.11
	Turkey	1828	1829	24	400	86	NG	MD	NR	80	3.33
					1600					130	

WAR	SIDE	BEGAN	END	POP	CMBT	RISK	KDESP	DEND	RESULT	LOSSES	INT
Mexican-Spanish War	Mexico	1829	1829	5.5	50	64	SU	MD	NR	3	0.55
	Spain	1829	1829	13.6	100	130	MP	MV	IR	1	0.07
					150					4	
Algerian War	Algeria	1830	1847	6	50	104	EX	MD	NR	4	0.67
	France	1830	1847	33	50	118	MP	MV	NR	10	0.30
					100					14	
Belgian Revolt	Belgium	1830	1833	4	25	108	NG	MV	IR	2	0.50
	France	1830	1833	33	50	103	MP	MV	IR	1	0.03
	Netherlands	1830	1833	3	50	14	NG	MD	NR	10	3.33
					125					13	
Cambodian War I	Cambodia	1831	1834	2	20	90	NG	MD	NR	7	3.50
	Thailand	1831	1834	3.6	50	180	MP	MV	NR	15	4.17
					70					22	
Black Hawk War	Fox/Sac	1832	1832	0.1	20	120	EX	CS	DI	5	50.00
	U.S.A.	1832	1832	15	25	68	MP	MV	IR	3	0.20
					45					8	
Egyptian War	Egypt	1832	1833	17	100	74	NG	MV	IR	5	0.29
	Turkey	1832	1833	24	400	135	EX	MD	NR	10	0.42
					500					15	
Bantu-Boer War	Bantu	1834	1837	1.5	150	105	NG	MD	NR	50	33.33
	Boers	1834	1837	0.07	7	101	MP	MV	NR	3	42.86
					157					53	
Carlist War	Britain	1834	1839	22	40	112	NG	MV	IR	10	0.45
	Carlists	1834	1839	0.05	10	151	NG	MD	NR	2	40.00
	France	1834	1839	34	25	88	NG	MV	IR	5	0.15
	Portugal	1834	1839	3.2	30	76	NG	MV	IR	5	1.56
	Spain	1834	1839	14	120	72	NG	MV	IR	10	0.71
					225					32	
Seminole War	Seminole	1835	1843	0.2	15	103	EX	CS	DI	3	15.00
	U.S.A.	1835	1843	15	50	68	MP	MV	IR	10	0.67
					65					13	
Texas War	Mexico	1835	1836	6	60	90	NG	MD	NR	1	0.17
	Texas	1835	1836	0.2	10	108	MP	MV	IR	1	5.00
					70					2	

TWO HUNDRED YEARS OF WAR

WAR	SIDE	BEGAN	END	POP	CMBT	RISK	KDESP	DEND	RESULT	LOSSES	INT
Afghan War	Afghanistan	1836	1838	5	85	21	MP	MV	NR	1	0.20
	Iran	1836	1838	7	100	125	EX	MD	NR	2	0.29
					185					3	
Peru-Bolivia Confed	Bolivia	1836	1839	1	80	27	NG	MD	NR	2	2.00
	Chile	1836	1839	4	50	75	MP	MV	IR	4	1.00
	Peru	1836	1839	1.7	15	75	EX	MD	NR	1	0.59
					145					7	
Pirate War	Britain	1837	1860	23	40	47	MP	MV	IR	14	0.61
	Netherlands	1837	1860	3	50	108	MP	MV	IR	10	3.33
	Pirates	1837	1860	0.2	3	105	NG	MD	NR	1	5.00
	Spain	1837	1860	14.1	120	121	MP	MV	IR	25	1.77
					213					50	
Afghan War	Afghanistan	1838	1842	5	85	126	EX	MD	NR	25	5.00
	Britain	1838	1842	23	50	56	MP	MV	NR	20	0.87
					135					45	
Burmese Civil War	Burma	1838	1845	10	50	30	MP	MV	NR	10	1.00
	Rebels	1838	1845	0.4	40	130	EX	MD	NR	10	25.00
					90					20	
Franco-Mexican War	France	1838	1839	34	25	49	MP	MV	IR	1	0.03
	Mexico	1838	1839	6.8	60	90	EX	MD	NR	1	0.15
					85					2	
Zulu-Boer War	Boers	1838	1840	0.07	7	90	MP	MV	NR	2	28.57
	Zulu	1838	1840	2	100	120	EX	MD	NR	40	20.00
					107					42	
Arabian War	Arabs	1839	1845	5.5	50	74	EX	MD	NR	15	2.73
	Britain	1839	1845	23	25	117	MP	MV	IR	5	0.22
					75					20	
Bali War	Bali	1839	1849	1	25	123	NG	MD	NR	10	10.00
	Netherlands	1839	1849	3	50	75	MP	MV	IR	7	2.33
					75					17	
C Amer Confederation	C Amer Confed	1839	1840	2	25	10	EX	MD	NR	5	2.50
	Rebels	1839	1840	0.15	5	108	MP	MV	NR	1	6.67
					30					6	

WAR	SIDE	BEGAN	END	POP	CMBT	RISK	KDESP	DEND	RESULT	LOSSES	INT
Egyptian War	Austria	1839	1841	33	600	76	MP	MV	IR	1	0.03
	Britain	1839	1841	23	60	64	MP	MV	IR	10	0.43
	Egypt	1839	1841	18	100	101	NG	MV	IR	20	1.11
	Turkey	1839	1841	24	400	43	NG	MD	NR	10	0.42
					1160					41	
Khivan War	Khivans	1839	1847	1	35	105	NG	MD	NR	2	2.00
	Russia	1839	1847	53	1200	58	MP	MV	IR	1	0.02
					1235					3	
Opium War	Britain	1839	1842	23	50	192	MP	MV	NR	10	0.43
	China	1839	1842	390	2000	108	NG	MD	NR	30	0.08
					2050					40	
Spanish Rebellion	Rebels	1840	1843	0.5	10	118	EX	MD	NR	4	8.00
	Spain	1840	1843	14.5	120	29	MP	MV	IR	35	2.41
					130					39	
Kwara War	Ethiopia	1841	1847	4	100	90	EX	MD	NR	25	6.25
	Kwara	1841	1847	0.5	40	74	MP	MV	NR	13	26.00
					140					38	
Peruvian-Bolivian War	Bolivia	1841	1841	2	80	113	MP	MV	IR	1	0.50
	Peru	1841	1841	2	20	52	EX	MD	NR	1	0.50
					100					2	
Vietnam War	Cambodia	1841	1845	3	25	123	MP	MV	NR	6	2.00
	Thailand	1841	1845	3.8	50	105	MP	MV	NR	20	5.26
	Vietnam	1841	1845	5	50	247	EX	MD	NR	10	2.00
					125					36	
Natal War	Boers	1842	1843	0.1	10	130	NG	MD	NR	3	30.00
	Britain	1842	1843	24	25	51	MP	MV	IR	4	0.17
					35					7	
Maori War	Maori	1843	1848	1	100	105	NG	MD	NR	18	18.00
	New Zealand	1843	1848	0.15	5	110	NG	MV	IR	2	13.33
					105					20	

TWO HUNDRED YEARS OF WAR

WAR	SIDE	BEGAN	END	POP	CMBT	RISK	KDESP	DEND	RESULT	LOSSES	INT
Rosas War	Argentina	1843	1852	1	70	105	NG	MD	NR	25	25.00
	Brazil	1843	1852	6	100	140	NG	MV	IR	2	0.33
	Britain	1843	1852	25	25	48	MP	MV	IR	1	0.04
	France	1843	1852	35	25	38	MP	MV	IR	1	0.03
	Uruguay	1843	1852	1	20	113	NG	MD	NR	2	2.00
					240					31	
Sind War	Baluchis	1843	1843	1	30	108	NG	MD	NR	6	6.00
	Britain	1843	1843	25	25	100	MP	MV	IR	2	0.08
					55					8	
Santo Domingo	Haiti	1844	1844	0.06	3	118	NG	MD	NR	1	16.67
	Rebels	1844	1844	0.1	10	108	MP	MV	IR	1	10.00
					13					2	
Sikh War	Britain	1845	1846	26	20	96	EX	MD	NR	4	0.15
	Sikhs	1845	1846	4	100	100	MP	MV	NR	10	2.50
					120					14	
Kaffir Wars	Britain	1846	1878	26	50	107	MP	MV	IR	16	0.62
	Kaffirs	1846	1878	1	120	113	NG	MD	NR	40	40.00
					170					56	
Mexican War	Mexico	1846	1848	7.7	60	19	NG	MD	NR	6	0.78
	U.S.A.	1846	1848	16	40	108	MP	MV	IR	11	0.69
					100					17	
German Revolt	Germany	1847	1848	26	500	56	MP	MV	IR	35	1.35
	Rebels	1847	1848	0.5	18	118	EX	MD	NR	3	6.00
					518					38	
Sino-Turkomen War	China	1847	1847	400	2000	130	MP	MV	NR	40	0.10
	Turkomen	1847	1847	2	35	105	EX	MD	NR	10	5.00
					2035					50	
Austrian Civil War	France	1848	1849	35	370	120	MP	MV	IR	20	0.57
	Republicans	1848	1849	1	35	63	NG	MD	NR	4	4.00
	Russia	1848	1849	68	1200	81	NG	MV	IR	15	0.22
					1605					39	
Austro-Sardinian War	Austria	1848	1849	35	600	120	MP	MV	IR	20	0.57
	Italy	1848	1849	25	250	42	NG	MD	NR	20	0.80
					850					40	

WAR	SIDE	BEGAN	END	POP	CMBT	RISK	KDESP	DEND	RESULT	LOSSES	INT
First Schleswig War	Denmark	1848	1850	1.8	50	70	NG	MD	NR	2.5	1.39
	Germany	1848	1850	27	500	144	MP	MV	NR	3.5	0.13
	Sweden	1848	1850	5	100	130	MP	MV	IR	25	5.00
					650					31	
Roman Republic War	Austria	1848	1849	35	600	76	NG	MV	IR	35	1.00
	France	1848	1849	36	370	110	MP	MV	IR	7	0.19
	Italy	1848	1849	25	250	36	EX	MD	NR	30	1.20
					1220					72	
Sikh War	Britain	1848	1849	27	50	51	MP	MV	IR	2	0.07
	Sikhs	1848	1849	4	100	108	NG	MD	NR	10	2.50
					150					12	
Java Revolt	Indonesia	1849	1849	85	100	79	NG	MD	NR	7	0.08
	Netherlands	1849	1849	4	50	105	MP	MV	IR	3	0.75
					150					10	
Afghan Civil War	Afghanistan	1855	1855	6	100	77	MP	MV	NR	30	5.00
	Rebels	1855	1855	0.4	50	108	NG	MD	NR	10	25.00
					150					40	
Indian Wars	American Indian	1850	1891	1	50	90	EX	CS	DI	10	10.00
	U.S.A.	1850	1891	16	50	78	MP	MV	IR	15	0.94
					100					25	
Syr Darya War	Russia	1850	1854	70	1200	225	MP	MV	IR	2	0.03
	Turkestan	1850	1854	2	150	92	NG	MD	NR	10	5.00
	Turkomen	1850	1854	2	35	108	NG	MD	NR	10	5.00
					1385					22	
Taiping Rebellion	China	1850	1881	400	2000	108	MP	MV	NR	8000	20.00
	Rebels	1850	1881	70	1000	126	EX	MD	NR	12000	171.43
					3000					20000	
Vietnam War	France	1851	1895	36	40	130	MP	MV	NR	20	0.56
	Vietnam	1851	1895	6	50	107	NG	MD	NR	20	3.33
					90					40	
Burmese War	Britain	1852	1853	28	50	84	MP	MV	IR	15	0.54
	Burma	1852	1853	13	50	105	NG	MD	NR	12	0.92
					100					27	

TWO HUNDRED YEARS OF WAR

WAR	SIDE	BEGAN	END	POP	CMBT	RISK	KDESP	DEND	RESULT	LOSSES	INT
Montenegro War	Montenegro	1852	1853	0.3	30	98	MP	MV	NR	5	16.67
	Turkey	1852	1853	25	400	98	EX	MD	NR	7	0.28
					430					12	
Crimean War	Austria	1853	1856	36	600	97	MP	MV	IR	50	1.39
	Britain	1853	1856	29	250	157	MP	MV	IR	30	1.03
	France	1853	1856	37	400	88	MP	MV	IR	27	0.73
	Russia	1853	1856	74	1200	225	NG	MD	NR	144	1.95
	Sardinia	1853	1856	1	10	97	MP	MV	IR	2	2.00
	Turkey	1853	1856	25	400	98	MP	MV	IR	45	1.80
					2860					298	
Abyssinian Civil War	Ethiopia	1854	1856	4	100	72	MP	MV	NR	6	1.50
	Rebels	1854	1856	0.4	10	113	EX	MD	NR	3	7.50
					110					9	
Spanish Revolution	Rebels	1854	1876	0.5	50	108	EX	MD	NR	9	18.00
	Spain	1854	1876	15.2	120	101	NG	MV	IR	25	1.64
					170					34	
Tukulor War	France	1854	1864	37	25	17	MP	MV	IR	8	0.22
	Senegal	1854	1864	0.7	50	123	NG	MD	NR	10	14.29
					75					18	
Afghan War	Afghanistan	1856	1857	6	90	126	NG	MV	IR	18	3.00
	Britain	1856	1857	30	50	58	MP	MV	NR	1	0.03
	Iran	1856	1857	8	100	181	NG	MD	NR	2	0.25
					240					21	
Opium War	Britain	1856	1860	30	50	83	MP	MV	NR	4	0.13
	China	1856	1860	410	2000	72	NG	MD	NR	6	0.01
					2050					10	
Zulu Civil War	Rebels	1856	1856	0.5	20	108	EX	MD	NR	5	10.00
	Zulu	1856	1856	2.5	100	125	MP	MV	NR	25	10.00
					120					30	
Great Mutiny	Britain	1857	1858	30	60	84	MP	MV	IR	2	0.07
	India	1857	1858	250	500	101	NG	MD	NR	8	0.03
					560					10	

WAR	SIDE	BEGAN	END	POP	CMBT	RISK	KDESP	DEND	RESULT	LOSSES	INT
Mexican Civil War	France	1857	1877	37	30	106	EX	MD	NR	9	0.24
	Mexico	1857	1877	8	100	49	NG	MV	IR	30	3.75
	Rebels	1857	1877	0.6	60	157	EX	MD	NR	12	20.00
					190					51	
Basuto Wars	Basuto	1858	1871	1	70	130	NG	MD	NR	50	50.00
	Boers	1858	1871	0.2	10	104	MP	MV	NR	16	80.00
					80					66	
Italian Unification	Austria	1859	1859	37	600	126	NG	MD	NR	13	0.35
	France	1859	1859	38	400	106	MP	MV	IR	8	0.21
	Italy	1859	1859	28	250	45	MP	MV	IR	3	0.11
					1250					24	
Moroccan War	Morocco	1859	1860	3.2	40	97	EX	MD	NR	6	1.88
	Spain	1859	1860	16	140	45	NG	MV	IR	4	0.25
					180					10	
Colombian Civil War	Colombia	1860	1861	10	40	60	NG	MV	IR	15	1.50
	Rebels	1860	1861	0.6	10	105	EX	MD	NR	4	6.67
					50					19	
Herzegovina War	Herzegovina	1860	1862	1	25	65	NG	MD	NR	8	8.00
	Montenegro	1860	1862	0.33	10	65	NG	MD	NR	2	6.06
	Turkey	1860	1862	25	400	31	MP	MV	NR	3	0.12
					435					13	
Maori War	Maori	1860	1870	1	45	108	NG	MD	NR	20	20.00
	New Zealand	1860	1870	0.75	10	29	MP	MV	IR	3	4.00
					55					23	
U.S. Civil War	Rebels	1861	1865	9	2000	194	SU	MD	DI	400	44.44
	U.S.A.	1861	1865	22	3995	156	MP	MV	IR	300	13.64
					5995					700	
Boer Civil War	Boers	1862	1864	0.3	10	101	MP	MV	NR	3	10.00
	Rebels	1862	1864	0.15	10	105	EX	MD	NR	3	20.00
					20					6	
Franco-Mexican War	France	1862	1867	38	450	165	EX	MD	NR	8	0.21
	Mexico	1862	1867	9	100	97	NG	MV	IR	12	1.33
	U.S.A.	1865	1867	34	30	125	MP	MV	IR	10	0.29
					580					30	

TWO HUNDRED YEARS OF WAR

WAR	SIDE	BEGAN	END	POP	CMBT	RISK	KDESP	DEND	RESULT	LOSSES	INT
Greek Revolution	Greece	1862	1862	3.5	100	38	NG	MD	NR	2	0.57
	Rebels	1862	1862	0.25	5	108	MP	MV	IR	2	8.00
					105					4	
Afghan Civil War	Afghanistan	1863	1879	7	90	96	NG	MV	IR	25	3.57
	Rebels	1863	1879	0.5	25	130	EX	MD	NR	5	10.00
					115					30	
Ecuador-Colombia War	Colombia	1863	1863	11.4	40	125	MP	MV	IR	0.3	0.03
	Ecuador	1863	1863	4	5	20	EX	MD	NR	0.7	0.18
					45					1	
Japanese Civil War	Japan	1863	1868	35	300	101	MP	MV	IR	20	0.57
	Rebels	1863	1868	0.3	50	108	EX	MD	NR	10	33.33
					350					30	
Madagascar Revolution	Madagascar	1863	1863	2.5	10	62	NG	MD	NR	2	0.80
	Rebels	1863	1863	0.1	3	113	MP	MV	IR	1	10.00
					13					3	
Polish Revolution	Poland	1863	1864	16	100	162	NG	MD	NR	2	0.13
	Russia	1863	1864	87	1200	108	MP	MV	NR	5	0.06
					1300					7	
Lopez War	Argentina	1864	1870	2.25	100	45	MP	MV	IR	10	4.44
	Brazil	1864	1870	11	150	60	MP	MV	IR	100	9.09
	Paraguay	1864	1870	0.525	20	130	EX	CS	DI	304	579.05
	Uruguay	1864	1870	1	40	108	MP	MV	IR	10	10.00
					310					424	
Peruvian-Spanish War	Peru	1864	1866	2.5	25	34	MP	MV	IR	5	2.00
	Spain	1864	1866	16.4	140	84	NG	MD	NR	4	0.24
					165					9	
Second Schleswig War	Denmark	1864	1864	2	50	67	NG	MD	NR	3	1.50
	Germany	1864	1864	30	500	192	MP	MV	IR	1	0.03
					550					4	
Tukulor Civil Wars	Rebels	1864	1890	0.2	25	108	EX	MD	NR	10	50.00
	Senegal	1864	1890	0.8	100	86	NG	MV	IR	15	10.75
					125					25	

WAR	SIDE	BEGAN	END	POP	CMBT	RISK	KDESP	DEND	RESULT	LOSSES	INT
Bhutan War	Bhutan	1865	1865	0.7	50	101	NG	MD	NR	5	7.14
	Britain	1865	1865	32	50	56	MP	MV	NR	2	0.06
					100					7	
Chilean-Spanish	Chile	1865	1866	5	50	45	MP	MV	IR	1	0.20
	Spain	1865	1866	16.4	150	32	NG	MD	NR	0.3	0.02
					200					1.3	
Red Sea War	Egypt	1865	1875	21	100	130	MP	MV	IR	20	0.95
	Rebels	1865	1875	0.5	25	101	EX	MD	NR	10	20.00
					125					30	
Austro-Prussian War	Austria	1866	1866	40	600	108	NG	MD	NR	20	0.50
	Germany	1866	1866	30	500	154	MP	MV	IR	26	0.87
	Italy	1866	1866	30	300	22	NG	MV	IR	11	0.37
					1400					57	
Cambodian Revolt	Cambodia	1866	1867	3	25	28	NG	MV	IR	8	2.67
	Rebels	1866	1867	0.25	10	108	EX	MD	NR	3	12.00
					35					11	
Cretan Insurrection	Greece	1866	1868	4	100	108	EX	MD	NR	3	0.75
	Turkey	1866	1868	25	400	108	MP	MV	NR	4	0.16
					500					7	
Anglo-Abyssinian War	Britain	1867	1868	33	40	125	MP	MV	IR	0.4	0.01
	Ethiopia	1867	1868	4	100	68	NG	MD	NR	1	0.25
					140					1.4	
Papal States	France	1867	1870	38	70	135	MP	MV	IR	1	0.03
	Italy	1867	1870	30	300	72	NG	MD	NR	2	0.07
	Pope	1867	1870	0.2	20	97	NG	MV	IR	1	5.00
					390					4	
Abyssinian Civil War	Ethiopia	1868	1872	4	100	90	NG	MV	IR	30	7.50
	Rebels	1868	1872	0.4	50	113	EX	MD	NR	5	12.50
					150					35	
Ten Years War	Cuba	1868	1878	1.4	25	105	EX	MD	NR	15	10.71
	Spain	1868	1878	16.5	160	140	NG	MV	IR	40	2.42
					185					55	

TWO HUNDRED YEARS OF WAR

WAR	SIDE	BEGAN	END	POP	CMBT	RISK	KDESP	DEND	RESULT	LOSSES	INT
Riel Rebellion	Canada	1869	1870	8	50	14	MP	MV	IR	5	0.63
	Rebels	1869	1870	0.5	5	96	SU	MD	NR	0.5	1.00
					55					5.5	
Franco-Prussian War	France	1870	1871	38	500	113	NG	MD	NR	140	3.68
	Germany	1870	1871	32	550	173	MP	MV	IR	100	3.13
					1050					240	
Sudan War	Egypt	1871	1875	22	100	130	MP	MV	IR	11	0.50
	Sudan	1871	1875	6	25	64	NG	MD	NR	15	2.50
					125					26	
Ashanti War	Ashanti	1873	1874	2	60	108	NG	MD	NR	2	1.00
	Britain	1873	1874	34	50	51	MP	MV	NR	1	0.03
					110					3	
Formosa War	Japan	1874	1874	36	300	98	MP	MV	IR	25	0.69
	Taiwan	1874	1874	2.7	100	81	NG	MD	NR	20	7.41
					400					45	
Upper Nile War	Egypt	1874	1879	22	200	96	MP	MV	IR	21	0.95
	Upper Nile	1874	1879	1	60	108	NG	MD	NR	10	10.00
					260					31	
Abyssinian War	Egypt	1875	1879	23	200	126	EX	MD	NR	7	0.30
	Ethiopia	1875	1879	5	100	93	NG	MV	IR	30	6.00
					300					37	
Russo-Turkish War II	Bulgaria	1877	1878	3	40	93	NG	MV	IR	15	5.00
	Montenegro	1876	1878	0.35	25	111	NG	MD	NR	5	14.29
	Russia	1877	1878	97	1200	203	MP	MV	IR	120	1.24
	Serbia	1876	1878	6	40	90	NG	MD	NR	5	0.83
	Turkey	1876	1878	26	400	216	MP	MV	IR	10	0.38
					1705					155	
Satsuma Rebellion	Japan	1877	1877	37	300	123	MP	MV	IR	15	0.41
	Samurai	1877	1877	0.1	25	202	NG	MD	NR	6	60.00
					325					21	
Serbian War	Montenegro	1877	1878	0.35	25	97	NG	MV	IR	5	14.29
	Serbia	1877	1878	6	40	49	NG	MV	IR	7	1.17
	Turkey	1877	1878	26	400	111	EX	MD	NR	165	6.35
					465					177	

WAR	SIDE	BEGAN	END	POP	CMBT	RISK	KDESP	DEND	RESULT	LOSSES	INT
Afghan War	Afghanistan	1878	1880	8	100	108	EX	MD	NR	1.5	0.19
	Britain	1878	1880	36	40	140	MP	MV	NR	2.5	0.07
					140					4	
Shoa War	Ethiopia	1878	1882	5	100	101	MP	MV	IR	30	6.00
	Shoa	1878	1882	1	60	123	NG	MD	NR	10	10.00
					160					40	
Zulu War	Britain	1878	1879	36	10	64	EX	MD	NR	3	0.08
	Zulu	1878	1879	3	100	113	MP	MV	IR	1	0.33
					110					4	
War of the Pacific	Bolivia	1879	1884	3	80	17	NG	MD	NR	1	0.33
	Chile	1879	1884	6	50	120	MP	MV	IR	10	1.67
	Peru	1879	1884	2.75	40	102	NG	MD	NR	1	0.36
					170					12	
Boer War I	Boers	1880	1881	0.5	10	101	NG	MD	NR	3	6.00
	Britain	1880	1881	38	50	120	MP	MV	NR	8	0.21
					60					11	
Gun War	Basuto	1880	1881	1.5	120	108	NG	MD	NR	8	5.33
	Britain	1880	1881	38	50	56	MP	MV	IR	2	0.05
					170					10	
British Occupation	Britain	1881	1882	38	40	61	MP	MV	NR	5	0.13
	Egypt	1881	1882	23	200	90	NG	MD	NR	8	0.35
					240					13	
Mahdist War	Britain	1881	1899	39	60	125	MP	MV	IR	10	0.26
	Egypt	1881	1899	23	200	90	MP	MV	IR	4	0.17
	Ethiopia	1881	1899	5	100	90	MP	MV	IR	25	5.00
	Mahdi	1881	1899	5	100	130	SU	MD	NR	500	100.00
	Sudan	1881	1899	6	25	41	MP	MV	IR	7	1.17
					485					546	
Tunis War	France	1881	1881	39	20	78	MP	MV	IR	0.8	0.02
	Tunisia	1881	1881	1.4	25	108	NG	MD	NR	0.2	0.14
					45					1	

TWO HUNDRED YEARS OF WAR

WAR	SIDE	BEGAN	END	POP	CMBT	RISK	KDESP	DEND	RESULT	LOSSES	INT
Korean Civil War	China	1882	1900	430	3000	90	EX	MD	NR	100	0.23
	Japan	1882	1900	40	300	176	MP	MV	IR	20	0.50
	Korea	1882	1900	10.8	100	137	NG	MD	NR	40	3.70
	Rebels	1882	1900	1	50	176	NG	MD	NR	20	20.00
	Russia	1895	1900	125	1200	203	MP	MV	IR	5	0.04
					4650					185	
Madagascar War	France	1883	1885	39	10	39	MP	MV	IR	0.1	0.00
	Madagascar	1883	1885	2.7	10	104	NG	MD	NR	1	0.37
					20					1.1	
Serbian Revolution	Rebels	1883	1883	0.3	20	113	EX	MD	NR	3	10.00
	Serbia	1883	1883	6	40	58	MP	MV	IR	4	0.67
					60					7	
Zulu Civil War	Rebels	1883	1884	0.5	75	108	EX	MD	NR	16	32.00
	Zulu	1883	1884	3	100	77	MP	MV	IR	35	11.67
					175					51	
Conquest of Merv	Merv	1884	1885	1	30	67	NG	MD	NR	10	10.00
	Russia	1884	1885	105	1200	270	MP	MV	IR	15	0.14
					1230					25	
Sino-French War	China	1884	1885	432	3000	72	NG	MD	NR	10	0.02
	France	1884	1885	39	50	172	MP	MV	IR	5	0.13
					3050					15	
Burmese War	Britain	1885	1895	39	25	67	MP	MV	NR	4	0.10
	Burma	1885	1895	17	50	105	NG	MD	NR	2.5	0.15
					75					6.5	
Mandinga Wars	France	1885	1898	39	25	58	MP	MV	IR	3	0.08
	Mandinga	1885	1898	1	100	101	NG	MD	NR	40	40.00
					125					43	
Religious Wars	Moslems	1885	1889	10	25	134	NG	MV	IR	1	0.10
	Uganda	1885	1889	5	10	115	EX	MD	NR	2	0.40
					35					3	
Riel Rebellion	Canada	1885	1885	9	50	28	MP	MV	IR	5	0.56
	Rebels	1885	1885	0.5	5	90	SU	MD	NR	0.5	1.00
					55					5.5	

WAR	SIDE	BEGAN	END	POP	CMBT	RISK	KDESP	DEND	RESULT	LOSSES	INT
Serbo-Bulgarian War	Austria	1885	1886	42	600	245	MP	MV	IR	1	0.02
	Bulgaria	1885	1886	3.5	40	63	NG	MV	IR	2	0.57
	Serbia	1885	1886	6	40	25	NG	MD	NR	2	0.33
					680					5	
Slave Wars	Belgium	1885	1898	6	50	16	MP	MV	IR	4	0.67
	Britain	1885	1898	39	25	37	MP	MV	IR	3	0.08
	Slavers	1885	1898	0.05	5	108	NG	MD	NR	1	20.00
					80					8	
Zulu Rebellion	Britain	1887	1887	40	25	19	MP	MV	NR	2	0.05
	Zulu	1887	1887	3	120	109	EX	MD	NR	40	13.33
					145					42	
Arab Revolt	Germany	1888	1890	37	25	34	MP	MV	NR	0.5	0.01
	Rebels	1888	1890	2	3	108	EX	MD	NR	0.5	0.25
					28					1	
Abyssinian Civil War	Ethiopia	1889	1899	6	100	90	NG	MV	IR	10	1.67
	Rebels	1889	1899	0.4	10	120	EX	MD	NR	4	10.00
					110					14	
Dahomey War	Dahomey	1889	1890	1	50	63	NG	MD	NR	10	10.00
	France	1889	1890	39	50	26	MP	MV	IR	2	0.05
					100					12	
Wahehe War	Germany	1891	1893	41	50	38	MP	MV	IR	3	0.07
	Wahehe	1891	1893	1	30	123	NG	MD	NR	10	10.00
					80					13	
Dahomey War	Dahomey	1892	1892	1	50	105	NG	MD	NR	1	1.00
	France	1892	1892	40	50	26	MP	MV	IR	2	0.05
					100					3	
Bornu Rebellion	Bornu	1893	1893	15	125	117	EX	MD	NR	3	0.20
	Zobeir	1893	1893	1	40	112	MP	MV	IR	2	2.00
					165					5	
Matabele War	Britain	1893	1893	41	25	67	MP	MV	NR	2	0.05
	Mashona	1893	1893	0.3	19	126	NG	MD	NR	7	23.33
	Matabele	1893	1893	0.45	15	112	NG	MD	NR	3	6.67
					59					12	

TWO HUNDRED YEARS OF WAR

WAR	SIDE	BEGAN	END	POP	CMBT	RISK	KDESP	DEND	RESULT	LOSSES	INT
Naval Rebellion	Brazil	1893	1895	17	200	56	MP	MV	IR	25	1.47
	Rebels	1893	1895	0.25	5	113	EX	MD	NR	1	4.00
					205					26	
Riff War	Berbers	1893	1893	0.125	10	113	NG	MD	NR	1	8.00
	Spain	1893	1893	18.2	180	101	NG	MV	IR	2	0.11
					190					3	
Tuareg War	France	1893	1893	40	50	58	NG	MV	IR	2	0.05
	Tuareg	1893	1893	0.1	8	123	NG	MD	NR	3	30.00
					58					5	
Madagascar War	France	1894	1905	40	20	33	NG	MV	IR	6	0.15
	Madagascar	1894	1905	2.75	10	113	NG	MD	NR	1	0.36
					30					7	
Sino-Japanese	China	1894	1895	448	3000	162	EX	MD	NR	35	0.08
	Japan	1894	1895	43	300	215	MP	MV	IR	25	0.58
					3300					60	
Ashanti War	Ashanti	1895	1896	3	60	101	NG	MD	NR	1	0.33
	Britain	1895	1896	41	25	75	MP	MV	NR	5	0.12
					85					6	
Cuban Revolution	Cuba	1895	1898	1.6	25	108	MP	MV	IR	5	3.13
	Spain	1895	1898	18.2	180	86	EX	MD	NR	25	1.37
					205					30	
Italo-Abyssinian War	Ethiopia	1895	1896	7	100	79	MP	MV	IR	15	2.14
	Italy	1895	1896	33	300	115	EX	MD	NR	9	0.27
					400					24	
Malakand War	Britain	1896	1897	41	25	67	MP	MV	NR	2	0.05
	Rebels	1896	1897	2	10	108	EX	MD	NR	3	1.50
					35					5	
Matabele Revolt	Britain	1896	1896	41	25	27	MP	MV	IR	1	0.02
	Matabele	1896	1896	0.5	15	111	EX	MD	NR	2	4.00
					40					3	

WAR	SIDE	BEGAN	END	POP	CMBT	RISK	KDESP	DEND	RESULT	LOSSES	INT
Philippine Rebellion	Philippines	1896	1905	20	100	86	NG	MD	NR	25	1.25
	Spain	1896	1898	18.3	190	121	SU	MD	NR	10	0.55
	U.S.A.	1898	1898	75	50	108	MP	MV	IR	15	0.20
					340					50	
Zanzibar Rebellion	Britain	1896	1896	41	25	27	MP	MV	NR	1	0.02
	Zanzibar	1896	1896	0.2	25	101	NG	MD	NR	7	35.00
					50					8	
Batetela War	Batetela	1897	1900	0.3	25	123	EX	MD	NR	10	33.33
	Belgium	1897	1900	6.9	50	15	MP	MV	IR	3	0.43
					75					13	
Fulani War	Britain	1897	1903	41	25	43	MP	MV	IR	4	0.10
	Fulani	1897	1903	13	150	47	SU	MD	NR	30	2.31
					175					34	
Greco-Turkish War	Greece	1897	1897	4.5	100	45	NG	MD	NR	0.5	0.11
	Turkey	1897	1897	28	400	32	NG	MV	IR	1.5	0.05
					500					2	
Tirah War	Afridi	1897	1898	0.3	10	123	EX	MD	NR	3	10.00
	Britain	1897	1898	41	25	13	MP	MV	NR	2	0.05
					35					5	
Uganda Mutiny	Britain	1897	1901	41	25	19	MP	MV	NR	4	0.10
	Uganda	1897	1901	6	15	101	EX	MD	NR	25	4.17
					40					29	
Spanish-American War	Spain	1898	1898	18.4	200	96	EX	MD	NR	15	0.82
	U.S.A.	1898	1898	75	130	134	MP	MV	IR	5	0.07
					330					20	
Boer War II	Boers	1899	1902	1.2	35	36	EX	MD	NR	5	4.17
	Britain	1899	1902	42	50	138	MP	MV	NR	20	0.48
					85					25	

TWO HUNDRED YEARS OF WAR

WAR	SIDE	BEGAN	END	POP	CMBT	RISK	KDESP	DEND	RESULT	LOSSES	INT
Boxer Rebellion	Britain	1900	1901	41	5	115	MP	MV	NR	1	0.02
	China	1899	1901	450	4000	75	EX	MD	NR	35	0.08
	Japan	1900	1901	45	12	202	MP	MV	NR	1	0.02
	Rebels	1899	1901	1	80	108	EX	MD	NR	20	20.00
	Russia	1900	1901	136	100	194	MP	MV	NR	11	0.08
	U.S.A.	1900	1901	75	4	194	MP	MV	NR	1	0.01
					4201					69	
Chad-French Conquest	Chad	1899	1900	3	30	102	EX	MD	NR	1	0.33
	France	1899	1900	41	50	59	MP	MV	NR	2	0.05
					80					3	
Somalia War	Britain	1899	1920	42	25	168	NG	MD	NR	1	0.02
	Ethiopia	1899	1920	10	100	54	NG	MD	NR	1	0.10
	Italy	1899	1920	34	300	173	NG	MD	NR	2	0.06
	Rebels	1899	1920	5	50	110	MP	MV	NR	1	0.20
					475					5	
Achinese War	Indonesia	1900	1908	100	150	45	NG	MD	NR	25	0.25
	Netherlands	1900	1908	5.2	100	60	NG	MV	IR	4	0.77
					250					29	
Arabian Civil War	Arabia	1900	1925	6	80	105	EX	MD	NR	30	5.00
	Saudi Arabia	1900	1925	6	100	47	NG	MV	IR	50	8.33
					180					80	
Sahara War	France	1900	1900	41	50	21	NG	MV	IR	2	0.05
	Tribes	1900	1900	1	60	144	NG	MD	NR	15	15.00
					110					17	
Angolan Revolt	Angola	1902	1902	4	40	115	EX	MD	NR	2	0.50
	Portugal	1902	1902	5	40	84	MP	MV	NR	2	0.40
					80					4	
Hottentot Uprising	Germany	1903	1908	43	80	60	MP	MV	IR	6	0.14
	Tribes	1903	1908	1	100	108	EX	MD	NR	30	30.00
					180					36	
Nigerian War	Britain	1903	1904	42	50	93	MP	MV	NR	2	0.05
	Nigeria	1903	1904	19	30	74	EX	MD	NR	1	0.05
					80					3	

WAR	SIDE	BEGAN	END	POP	CMBT	RISK	KDESP	DEND	RESULT	LOSSES	INT
Panamanian Revolution	Colombia	1903	1903	15	50	113	EX	MD	NR	7	0.47
	Panama	1903	1903	0.5	10	38	MP	MV	IR	2	4.00
	U.S.A.	1903	1903	88	15	144	MP	MV	IR	1	0.01
					---					---	
					75					10	
Russo-Japanese War	Japan	1904	1905	45	400	151	MP	MV	IR	85	1.89
	Russia	1904	1905	136	2000	151	SU	MD	NR	125	0.92
					---					---	
					2400					210	
Cameroon Revolt	Germany	1905	1907	46	100	86	EX	MD	NR	30	0.65
	Tribes	1905	1907	2	100	126	MP	MV	IR	30	15.00
					---					---	
					200					60	
French Congo	France	1905	1905	41	10	74	MP	MV	NR	2	0.05
	Rebels	1905	1905	5	10	108	EX	MD	NR	3	0.60
					---					---	
					20					5	
Iranian Revolt	Britain	1905	1921	43	50	56	MP	MV	NR	6	0.14
	Iran	1905	1921	11	200	108	EX	MD	NR	60	5.45
	Rebels	1905	1921	1	50	105	MP	MV	NR	5	5.00
	Russia	1905	1921	137	2000	189	MP	MV	IR	50	0.36
					---					---	
					2300					121	
Nigerian War	Britain	1906	1906	43	25	93	MP	MV	NR	2	0.05
	Rebels	1906	1906	5	100	157	EX	MD	NR	10	2.00
					---					---	
					125					12	
Angolan War	Portugal	1907	1907	5.3	40	48	MP	MV	NR	5	0.94
	Rebels	1907	1907	2	50	141	EX	MD	NR	5	2.50
					---					---	
					90					10	
Honduran War	Honduras	1907	1907	1.4	10	23	SU	MD	NR	2	1.43
	Nicaragua	1907	1907	0.5	8	108	MP	MV	NR	2	4.00
					---					---	
					18					4	
Moroccan War	France	1908	1909	41	30	49	MP	MV	IR	8	0.20
	Morocco	1908	1909	6	80	108	EX	MD	NR	12	2.00
					---					---	
					110					20	
Honduran Civil War	Honduras	1909	1911	1.4	10	45	SM	MS	NR	3	2.14
	Rebels	1909	1911	0.15	25	108	SM	MS	NR	3	20.00
					---					---	
					35					6	

TWO HUNDRED YEARS OF WAR

WAR	SIDE	BEGAN	END	POP	CMBT	RISK	KDESP	DEND	RESULT	LOSSES	INT
Turkish Revolt	Armenians	1909	1913	4	25	101	EX	MD	NR	6	1.50
	Turkey	1909	1913	29	400	81	MP	MV	NR	3	0.10
					425					9	
Wadai War	France	1909	1911	41	50	53	MP	MV	IR	4	0.10
	Tribes	1909	1911	0.5	50	113	EX	MD	NR	8	16.00
					100					12	
Mexican Civil War	Mexico	1911	1914	15	100	111	EX	MD	NR	150	10.00
	Rebels	1911	1914	1	100	126	MP	MV	IR	25	25.00
					200					175	
Chinese Revolution	China	1911	1948	500	5000	51	EX	MD	NR	2000	4.00
	Japan	1911	1948	50	500	151	EX	MD	NR	150	3.00
	Rebels	1911	1948	20	1000	148	MP	MV	IR	200	10.00
					6500					2350	
Italo-Turkish War	Italy	1911	1912	36	300	30	MP	MV	IR	6	0.17
	Turkey	1911	1912	29	400	43	EX	MD	NR	14	0.48
					700					20	
Balkan War I	Bulgaria	1912	1913	4.1	60	252	MP	MV	NR	32	7.80
	Greece	1912	1913	4.8	100	105	EX	MD	NR	5	1.04
	Montenegro	1912	1913	0.7	40	141	EX	MD	NR	3	4.29
	Serbia	1912	1913	8	60	141	EX	MD	NR	15	1.88
	Turkey	1912	1913	29	420	144	EX	MD	NR	30	1.03
					680					85	
Riff War	Berbers	1912	1926	0.5	15	117	EX	MD	NR	5	10.00
	France	1912	1926	41	75	84	MP	MV	IR	16	0.39
	Spain	1912	1926	22	200	50	MP	MV	IR	15	0.68
					290					36	
U.S. Intervention	Cuba	1912	1919	3	25	47	SU	MD	NR	5	1.67
	Haiti	1912	1919	0.4	5	18	SU	MD	NR	2	5.00
	Honduras	1912	1919	1.5	10	17	SU	MD	NR	3	2.00
	Nicaragua	1912	1919	0.6	10	27	SU	MD	NR	3	5.00
	U.S.A.	1912	1919	96	25	125	SU	MV	IR	6	0.06
					75					19	

WAR	SIDE	BEGAN	END	POP	CMBT	RISK	KDESP	DEND	RESULT	LOSSES	INT
Balkan War II	Bulgaria	1913	1913	4.1	60	144	EX	MD	NR	18	4.39
	Greece	1913	1913	4.8	100	101	MP	MV	NR	12.5	2.60
	Montenegro	1913	1913	0.7	40	106	SU	MD	NR	2	2.86
	Romania	1913	1913	12	200	135	MP	MV	NR	1.5	0.13
	Serbia	1913	1913	8	80	141	MP	MV	NR	18.5	2.31
	Turkey	1913	1913	29	450	144	MP	MV	NR	20	0.69
					-----					-----	
					930					72.5	
Boer War III	Boers	1914	1914	1.5	85	172	EX	MD	NR	15	10.00
	Britain	1914	1914	44	50	133	MP	MV	NR	5	0.11
					-----					-----	
					135					20	
World War I	Arabs	1914	1918	3	50	36	MP	MV	IR	15	5.00
	Australia	1914	1918	8	50	37	MP	MV	IR	5	0.63
	Austria	1914	1918	50	7800	240	EX	MD	NR	1500	30.00
	Belgium	1914	1918	8	200	64	MP	MV	IR	80	10.00
	Britain	1914	1918	44	8900	230	MP	MV	IR	908	20.64
	Canada	1914	1918	10	100	58	MP	MV	IR	50	5.00
	France	1914	1918	42	8400	151	MP	MV	DI	1350	32.14
	Germany	1914	1918	55	8700	302	SU	MD	DI	2500	45.45
	Greece	1917	1918	5	120	86	MP	MV	IR	5	1.00
	Italy	1915	1918	37	5600	194	MP	MV	IR	650	17.57
	Japan	1914	1918	51	800	36	NG	NC	IR	0.3	0.01
	New Zealand	1914	1918	0.8	10	36	MP	MV	IR	5	6.25
	Portugal	1916	1918	5.5	50	82	MP	MV	IR	7	1.27
	Romania	1916	1917	13	200	111	SU	CS	IR	335	25.77
	Russia	1914	1918	135	12000	189	MP	MV	DI	1700	12.59
	S. Africa	1914	1918	7	35	101	MP	MV	IR	10	1.43
	Turkey	1914	1918	29	2850	130	EX	MD	NR	325	11.21
	U.S.A.	1917	1918	98	4355	173	MP	MV	IR	126	1.29
	Yugoslavia	1914	1918	10	200	130	MP	MV	IR	48	4.80
	Bulgaria	1915	1918	4.2	60	120	EX	MD	NR	14	3.33
					-----					------	
					60480					9633.3	
Armenian Terror	Armenians	1915	1922	5	25	26	EX	MD	NR	1000	200.00
	Turkey	1915	1922	29	450	50	MP	MV	IR	65	2.24
					-----					-----	
					475					1065	
Irish Civil War	Britain	1916	1921	44	10	160	NG	MD	NR	1	0.02
	Ireland	1916	1921	4.25	10	64	MP	MV	NR	1	0.24
	Rebels	1916	1921	0.5	7	113	EX	MD	NR	1	2.00
					---					---	
					27					3	
Russian Civil War	Rebels	1917	1921	30	1200	340	EX	MD	NR	1500	50.00
	Russia	1917	1921	135	3600	72	MP	MV	IR	350	2.59
					-----					-----	
					4800					1850	

TWO HUNDRED YEARS OF WAR

WAR	SIDE	BEGAN	END	POP	CMBT	RISK	KDESP	DEND	RESULT	LOSSES	INT
Afghan War	Afghanistan	1919	1919	11	125	120	EX	MD	NR	1	0.09
	Britain	1919	1919	44	50	34	MP	MV	NR	2	0.05
					175					3	
Greco-Turkish War	Greece	1919	1922	5.1	120	28	EX	MD	NR	30	5.88
	Turkey	1919	1922	29	450	72	MP	MV	NR	20	0.69
					570					50	
Hungarian War	Czechoslovakia	1919	1920	12.5	20	202	MP	MV	IR	1	0.08
	Hungary	1919	1920	7.2	100	45	EX	MD	NR	1	0.14
	Romania	1919	1920	13	250	247	MP	MV	IR	2	0.15
					370					4	
Russo-Polish War	Poland	1919	1920	28	200	56	MP	MV	IR	25	0.89
	Russia	1919	1920	133	3600	202	EX	MD	NR	105	0.79
					3800					130	
Waziristan Revolt	Britain	1919	1919	44	50	20	MP	MV	IR	2	0.05
	Masud	1919	1919	1	5	126	EX	MD	NR	2	2.00
					55					4	
Iraq Revolt	Britain	1920	1920	45	50	34	MP	MV	NR	3	0.07
	Iraq	1920	1920	3.75	75	108	EX	MD	NR	10	2.67
					125					13	
Druse Revolt	Druse	1925	1927	0.25	25	108	EX	MD	NR	5	20.00
	France	1925	1927	40	746	88	MP	MV	NR	4	0.10
					771					9	
Kurdish Revolt	Iran	1925	1932	15	250	72	MP	MV	IR	35	2.33
	Kurds	1925	1932	0.25	50	130	EX	MD	NR	10	40.00
	Turkey	1925	1932	30	500	105	MP	MV	IR	55	1.83
					800					100	
Indonesia Revolution	Indonesia	1926	1927	115	150	56	EX	MD	NR	5	0.04
	Netherlands	1926	1927	7.5	100	72	MP	MV	NR	3	0.40
					250					8	
Mexican Revolt	Mexico	1927	1929	21	100	63	MP	MV	IR	25	1.19
	Rebels	1927	1929	2	50	102	EX	MD	NR	10	5.00
					150					35	

WAR	SIDE	BEGAN	END	POP	CMBT	RISK	KDESP	DEND	RESULT	LOSSES	INT
Stalin Terror	Population	1927	1940	135	1000	36	SU	MD	NR	18000	133.33
	Russia	1927	1940	30	5000	144	MP	MV	IR	50	1.67
					6000					18050	
Chaco War	Bolivia	1928	1935	4	100	111	EX	MD	NR	80	20.00
	Paraguay	1928	1935	0.8	80	173	MP	MV	DI	200	250.00
					180					280	
Spanish Civil War	Germany	1936	1939	85	20	235	NG	MV	IR	2	0.02
	Italy	1936	1939	43	50	163	NG	MV	IR	10	0.23
	Rebels	1930	1939	5	50	221	MP	MV	IR	200	40.00
	Russia	1936	1939	170	50	432	NG	MD	NR	6	0.04
	Spain	1930	1939	25	200	194	EX	MD	NR	545	21.80
					370					763	
Manchurian War	China	1931	1939	640	6000	151	EX	MD	DI	800	1.25
	Japan	1931	1939	73	1000	227	MP	MV	IR	260	3.56
					7000					1060	
Italo-Ethiopian War	Ethiopia	1935	1936	28	100	75	EX	MD	NR	16	0.57
	Italy	1935	1936	39	330	120	MP	MV	IR	15	0.38
					430					31	
Arab Revolt	Britain	1936	1939	47	50	42	MP	MV	NR	2	0.04
	Rebels	1936	1939	10	100	108	EX	MD	NR	25	2.50
					150					27	
Russo-Japanese War	Japan	1938	1939	77	1000	130	EX	MD	NR	15	0.19
	Russia	1938	1939	170	5000	162	MP	MV	IR	4	0.02
					6000					19	
Russo-Finnish War	Finland	1939	1940	4	80	54	EX	MD	NR	40	10.00
	Russia	1939	1940	172	4000	130	MP	MV	IR	50	0.29
					4080					90	

TWO HUNDRED YEARS OF WAR

WAR	SIDE	BEGAN	END	POP	CMBT	RISK	KDESP	DEND	RESULT	LOSSES	INT
World War II	Albania	1939	1945	2	50	134	MP	MV	IR	25	12.50
	Australia	1939	1945	9	50	69	MP	MV	IR	30	3.33
	Belgium	1940	1945	8	60	93	MP	MV	IR	10	1.25
	Brazil	1944	1945	30	200	65	MP	MV	IR	1	0.03
	Britain	1939	1945	48	4200	202	MP	MV	IR	300	6.25
	Bulgaria	1941	1945	7	60	108	EX	MD	NR	50	7.14
	Canada	1939	1945	11	100	29	MP	MV	IR	40	3.64
	China	1941	1945	700	8000	148	MP	MV	DI	3000	4.29
	Denmark	1939	1945	4	50	29	MP	MV	IR	10	2.50
	Ethiopia	1939	1945	30	100	63	MP	MV	IR	5	0.17
	Finland	1941	1945	4	80	151	MP	MV	IR	42	10.50
	France	1939	1945	41	6000	194	MP	MV	DI	500	12.20
	Germany	1939	1945	85	10000	529	EX	MD	DI	7000	82.35
	Greece	1940	1945	7	140	67	MP	MV	IR	10	1.43
	Hungary	1941	1945	9.2	100	65	SU	MD	NR	40	4.35
	Iran	1939	1945	26	300	63	MP	MV	IR	45	1.73
	Iraq	1939	1945	4.5	100	63	MP	MV	IR	25	5.56
	Italy	1940	1945	43.6	4500	156	EX	MD	NR	250	5.73
	Japan	1941	1945	71	7400	323	EX	MD	DI	3000	42.25
	Netherlands	1940	1945	8.7	100	72	MP	MV	IR	6.2	0.71
	New Zealand	1939	1945	1.8	60	56	MP	MV	IR	17.3	9.61
	Norway	1940	1945	2.9	50	56	MP	MV	IR	5	1.72
	Poland	1939	1945	33	300	154	MP	MV	IR	6000	181.82
	Romania	1941	1945	20	260	101	EX	MD	NR	300	15.00
	Russia	1941	1952	170	20000	340	MP	MV	DI	25000	147.06
	S. Africa	1939	1945	10	50	44	MP	MV	IR	8.7	0.87
	Thailand	1939	1945	16	150	56	MP	MV	IR	20	1.25
	U.S.A.	1941	1945	130	16000	130	MP	MV	IR	408	3.14
	Yugoslavia	1941	1945	15.4	500	194	MP	MV	IR	1500	97.40
					78960					47648.2	
Greek Civil War	Greece	1944	1949	7.2	150	130	MP	MV	IR	55	7.64
	Rebels	1944	1949	0.5	50	167	EX	MD	NR	10	20.00
					200					65	
Arab-Israeli War	Britain	1945	1948	50	25	75	NG	MD	NR	1	0.02
	Israel	1945	1948	2	140	147	MP	MV	NR	3	1.50
					165					4	
Burmese Rebellion	Britain	1945	1946	50	40	67	NG	MD	NR	3	0.06
	Rebels	1945	1946	1	80	137	MP	MV	NR	10	10.00
					120					13	
Indonesian War	Indonesia	1945	1949	130	200	64	MP	MV	IR	5	0.04
	Netherlands	1945	1949	8.4	100	88	EX	MD	NR	2	0.24
					300					7	

WAR	SIDE	BEGAN	END	POP	CMBT	RISK	KDESP	DEND	RESULT	LOSSES	INT
Iran Revolt	Iran	1945	1946	28	300	126	MP	MV	NR	20	0.71
	Rebels	1945	1946	2	10	123	EX	MD	NR	4	2.00
	Russia	1945	1946	180	20000	144	EX	MD	NR	3	0.02
					20310					27	
Huk Rebellion	Philippines	1946	1954	40	75	144	MP	MV	NR	30	0.75
	Rebels	1946	1954	0.5	50	109	EX	MD	NR	5	10.00
					125					35	
Indochina War	China	1946	1954	730	4000	126	MP	MV	IR	10	0.01
	France	1946	1954	40	100	162	EX	MD	NR	15	0.38
	Vietminh	1946	1954	5	80	109	MP	MV	IR	5	1.00
					4180					30	
Indian Civil War	Hindus	1947	1948	25	150	96	MP	MV	IR	10	0.40
	Moslems	1947	1948	100	50	100	EX	MD	NR	15	0.15
					200					25	
Indo-Pakistani War	India	1947	1948	480	1000	162	MP	MV	NR	35	0.07
	Pakistan	1947	1948	70	300	108	EX	MD	NR	25	0.36
					1300					60	
Kashmir War	India	1947	1949	480	1000	105	MP	MV	IR	3	0.01
	Pakistan	1947	1949	70	300	75	EX	MD	NR	5	0.07
					1300					8	
Madagascar Revolution	France	1947	1948	41	10	88	MP	MV	IR	2	0.05
	Madagascar	1947	1948	6	15	150	EX	MD	NR	2	0.33
					25					4	
Malaysian Rebellion	Britain	1947	1960	50	25	154	MP	MV	NR	2	0.04
	Rebels	1947	1960	3	20	108	EX	MD	NR	1	0.33
					45					3	
Trieste Incident	Italy	1947	1953	45	350	60	SM	MS	IR	0.1	0.00
	Yugoslavia	1947	1953	16	500	73	SM	MS	IR	0.1	0.01
					850					0.2	

TWO HUNDRED YEARS OF WAR

WAR	SIDE	BEGAN	END	POP	CMBT	RISK	KDESP	DEND	RESULT	LOSSES	INT
Arab-Israeli War	Egypt	1948	1949	35	300	172	EX	MD	NR	2	0.06
	Israel	1948	1949	2.2	140	149	MP	MV	NR	6	2.73
	Jordan	1948	1949	1	60	108	EX	MD	NR	1	1.00
	Palestine	1948	1949	2.25	50	99	EX	MD	NR	3	1.33
	PLO	1948	1987	2.25	10	151	UN	MS	NR	3	1.33
	Syria	1948	1949	6	300	144	EX	MD	NR	1	0.17
					860					16	
Burmese Revolution	Burma	1948	1987	30	125	64	UN	MS	NR	50	1.67
	Rebels	1948	1987	1	100	139	UN	MS	NR	20	20.00
					225					70	
Colombian Rebellion	Colombia	1948	1958	17	66	83	MP	MV	NR	15	0.88
	Rebels	1948	1958	1	10	108	EX	MD	NR	4	4.00
					76					19	
Sino-Taiwanese War	China	1948	1965	750	4000	58	SM	MD	NR	2	0.00
	Taiwan	1948	1965	7	300	79	SM	MV	IR	2	0.29
					4300					4	
Congo War	Rebels	1949	1967	1	50	108	EX	MD	NR	7	7.00
	Zaire	1949	1967	25	40	88	MP	MV	NR	100	4.00
					90					107	
Libyan Revolt	Britain	1949	1951	52	25	47	EX	MD	NR	1	0.02
	Rebels	1949	1951	1.7	100	115	MP	MV	IR	5	2.94
					125					6	
Thai Rebellion	Rebels	1949	1951	0.5	10	113	EX	MD	NR	3	6.00
	Thailand	1949	1951	19	150	115	MP	MV	NR	10	0.53
					160					13	
Communist Terror	China	1950	1958	800	4000	196	MP	MV	IR	100	0.13
	Population	1950	1958	520	1000	40	EX	MD	NR	20000	38.46
					5000					20100	
Indochina War	Cambodia	1950	1954	6	75	70	MP	MV	IR	30	5.00
	France	1950	1954	42	50	140	EX	MD	NR	10	0.24
					125					40	
Indonesian Civil War	Indonesia	1950	1961	140	200	78	MP	MV	IR	15	0.11
	Rebels	1950	1961	2	50	118	EX	MD	NR	10	5.00
					250					25	

WAR	SIDE	BEGAN	END	POP	CMBT	RISK	KDESP	DEND	RESULT	LOSSES	INT
Korean War	China	1950	1953	800	4000	148	EX	MD	NR	900	1.13
	N. Korea	1950	1953	15	230	224	SU	MD	DI	1500	100.00
	S. Korea	1950	1953	15	100	151	MP	MV	DI	1500	100.00
	U.S.A.	1950	1953	150	500	113	MP	MV	IR	54	0.36
					4830					3954	
Buraimi War	Oman	1952	1955	0.6	15	113	MP	MV	IR	6	10.00
	Saudi Arabia	1952	1955	8	100	90	SU	MD	NR	8	1.00
					115					14	
Cypriot War	Britain	1952	1959	55	20	120	MP	MV	NR	2	0.04
	Greece	1952	1959	7.6	150	108	NG	MD	NR	6	0.79
					170					8	
Mau Mau War	Britain	1952	1956	55	51	125	MP	MV	NR	4	0.07
	Kenya	1952	1956	5	120	126	EX	MD	NR	40	8.00
					171					44	
East German Revolt	Rebels	1953	1953	14	1000	100	SU	MD	NR	1	0.07
	Russia	1953	1953	183	10000	118	MP	MV	IR	1	0.01
					11000					2	
Laotian Rebellion	Laos	1953	1987	3.7	53.7	108	UN	MS	NR	30	8.11
	Rebels	1953	1987	0.5	50	163	UN	MS	NR	20	40.00
	Vietnam	1953	1987	26	1000	221	UN	MS	NR	55	2.12
					1103.7					105	
Moroccan Rebellion	France	1953	1955	43	10	69	EX	MD	NR	2	0.05
	Rebels	1953	1955	1	50	115	MP	MV	IR	5	5.00
					60					7	
Nepal Rebellion	India	1953	1953	518	1000	120	MP	MV	IR	5	0.01
	Nepal	1953	1953	9	25	60	MP	MV	IR	3	0.33
	Rebels	1953	1953	0.2	10	137	EX	MD	NR	4	20.00
					1035					12	
Syrian Revolt	Druse	1953	1954	0.5	20	130	EX	MD	NR	2	4.00
	Syria	1953	1954	6	300	63	MP	MV	NR	2	0.33
					320					4	
Algerian War	France	1954	1962	44	60	84	EX	MD	NR	15	0.34
	Rebels	1954	1962	10	30	105	MP	MV	IR	10	1.00
					90					25	

TWO HUNDRED YEARS OF WAR

WAR	SIDE	BEGAN	END	POP	CMBT	RISK	KDESP	DEND	RESULT	LOSSES	INT
Nagaland War	India	1954	1987	520	1000	86	UN	MS	NR	30	0.06
	Nagaland	1954	1987	0.1	25	105	UN	MS	NR	4	40.00
					1025					34	
Sudan Revolt	Rebels	1955	1972	0.5	5	125	EX	MD	NR	2	4.00
	Sudan	1955	1972	15	40	126	MP	MV	NR	15	1.00
					45					17	
Arab-Israeli War	Britain	1956	1956	56	2	207	MP	MV	NR	0.02	0.00
	Egypt	1956	1956	37	300	181	EX	MD	NR	3	0.08
	France	1956	1956	45	1	151	MP	MV	NR	0.01	0.00
	Israel	1956	1956	3	175	161	MP	MV	NR	0.2	0.07
					478					3.23	
Cameroon Rebellion	Cameroon	1956	1959	5.6	50	45	NG	MV	IR	20	3.57
	France	1956	1959	45	10	47	EX	MD	NR	3	0.07
					60					23	
Sri Lanka War	Tamils	1956	1961	1.5	4	123	SU	MD	NR	10	6.67
	Sri Lanka	1956	1961	10	80	22	MP	MV	IR	13	1.30
					84					23	
Cuban Revolution	Cuba	1956	1959	7	100	78	SU	MD	NR	1	0.14
	Rebels	1956	1959	1	4	125	MP	MV	IR	1	1.00
					104					2	
Hungarian Revolt	Hungary	1956	1956	10	106	86	SU	MD	NR	25	2.50
	Russia	1956	1956	193	10000	173	MP	MV	IR	7	0.04
					10106					32	
Polish Revolt	Rebels	1956	1957	30	1000	115	NG	MD	NR	1	0.03
	Russia	1956	1957	193	10000	108	MP	MV	NR	1	0.01
					11000					2	
Sino-Burmese War	Burma	1956	1956	40	186	46	NG	MD	NR	8	0.20
	China	1956	1956	830	4000	108	MP	MV	NR	5	0.01
					4186					13	
Tibet War	China	1956	1959	830	4000	72	MP	MV	NR	4	0.00
	Tibet	1956	1959	8	50	49	EX	MD	NR	6	0.75
					4050					10	

WAR	SIDE	BEGAN	END	POP	CMBT	RISK	KDESP	DEND	RESULT	LOSSES	INT
Ifni Revolt	Morocco	1957	1958	10	100	45	EX	MD	NR	5	0.50
	Spain	1957	1958	29	200	48	MP	MV	IR	3	0.10
					300					8	
Syrian War	Syria	1957	1957	6	300	96	EX	MD	NR	3	0.50
	Turkey	1957	1957	35	550	63	MP	MV	IR	2	0.06
					850					5	
Tunisian Revolt	France	1957	1962	46	10	90	EX	MD	NR	4	0.09
	Tunisia	1957	1962	6	25	57	MP	MV	NR	10	1.67
					35					14	
Colombian Civil War	Colombia	1958	1987	18	66	80	UN	MS	NR	15	0.83
	Rebels	1958	1987	1	10	125	UN	MS	NR	3	3.00
					76					18	
Lebanese Rebellion	Lebanon	1958	1958	2.4	15	86	MP	MV	NR	3	1.25
	Rebels	1958	1958	0.5	10	146	EX	MD	NR	2	4.00
	U.S.A.	1958	1958	187	35	130	MP	MV	IR	0.1	0.00
					60					5.1	
Rwanda Civil War	Hutu	1959	1961	5.5	50	134	MP	MV	IR	8	1.45
	Tutsi	1959	1961	0.25	25	134	SU	MD	NR	8	32.00
					75					16	
Tibet War	China	1959	1974	850	4000	98	MP	MV	NR	10	0.01
	Tibet	1959	1974	8	50	32	EX	MD	NR	6	0.75
					4050					16	
Guatemalan Rebellion	Guatemala	1960	1987	8.4	31.7	83	UN	MS	NR	10	1.19
	Rebels	1960	1987	0.25	8	121	UN	MS	NR	2	8.00
					39.7					12	
Angolan War	Angola	1961	1974	5	100	130	MP	MV	NR	30	6.00
	Portugal	1961	1974	9	73	75	EX	MD	NR	9	1.00
					173					39	
Eritrean War	Cuba	1975	1987	8.7	150	144	UN	MS	NR	5	0.57
	Eritrea	1961	1987	2.5	15	108	UN	MS	NR	50	20.00
	Ethiopia	1961	1987	42	217	104	UN	MS	NR	75	1.79
					382					130	

TWO HUNDRED YEARS OF WAR

WAR	SIDE	BEGAN	END	POP	CMBT	RISK	KDESP	DEND	RESULT	LOSSES	INT
Nepal Civil War	Nepal	1961	1961	11	25	80	MP	MV	NR	5	0.45
	Rebels	1961	1961	0.5	10	125	EX	MD	NR	3	6.00
					35					8	
Niger Civil War	Niger	1961	1974	5	100	74	MP	MV	NR	25	5.00
	Rebels	1961	1974	1	50	130	EX	MD	NR	10	10.00
					150					35	
Syrian Revolt	Rebels	1961	1966	0.5	15	125	MP	MV	IR	3	6.00
	Syria	1961	1966	8	300	78	EX	MD	NR	2	0.25
					315					5	
Yemen War	Egypt	1961	1970	39	400	120	EX	MD	NR	10	0.26
	Rebels	1961	1970	0.5	40	126	MP	MV	NR	10	20.00
	Yemen	1961	1970	5.7	50	97	EX	MD	NR	10	1.75
					490					30	
Algerian Revolt	France	1962	1965	48	10	65	NG	MD	NR	2	0.04
	Rebels	1962	1965	10	20	130	MP	MV	IR	7	0.70
					30					9	
Cameroon Rebellion	Cameroon	1962	1971	8	50	64	MP	MV	IR	15	1.88
	Rebels	1962	1971	0.5	25	105	EX	MD	NR	4	8.00
					75					19	
Guinea-Bissau War	Guinea-Bissau	1962	1974	0.25	20	120	EX	MD	NR	4	16.00
	Portugal	1962	1974	9	73	40	MP	MV	IR	5	0.56
					93					9	
Mozambique War	Mozambique	1962	1974	11	15	97	MP	MV	IR	25	2.27
	Portugal	1962	1974	9	73	58	EX	MD	NR	10	1.11
					88					35	
Sino-Indian	China	1962	1963	890	4000	115	MP	MV	NR	3	0.00
	India	1962	1963	600	1000	108	EX	MD	NR	4	0.01
					5000					7	
Algerian-Moroccan War	Algeria	1963	1964	16	100	32	EX	MD	NR	8	0.50
	Morocco	1963	1964	13	120	105	MP	MV	IR	4	0.31
					220					12	

WAR	SIDE	BEGAN	END	POP	CMBT	RISK	KDESP	DEND	RESULT	LOSSES	INT
Cypriot War	Greece	1963	1964	8	150	86	MP	MV	NR	2	0.25
	Turkey	1963	1964	40	600	130	SM	MD	NR	2	0.05
					750					4	
Dahomey Revolt	Dahomey	1963	1972	2	100	126	MP	MV	IR	25	12.50
	Rebels	1963	1972	0.35	50	108	SU	MD	NR	10	28.57
					150					35	
Dhofar Rebellion	Oman	1963	1987	0.75	21	32	UN	MS	NR	15	20.00
	Rebels	1963	1987	0.3	10	135	UN	MS	NR	3	10.00
	S. Yemen	1963	1987	2.25	50	121	UN	MS	NR	20	8.89
					81					38	
Indonesian War	Indonesia	1963	1966	153	200	120	EX	MD	NR	20	0.13
	Malaysia	1963	1966	13	80	88	MP	MV	NR	25	1.92
					280					45	
New Huk War	Philippines	1964	1974	50	110	90	MP	MV	NR	20	0.40
	Rebels	1964	1974	0.5	20	108	EX	MD	NR	6	12.00
					130					26	
Ogaden War	Cuba	1975	1987	8.7	150	135	UN	MS	NR	2	0.23
	Ethiopia	1964	1987	42	217	90	UN	MS	NR	15	0.36
	Rebels	1964	1987	1	50	108	UN	MS	NR	5	5.00
	Somalia	1964	1987	5	50	144	UN	MS	NR	15	3.00
					467					37	
Thailand War	Cambodia	1964	1987	6.5	75	147	UN	MS	NR	120	18.46
	Thailand	1964	1987	40	235	75	UN	MS	NR	80	2.00
					310					200	
Chad War	Chad	1965	1987	5	50	130	UN	MS	NR	6	1.20
	France	1965	1987	52	5	118	UN	MS	NR	1	0.02
	Libya	1965	1987	3.55	73	105	UN	MS	NR	8	2.25
	Nigeria	1965	1987	80	94	108	UN	MS	NR	6	0.08
	Rebels	1965	1987	1	50	122	UN	MS	NR	5	5.00
	Zaire	1965	1987	30	48	113	UN	MS	NR	8	0.27
					320					34	
Communist Revolt	Indonesia	1965	1965	155	200	96	MP	MV	NR	4	0.03
	Rebels	1965	1965	2	20	138	EX	MD	NR	3	1.50
					220					7	

TWO HUNDRED YEARS OF WAR

WAR	SIDE	BEGAN	END	POP	CMBT	RISK	KDESP	DEND	RESULT	LOSSES	INT
Thai Rebellion	Rebels	1965	1987	1	50	212	UN	MS	NR	15	15.00
	Thailand	1965	1987	40	235	88	UN	MS	NR	100	2.50
					285					115	
Vietnam War	China	1961	1975	900	4000	84	NG	MV	IR	10	0.01
	N. Vietnam	1956	1975	21	500	132	MP	MV	IR	1000	47.62
	S. Korea	1965	1975	40	200	120	SU	MD	NR	10	0.25
	S. Vietnam	1956	1975	15	200	132	NG	MD	NR	1000	66.67
	U.S.A.	1961	1975	202	500	194	NG	MD	NR	50	0.25
					5400					2070	
Cultural Revolution	China	1966	1977	910	4000	51	MP	MV	IR	10000	10.99
	Rebels	1966	1977	30	2000	202	EX	MD	NR	1000	33.33
					6000					11000	
Namibian Revolution	S. Africa	1966	1987	27	106	121	UN	MS	NR	8	0.30
	SWAPO	1966	1987	1	50	141	UN	MS	NR	5	5.00
					156					13	
Biafran War	Biafra	1967	1970	10	100	126	EX	MD	NR	100	10.00
	Nigeria	1967	1970	82	94	104	MP	MV	IR	25	0.30
					194					125	
Sierra Leone	Rebels	1967	1971	0.4	7	120	EX	MD	NR	3	7.50
	Sierra Leone	1967	1971	3	25	30	MP	MV	IR	8	2.67
					32					11	
Six Day War	Egypt	1967	1967	40	400	148	SU	MD	NR	10	0.25
	Iraq	1967	1967	10	250	168	SU	MD	NR	2	0.20
	Israel	1967	1967	3.8	200	123	MP	MV	NR	2	0.53
	Jordan	1967	1967	1.5	60	52	EX	MD	NR	5	3.33
	Syria	1967	1967	8	300	118	SU	MD	NR	1	0.13
					1210					20	
Tupamaros Terror	Tupamaros	1967	1973	0.5	10	76	EX	MD	NR	2	4.00
	Uruguay	1967	1973	2.6	25	53	MP	MV	IR	7	2.69
					35					9	
Czech Invasion	Rebels	1968	1968	14	500	153	SU	MD	NR	1	0.07
	Russia	1968	1968	235	8000	144	MP	MV	IR	1	0.00
					8500					2	

WAR	SIDE	BEGAN	END	POP	CMBT	RISK	KDESP	DEND	RESULT	LOSSES	INT
Dhofar Revolt	Oman	1968	1974	0.8	21	105	MP	MV	IR	7	8.75
	Rebels	1968	1974	0.5	50	118	EX	MD	NR	5	10.00
	S. Yemen	1968	1969	3	50	108	EX	MD	NR	9	3.00
					121					21	
Malaysian Rebellion	Malaysia	1968	1987	16	110	90	UN	MS	NR	26	1.63
	Rebels	1968	1987	1	14	113	UN	MS	NR	4	4.00
					124					30	
Yemen Rebellion	Rebels	1968	1969	0.35	50	115	MP	MV	NR	5	14.29
	S. Yemen	1968	1969	3	50	78	EX	MD	NR	9	3.00
					100					14	
Iran-Iraq War	Iran	1969	1970	38	305	151	MP	MV	NR	10	0.26
	Iraq	1969	1970	10	300	206	EX	MD	NR	5	0.50
					605					15	
Lebanese Civil War	Lebanon	1969	1969	2.6	16	75	MP	MV	NR	5	1.92
	PLO	1969	1969	4.4	16	120	EX	MD	NR	3	0.68
					32					8	
Sudanese Rebellion	Rebels	1969	1971	1	10	126	MP	MD	NR	3	3.00
	Sudan	1969	1971	20	50	53	EX	MV	NR	15	0.75
					60					18	
Ulster Rebellion	Britain	1969	1987	58	14	77	UN	MS	NR	6	0.10
	Rebels	1969	1987	0.5	10	103	UN	MS	NR	5	10.00
					24					11	
West Irian War	Indonesia	1969	1987	161	278	67	UN	MS	NR	25	0.16
	West Irian	1969	1987	0.7	20	108	UN	MS	NR	5	7.14
					298					30	
Cambodian Civil War	Cambodia	1970	1975	6.8	75	202	EX	MD	NR	25	3.68
	Rebels	1970	1975	0.75	50	160	MP	MV	NR	20	26.67
					125					45	
PLO Revolt	Jordan	1970	1971	1.7	60	80	MP	MV	NR	3	1.76
	PLO	1970	1971	4.5	16	108	EX	MD	NR	2	0.44
					76					5	

TWO HUNDRED YEARS OF WAR

WAR	SIDE	BEGAN	END	POP	CMBT	RISK	KDESP	DEND	RESULT	LOSSES	INT
Polish Revolt	Poland	1970	1970	35	300	130	MP	MV	NR	1	0.03
	Rebels	1970	1970	34	1000	115	NG	MD	NR	1	0.03
					1300					2	
Syrian-Jordanian War	Jordan	1970	1970	1.7	60	86	MP	MV	NR	2	1.18
	Syria	1970	1970	9	350	134	EX	MD	NR	3	0.33
					410					5	
Burundi Terror	Hutu	1970	1972	6	50	45	MP	MV	NR	200	33.33
	Tutsi	1970	1972	0.75	50	54	EX	MD	NR	50	66.67
					100					250	
Indo-Pakistani War	India	1971	1971	700	1260	180	MP	MV	NR	20	0.03
	Pakistan	1971	1971	84	400	86	EX	MD	NR	4	0.05
					1660					24	
Moroccan Rebellion	Morocco	1971	1973	17	120	63	MP	MV	IR	10	0.59
	Rebels	1971	1973	0.7	25	130	EX	MD	NR	4	5.71
					145					14	
Uganda Terror	Population	1971	1987	11	50	43	EX	MD	NR	100	9.09
	Uganda	1971	1987	14	18	100	MP	MV	IR	75	5.36
					68					175	
Zimbabwe Rebellion	Rebels	1971	1980	1	100	120	MP	MV	NR	10	10.00
	Rhodesia	1971	1980	6.2	100	51	EX	MD	NR	35	5.65
					200					45	
Pakistani Rebellion	Pakistan	1972	1987	95	483	78	UN	MS	NR	25	0.26
	Rebels	1972	1987	5	20	113	UN	MS	NR	6	1.20
					503					31	
Philippine Rebellion	Moros	1972	1987	0.75	50	158	UN	MS	NR	10	13.33
	Philippines	1972	1987	55	115	150	UN	MS	NR	50	0.91
	Rebels	1972	1987	2	10	180	UN	MS	NR	3	1.50
					175					63	
Yemen War	N. Yemen	1972	1987	8	36.5	108	UN	MS	NR	12	1.50
	S. Yemen	1972	1987	3.5	50	90	UN	MS	NR	15	4.29
					86.5					27	

WAR	SIDE	BEGAN	END	POP	CMBT	RISK	KDESP	DEND	RESULT	LOSSES	INT
Iran-Iraq War	Iran	1973	1975	40	305	64	MP	MV	IR	15	0.38
	Iraq	1973	1975	11	400	235	NG	MD	NR	6	0.55
					705					21	
Lebanon	Lebanon	1973	1973	2.7	17	48	NG	MV	DI	8	2.96
	PLO	1973	1973	4.6	16	108	EX	MD	NR	5	1.09
					33					13	
Yom Kippur War	Egypt	1973	1973	43	400	216	EX	MD	NR	5	0.12
	Iraq	1973	1973	11	400	196	SU	MD	NR	5	0.45
	Israel	1973	1973	4.2	200	136	MP	MV	NR	4	0.95
	Jordan	1973	1973	1.75	60	130	SU	MD	NR	1	0.57
	Syria	1973	1973	9	350	157	EX	MD	NR	8	0.89
					1410					23	
Cypriot War	Cyprus	1974	1974	0.08	5	95	SM	MD	NR	1	12.50
	Turkey	1974	1974	44	600	108	MP	MV	NR	1	0.02
					605					2	
Ethiopian War	Cuba	1974	1987	8.6	150	138	UN	MS	NR	3	0.35
	Ethiopia	1974	1987	42	217	108	UN	MS	NR	25	0.60
	Rebels	1974	1987	2	25	113	UN	MS	NR	10	5.00
					392					38	
Angolan War	Angola	1975	1987	8	100	118	UN	MS	NR	50	6.25
	Cuba	1975	1987	8.7	150	108	UN	MS	NR	5	0.57
	Rebels	1975	1987	2	40	130	UN	MS	NR	15	7.50
	S. Africa	1975	1987	29	106	101	UN	MS	NR	3	0.10
					396					73	
Cambodian Terror	Cambodia	1975	1978	7	75	126	MP	MV	IR	100	14.29
	Population	1975	1978	6	100	33	EX	MD	NR	2000	333.33
					175					2100	
Lebanese Civil War	Israel	1982	1987	4.3	200	144	UN	MS	NR	0.5	0.12
	Lebanon	1975	1987	2.8	17.4	157	UN	MS	NR	10	3.57
	Syria	1975	1987	11	380	147	UN	MS	NR	20	1.82
	Warlords	1975	1987	0.5	25	205	UN	MS	NR	10	20.00
					622.4					40.5	
Mozambique War	Cuba	1975	1987	8.7	150	130	UN	MS	NR	3	0.34
	Mozambique	1975	1987	12.3	15.8	48	UN	MS	NR	5	0.41
	Rebels	1975	1987	1	10	130	UN	MS	NR	4	4.00
					175.8					12	

TWO HUNDRED YEARS OF WAR

WAR	SIDE	BEGAN	END	POP	CMBT	RISK	KDESP	DEND	RESULT	LOSSES	INT
S. Africa Rebellion	Rebels	1975	1987	10	100	137	UN	MS	NR	5	0.50
	S. Africa	1975	1987	29	106	120	UN	MS	NR	10	0.34
					206					15	
Sahara War	Morocco	1975	1987	22	149	83	UN	MS	NR	7	0.32
	Rebels	1975	1987	1	15	189	UN	MS	NR	4	4.00
					164					11	
Syrian Revolt	Rebels	1975	1982	0.5	5	122	EX	MD	NR	2	4.00
	Russia	1975	1982	270	7000	98	MP	NC	NR	0	0.00
	Syria	1975	1982	11	380	98	MP	MV	NR	10	0.91
					7385					12	
Timor War	Indonesia	1975	1987	161	278	83	UN	MS	NR	125	0.78
	Timor	1975	1987	12	30	104	UN	MS	NR	6	0.50
					308					131	
Afghan War	Afghanistan	1978	1987	16	125	104	UN	MS	NR	50	3.13
	Rebels	1978	1987	3	100	232	UN	MS	NR	35	11.67
	Russia	1978	1987	276	5300	219	UN	MS	NR	50	0.18
					5525					135	
Cambodian War	Cambodia	1978	1987	7	75	58	UN	MS	NR	150	21.43
	Rebels	1978	1987	0.6	80	120	UN	MS	NR	20	33.33
	Vietnam	1978	1987	44	1000	144	UN	MS	NR	125	2.84
					1155					295	
Zaire Rebellion	Rebels	1978	1987	1	20	125	UN	MS	NR	5	5.00
	Zaire	1978	1987	32	48	90	UN	MS	NR	20	0.63
					68					25	
El Salvador Civil War	El Salvador	1979	1987	4.3	41	102	UN	MS	NR	10	2.33
	Rebels	1979	1987	0.5	20	126	UN	MS	NR	7	14.00
	U.S.A.	1979	1987	240	2151	88	UN	MS	NR	0	0.00
					2212					17	
Iranian Revolution	Iran	1979	1987	43	305	165	UN	MS	NR	70	1.63
	Rebels	1979	1987	10	50	202	UN	MS	NR	20	2.00
					355					90	

WAR	SIDE	BEGAN	END *	POP	CMBT	RISK	KDESP	DEND	RESULT	LOSSES	INT
Kurdistan War	Iran	1979	1987	43	305	108	UN	MS	NR	7	0.16
	Iraq	1979	1987	12	450	105	UN	MS	NR	6	0.50
	Kurds	1979	1987	0.3	50	112	UN	MS	NR	5	16.67
	Turkey	1979	1987	49	630	86	UN	MS	NR	5	0.10
					1435					23	
Sino-Vietnamese War	China	1979	1987	1055	4000	126	UN	MS	NR	30	0.03
	Vietnam	1979	1987	45	1000	84	UN	MS	NR	60	1.33
					5000					90	
Ugandan Rebellion	Rebels	1979	1987	5	20	125	UN	MS	NR	5	1.00
	Uganda	1979	1987	14.7	18	83	UN	MS	NR	3	0.20
					38					8	
Central American War	Honduras	1980	1987	4.4	16.6	45	UN	MS	NR	5	1.14
	Nicaragua	1980	1987	3.2	62.8	113	UN	MS	NR	10	3.13
					79.4					15	
Honduran Rebellion	Honduras	1980	1987	4.4	16.6	56	UN	MS	NR	3	0.68
	Rebels	1980	1987	0.25	5	156	UN	MS	NR	2	8.00
					21.6					5	
Iran-Iraq War	Iran	1980	1987	43	500	252	UN	MS	NR	400	9.30
	Iraq	1980	1987	13	520	202	UN	MS	NR	100	7.69
					1020					500	
Mozambique Rebellion	Mozambique	1980	1987	12.3	15.8	75	SM	MS	NR	4	0.33
	Rebels	1980	1987	0.5	10	130	UN	MS	NR	4	8.00
					25.8					8	
Peruvian Rebellion	Peru	1980	1987	16	128	80	UN	MS	NR	5	0.31
	Rebels	1980	1987	0.4	8	114	UN	MS	NR	3	7.50
					136					8	
Polish Revolt	Poland	1980	1987	37.5	319	81	UN	NC	NR	1	0.03
	Russia	1980	1987	276	5300	88	UN	NC	NR	0	0.00
	Workers	1980	1987	35	100	86	UN	NC	NR	2	0.06
					5719					3	
Zimbabwe Rebellion	Rebels	1980	1987	1	15	120	UN	MS	NR	5	5.00
	Zimbabwe	1980	1987	8.5	42	96	UN	MS	NR	4	0.47
					57					9	

TWO HUNDRED YEARS OF WAR

WAR	SIDE	BEGAN	END	POP	CMBT	RISK	KDESP	DEND	RESULT	LOSSES	INT
Nicaraguan Insurgency	Cuba	1981	1987	9	162	78	UN	MS	NR	1	0.11
	Nicaragua	1981	1987	3.2	62.8	126	UN	MS	NR	25	7.81
	Rebels	1981	1987	0.5	20	156	UN	MS	NR	8	16.00
					244.8					34	
Falklands War	Argentina	1982	1982	27	108	140	SU	MD	NR	1	0.04
	Britain	1982	1982	60	20	121	MP	MV	IR	1	0.02
					128					2	
PLO Terror	Arafat	1983	1987	1	8	108	UN	MS	NR	2	2.00
	Rebels	1983	1987	1	25	157	UN	MS	NR	8	8.00
					33					10	
Sri Lankian Rebellion	Sinhalese	1983	1987	14.4	37.6	48	UN	MS	NR	3	0.21
	Tamils	1983	1987	1.8	10	105	UN	MS	NR	2	1.11
					47.6					5	
Sudanese Revolt	Rebels	1983	1987	1	20	130	UN	MS	NR	5	5.00
	Sudan	1983	1987	23.5	56.6	78	UN	MS	NR	10	0.43
					76.6					15	
Totals and Averages					466.992	106				163,026	8

FIVE PAST WARS

WAR	Stalin Terror		Russian Civil War		Taiping Rebellion		U.S. Civil War		Franco-Prussian War	
SIDE	Russia	Population	Russia	Rebels	China	Rebels	U.S.A.	Rebels	France	Germany
REGION	3	3	3	3	2	2	7	7	4	4
BEGAN	1927	1927	1917	1917	1850	1850	1861	1861	1870	1870
END	1940	1940	1921	1921	1881	1881	1865	1865	1871	1871
POP	30	135	135	30	400	70	22	9	38	32
SCALE	2	2	4	4	6	6	8	8	7	7
DUR	14	14	5	3	32	32	5	5	2	2
GOV	SD	SD	SD	IN	AM	IN	DM	IN	CD	CM
GSTAB	8	1	6	8	6	8	9	8	7	8
SUPT	1	1	1	2	2	2	4	5	3	5
PWRSTAT	9	3	9	3	7	3	7	3	7	8
LADV	3	2	8	9	7	8	8	5	6	7
SADV	3	1	5	8	5	6	8	6	6	3
CMBT	5000	1000	3600	1200	2000	1000	3995	2000	500	550
QUAL	7	1	7	3	6	3	7	6	7	9
PWR	3500	100	2520	360	1200	300	2797	1200	350	495
POPINV	6	1	1	9	6	9	9	9	8	8
PI	3	8	6	4	4	5	5	4	4	5
SG	6	4	5	6	6	7	6	6	6	5
NO	5	4	4	7	4	6	6	6	5	6
AC	4	5	4	7	6	5	6	6	5	6
HI	9	6	9	9	6	6	6	6	6	8
DU	4	6	6	6	5	5	6	6	5	6
RISK	144	36	72	340	108	126	156	194	113	173
TYPE	C	C	R	R	R	R	R	R	T	T
ISTAB	ID	ID	ID	ID	ID	ID	ID	ID	LG	SS
INIT	AT	DF	DF	AT	TE	AT	DF	AT	AT	AT
KDESP	MP	SU	MP	EX	MP	EX	MP	SU	NG	MP
DEND	MV	MD	MV	MD	MV	MD	MV	MD	MD	MV
RESULT	IR	NR	IR	NR	NR	NR	IR	DI	NR	IR
LOSSES	50	18000	350	1500	8000	12000	300	400	140	100
INT	2	133	3	50	20	171	14	44	4	3
CONCEN	0	3	10	10	1	5	3	9	2	2
INV	1008	504	1080	540	9408	5184	2240	1080	686	784
EFRT	4	6	6	9	7	9	8	9	7	7

WARS THAT NEVER HAPPENED

WAR	SIDE	BEGAN	POP	COMBT	RISK	TYPE	ESCP
Franco-American	France	1790	28	50	59	T	5
	U.S.A.	1790	6	50	67	T	5

				100			
Canada	Canada	1815	8	50	72	T	◆
	U.S.A.	1815	75	300	60	T	◆

				350			
Gibraltar	Britain	1815	17	250	65	T	2
	Spain	1815	12	100	48	T	2

				350			
India	Britain	1858	30	250	97	T	◆
	India	1858	250	500	75	T	◆

				750			
Britain	Britain	1860	32	250	60	T	◆
	France	1860	38	400	77	T	◆

				650			
Germany	France	1872	38	500	84	T	5
	Germany	1872	32	550	90	T	5

				1050			
Germany	Britain	1885	39	250	113	T	5
	Germany	1885	37	550	92	T	5

				800			
Afghanistan	Afghanistan	1920	16	47	90	T	◆
	Iran	1920	15	250	72	T	◆

				297			
Alexandretta	Syria	1920	5	200	47	T	3
	Turkey	1920	29	450	40	T	3

				650			
Kurdistan	Kurds	1920	0.3	10	88	T	5
	Rebels	1920	0.5	5	70	T	5

				15			

WAR	SIDE	BEGAN	POP	COMBT	RISK	TYPE	ESCP
Balkan	Bulgaria	1945	9	148	48	T	4
	Greece	1945	7.2	150	72	T	4
	Yugoslavia	1945	16	500	75	T	4
				798			
Czech-Hungarian	Czechoslovakia	1945	15	203	84	T	4
	Hungary	1945	9.2	100	63	T	4
				303			
Czech-Russian	Czechoslovakia	1945	15	203	77	T	4
	Russia	1945	276	5300	75	T	2
				5503			
German-Polish	Germany	1945	61.2	478	78	T	4
	Poland	1945	33	300	84	T	5
				778			
Hungarian-Romanian	Hungary	1945	9.2	100	63	T	4
	Romania	1945	20	260	48	T	3
				360			
Polish-Czech	Czechoslovakia	1945	15	203	67	T	4
	Poland	1945	33	300	88	T	5
				503			
Polish-Russian	Poland	1945	33	300	108	T	5
	Russia	1945	276	5300	80	T	2
				5600			
Romanian-Russian	Romania	1945	20	260	72	T	3
	Russia	1945	276	5300	75	T	2
				5560			
Russia	Russia	1945	276	5300	88	T	2
	U.S.A.	1945	140	2151	86	T	2
				7451			
Sudan	Egypt	1945	35	300	94	T	4
	Sudan	1945	13	50	58	T	4
				350			

WARS THAT NEVER HAPPENED

WAR	SIDE	BEGAN	POP	COMBT	RISK	TYPE	ESCP
Yugoslavia	Separatists	1945	1	10	86	S	4
	Yugoslavia	1945	16	500	88	S	4

				510			
Baluchistan	Baluchis	1948	4	75	75	T	5
	Tribes	1948	1	25	27	T	5

				100			
Vietnam	U.S.A.	1948	150	1500	75	T	9
	Vietnam	1948	26	150	80	T	9

				1650			
China	China	1953	830	3900	75	T	4
	U.S.A.	1953	220	2500	111	T	4

				6400			
China	China	1958	850	3900	86	R	4
	Russia	1958	276	5300	90	R	4

				9200			
France	France	1958	46	350	58	T	4
	Rebels	1958	0.1	2	69	T	4

				352			
Latin America	Cuba	1960	7	130	59	T	6
	U.S.A.	1960	190	2300	79	T	4

				2430			
Cuba	Cuba	1962	7.1	161	70	T	4
	U.S.A.	1962	240	2151	48	T	4

				2312			
Libya	Egypt	1970	43	400	75	T	7
	Libya	1970	3.5	70	75	T	7

				470			
Morocco	Algeria	1970	22	170	38	T	5
	Morocco	1970	17	120	50	T	5

				290			

WAR	SIDE	BEGAN	POP	COMBT	RISK	TYPE	ESCP
Vietnam	China	1975	1055	3900	88	T	6
	Vietnam	1975	44	1000	94	T	6

				4900			
Averages and Totals				60,832	74		4.3

FUTURE WARS

WAR	SIDE	BEGAN	POP	COMBT	RISK	TYPE	ESCP
India	Hindus	1400	25	100	72	S	4
	Moslems	1400	50	25	106	S	5
				125			
Iraq-Syria	Iraq	1600	13	520	67	T	5
	Syria	1600	11	402	81	T	5
				922			
Kurdistan	Iran	1600	43	305	73	T	4
	Iraq	1600	13	520	81	T	4
	Kurds	1600	0.1	3	75	T	5
	Turkey	1600	49	630	94	T	5
				1458			
Rwanda Civil War	Hutu	1700	0.1	50	28	R	2
	Tutsi	1700	0.1	10	47	R	2
				60			
Maranon	Ecuador	1800	10	42	25	T	2
	Peru	1800	16	128	38	T	2
				170			
S China Sea	China	1800	1055	3900	67	T	3
	Vietnam	1800	44	1027	86	T	4
				4927			
Falklands War	Argentina	1820	30	108	101	T	3
	Britain	1820	56	327	79	T	2
				435			
Zimbabwe	Rebels	1852	0.1	10	105	R	4
	Zimbabwe	1852	8.5	42	90	R	8
				52			
Moro Rebellion	Moros	1898	0.1	5	112	R	4
	Philippines	1898	50	115	72	R	3
				120			

WAR	SIDE	BEGAN	POP	COMBT	RISK	TYPE	ESCP
Cyprus	Greece	1900	10.3	201	108	T	2
	Greeks	1900	0.01	5	94	T	4
	Turkey	1900	49	630	125	T	2
	Turks	1900	0.05	15	102	T	5
				851			
Kosovo	Albania	1900	2	40.4	70	T	2
	Yugoslavia	1900	23.3	241	105	T	2
				281.4			
Malta	Libya	1900	3.55	73	104	T	2
	Malta	1900	0.4	0.7	63	T	5
				73.7			
S Africa	Rebels	1900	1	50	131	R	6
	S. Africa	1900	29	106	130	R	4
				156			
Sino-Soviet	China	1900	1055	3900	117	T	3
	Russia	1900	276	5300	112	T	4
				9200			
Yugoslavia	Separatists	1900	1	10	113	S	2
	Yugoslavia	1900	23.3	241	101	S	3
				251			
Beagle Channel	Argentina	1902	30	108	90	T	1
	Chile	1902	12	101	75	T	1
				209			
Tacna-Arica	Rebels	1910	0.02	5	101	R	1
	Tacna-Arica	1910	0.5	10	74	R	1
				15			
Honduran Civil War	Honduras	1911	4.4	17	72	R	2
	Rebels	1911	0.005	3	113	R	6
				20			
Honduran War	Honduras	1911	4.4	17	65	T	2
	Nicaragua	1911	3.2	63	80	T	2
				80			

FUTURE WARS

WAR	SIDE	BEGAN	POP	COMBT	RISK	TYPE	ESCP
U.S. Intervention	Cuba	1919	9.8	161	60	T	4
	Honduras	1919	4.4	17	69	T	2
	Nicaragua	1919	3.2	63	90	T	4
	U.S.A.	1919	240	2151	83	T	2

				2392			
Aegean	Greece	1921	10.3	201	90	T	4
	Turkey	1921	49	630	94	T	4

				831			
Irish Civil War	Ireland	1921	4.25	13	67	R	2
	Rebels	1921	0.1	3	105	R	2

				16			
Mexican Revolt	Mexico	1929	79	129	126	R	2
	Rebels	1929	0.5	25	123	R	2

				154			
U.S.A.-Russia	Russia	1945	276	5300	120	T	9
	U.S.A.	1945	240	2151	150	T	9

				7451			
World War III	Australia	1945	15.6	70	53	T	9
	Belgium	1945	10	91	88	T	9
	Britain	1945	56	327	93	T	9
	Bulgaria	1945	9	149	90	T	9
	Canada	1945	25.1	90	53	T	9
	China	1945	1055	3900	105	T	9
	Czechoslovakia	1945	15.6	203	42	T	9
	Denmark	1945	5.1	50	42	T	9
	France	1945	52	476	83	T	9
	Germany	1945	61	478	98	T	9
	Greece	1945	10.3	201	59	T	9
	Holland	1945	14.5	106	26	T	9
	Hungary	1945	10.8	106	93	T	9
	Italy	1945	57.1	385	80	T	9
	Japan	1945	122	243	84	T	9
	Norway	1945	4.1	50	70	T	9
	Poland	1945	37.5	319	108	T	9
	Romania	1945	23.5	190	84	T	9
	Russia	1945	276	5300	114	T	9
	Turkey	1945	49	630	74	T	9
	U.S.A.	1945	240	2151	158	T	9

				15515			

WAR	SIDE	BEGAN	POP	COMBT	RISK	TYPE	ESCP
Indo-Pakistan War	India	1948	600	1260	120	T	7
	Pakistan	1948	84	483	101	T	6

				1743			
Malaysia	Malaysia	1948	16	110	72	R	2
	Rebels	1948	0.1	6	101	R	2

				116			
Nepal Civil War	Nepal	1948	11	25	90	R	2
	Rebels	1948	0.05	10	108	R	2

				35			
Sino-Taiwan	China	1948	1055	3900	48	T	2
	Taiwan	1948	20	444	104	T	5

				4344			
Syria-Israel	Israel	1948	4.2	142	105	T	5
	Jordan	1948	1.75	70	90	T	5
	Syria	1948	11	402	126	T	5

				614			
Indonesia	Indonesia	1950	155	278	86	R	2
	Rebels	1950	0.2	10	101	R	2

				288			
Korea	N. Korea	1953	20.1	838	130	T	4
	S. Korea	1953	42	598	118	T	4
	U.S.A.	1953	240	2151	100	T	6

				3587			
Tibet War	China	1958	1055	3900	80	T	1
	Tibet	1958	8	25	75	T	1

				3925			
Colombia	Colombia	1960	20.1	66.2	78	R	2
	Rebels	1960	0.01	5	113	R	4

				71.2			
Laos	Laos	1960	3.7	54	60	R	2
	Rebels	1960	0.2	6	101	R	2
	Vietnam	1960	44	1027	86	R	4

				1087			

FUTURE WARS

WAR	SIDE	BEGAN	POP	COMBT	RISK	TYPE	ESCP
Oman	Oman	1960	1.3	21.5	33	T	4
	U.A.E	1960	1.4	43	25	T	4
				64.5			
Timor	Rebels	1960	0.01	5	105	R	2
	Timor	1960	12	30	96	R	2
				35			
West Sahara	Rebels	1960	0.05	1	105	R	3
	West Sahara	1960	0.5	10	65	R	3
				11			
Yemen	N. Yemen	1960	8	36.5	94	R	4
	S. Yemen	1960	3.5	27.5	84	R	5
				64			
Zaire	Rebels	1961	0.1	5	117	R	3
	Zaire	1961	32	48	78	R	2
				53			
Congo War	Rebels	1965	1	6	117	R	2
	Zaire	1965	32	48	75	S	2
				54			
Thailand	Rebels	1965	0.02	10	112	R	4
	Thailand	1965	52	235	81	R	4
				245			
Guatemala	Guatemala	1970	8.4	32	50	R	4
	Rebels	1970	0.01	3	113	R	4
				35			
Belize	Britain	1972	56	327	88	T	1
	Guatemala	1972	8.4	32	40	T	1
				359			
Guyana	Guyana	1972	0.844	6.6	83	R	1
	Rebels	1972	0.01	1	101	R	1
	Suriname	1972	0.4	2	63	R	1
	Venezuela	1972	18.3	49	78	R	1
				58.6			

WAR	SIDE	BEGAN	POP	COMBT	RISK	TYPE	ESCP
Nigerian Civil War	Nigeria	1972	70	94	67	S	2
	Separatists	1972	5	10	117	S	3
				104			
Sudan	Rebels	1972	0.01	6	101	R	2
	Sudan	1972	23.5	56	53	R	2
				62			
Cameroon Rebellion	Cameroon	1975	9.6	7.3	90	R	3
	Rebels	1975	0.005	2.5	109	R	3
				9.8			
Syria	Rebels	1975	0.05	2	112	R	1
	Syria	1975	11	402	90	R	4
				404			
Vietnam	Rebels	1975	0.05	5	125	R	2
	Vietnam	1975	44	1027	104	R	2
				1032			
Burundi Civil War	Burundi	1978	10	5	84	R	1
	Rebels	1978	29	25	100	R	1
				30			
Libya	Egypt	1978	48.5	445	100	T	2
	Libya	1978	3.55	73	123	T	4
	Sudan	1978	23.5	56	90	T	3
				574			
Dhofar Revolt	Oman	1979	1.3	21.5	86	R	2
	Rebels	1979	0.02	4	126	R	2
				25.5			
Honduras	Honduras	1979	4.4	17	60	R	2
	Rebels	1979	0.05	3	113	R	2
				20			
Suriname	Rebels	1980	0.01	0.5	105	R	2
	Suriname	1980	0.4	2	84	R	2
				2.5			
Averages and Totals				64,818	89		3.9

FIVE FUTURE WARS

WAR	U.S.-Russian		Honduras-Nicaragua		Mexican Revolt		Iraq-Syria		South Africa	
SIDE	U.S.A.	Russia	Honduras	Nicaragua	Rebels Mexico	Mexico	Iraq	Syria	Rebels	Government
REGION	4	3	7	7	7	7	6	6	1	1
BEGAN	1945	1945	1911	1911	1929	1929	1600	1600	1900	1900
END	1987	1987	1987	1987	1987	1987	1987	1987	1987	1987
POP	240	276	3.2	3.2	.5	.5	13	11	5	29
SCALE	9	9	3	3	1	1	5	5	2	2
DUR	43	43	77	77	59	59	388	388	88	88
GOV	DM	SD	DM	SD	IN	DM	CD	MD	IN	DM
GSTAB	9	9	6	5	6	5	5	6	8	7
SUPT	1	1	4	7	1	3	7	6	6	3
PWRSTAT	9	9	1	2	7	4	6	4	1	7
LADV	8	8	5	5	2	6	5	5	7	6
SADV	1	1	4	4	5	6	6	4	2	3
CMBT	2151	5300	17	63	25	129	520	402	50	106
QUAL	8	7	5	5	2	4	4	5	2	7
PWR	1721	3710	9	32	5	52	208	201	10	74
POPINV	7	8	5	7	8	4	8	8	8	7
PI	2	3	6	3	5	5	5	5	4	4
SG	6	6	3	6	5	5	7	6	7	6
NO	5	5	6	5	7	7	5	7	6	4
AC	5	5	6	4	5	6	6	6	5	6
HI	5	9	6	5	7	6	4	6	5	6
DU	4	4	6	4	6	5	4	4	5	6
RISK	150	120	65	80	123	126	67	81	131	130
TYPE	T	T	T	T	R	R	T	T	R	R
INT	112	52	258	51	20	612	25	27	20	273
ESCP	9	9	2	2	2	2	5	5	6	4
CONCEN	2	1	3	.6	.3	10	.1	.1	.2	3
INV	30618	30618	2736	2736	290	1392	58050	81270	870	3654
EFRT	9	9	3	3	5	4	5	7	5	3

Trends in the Data Base (Just to Get You Started)

Overwhelmed by all the numbers in the data base? We've picked out some patterns and nuggets to show how you can turn a blizzard of numbers into a useful trend.

You, too, can become adept at predicting how wars and warlike situations will develop. Military analysts call this risk analysis. Although the techniques can become complex, you use the basic theory daily. Say you drive over the same road year-round. You learn which portions of the road become treacherous when wet or icy. You analyze your experience and take appropriate action. You've done a risk analysis of the road. If you don't heed your analysis, you may have an accident, perhaps fatal. We have applied the same kind of thinking to war and peace. Here we will show you the road, and how to spot the danger spots.

Put simply, you need to follow these steps to do a risk analysis of any conflict:

1. **Examine past wars.** This is your best source of information. We provide ample information on past wars in the data base and elsewhere.

2. **Compile information on current and potential wars.** These are the ones you are trying to do something about. Again, we have done a lot of your work for you, although this is an ongoing process which you will have to continue.

3. **Determine patterns.** They are there. We will point out many patterns, although you will eventually have to continue this ongoing work on your own.

4. Isolate patterns of how wars end. We do this for you, at least for the wars that have ended during the last two centuries.

5. Isolate behavior that avoids wars. We do this for you, at least for the wars that have ended during the last two centuries.

6. Compare patterns to current potential wars and determine what can be done. This is applying the lessons of the past.

The above will not seem so cryptic once you have examined these examples from the data base.

1. EXAMINE PAST WARS

Each nation has a style of warfare. Examine past wars for broad and repetitive trends. Do not be misled by tasty trivia. Some trends are nearly universal. For example, armies that have not fought for years launch their first offensive of a war with disastrous results. The Russian Army is particularly prone to this. Another trend is that weapons untried in combat have unpredictable effects. Often, the side with fewer of them, but a better guess at their correct employment, will prevail. Germany's use of armored vehicles in World War II is an example. All of Germany's opponents had more, but Germany used them more efficiently. If you want an idea of how an army will perform in its next war, look at how it did its last few times out.

2. COMPILE INFORMATION ON CURRENT AND POTENTIAL WARS

We have done this in the data base at the end of the book.

3. DETERMINE PATTERNS

Here are examples to get you started.

▪ There were 409 wars between 1786 and 1986. About 54 percent were territorial conflicts, the remainder were internal affairs (93 percent revolutions, 4 percent secessions, 3 percent civil terror).

▪ Aggressors generally lose. They are twice as likely to be defeated as defenders.

▪ Secessions are more likely to be in smaller nations and are the least likely type of war to succeed. Large nations get that way by keeping separatism under control.

▪ Compare wars since 1945 to those previously. They have been more numerous, longer-lasting and of lower intensity. These conflicts have been primarily in the less developed nations of Africa, Asia and the Middle East. Most were internal disorders and used low-quality combat forces. Worst of all, these wars frequently became stalemated and did not resolve issues.

The following charts showed these trends.

THE INTENSITY OF WAR THROUGHOUT HISTORY

There has been no letup in war deaths, or the number of participants. Troops and Average Losses in thousands, Total Losses in millions.

		Period			
	All Periods	1786 1815	1815 1900	1900 1945	1945 1987
Avg Troops	462	205	197	1333	541
Cmbt Power	310	126	121	811	356
Avg Losses	161	75	64	496	140
Tot Losses	163	8	27	84	44
Intensity	8	9	7	12	6

Combat Power: Calculated by multiplying the Avg Troops number by the quality value assigned to that participant's troops. It gives a better indication of overall combat capability.

Intensity: Average losses per million population for each participant in each war. This indicates the relative impact of warfare on participants.

IMPACT OF WARS BY REGION

The number and intensity of wars, as well as losses, varies greatly from region to region.

	% Wars	% Participants	% Killed	% People	V Index
Africa	22	19	2	7	28
East Asia	16	15	44	46	95
Russia	8	9	39	13	300
Europe	11	16	11	7	142
India, etc.	9	7	1	15	6
Mideast	20	21	2	8	37
Americas	14	13	1	4	25
	100%	100%	100%	100%	

% Wars is the percentage of wars that occurred in each region during the last two hundred years.

% Participants is the percentage of nations or groups that participated in a war found in that region. For example, 195 of the thousand total participants fought their wars in Africa (rounded to 20 percent).

% Killed is the percentage of the total war deaths that occurred in each region.

% People is the average portion of world population for each region over two centuries. The population has grown at vastly different rates over this period, so this is an approximate number.

The V Index shows the relative amount of war losses among the population in each region. Obviously, the place to go to avoid death from wars is India. The most dangerous place is Russia.

WARS IN AFRICA

Africa has lots of wars between lots of groups, but not nearly as many casualties. (Forces and losses are in thousands.)

Period	Wars	Groups Fighting	Forces Involved Per Group	Average Losses Per Group
1786-1815	8	17	67	21
1815-1900	42	88	55	10
1900-1945	11	21	70	9
1945-1986	28	67	66	21
All Africa	89	193	62	15
All World	409	1011	462	161

WARS IN EAST ASIA

East Asia (China and its neighbors) has been the deadliest region in the past two centuries for sheer volume of deaths.

Period	Wars	Combat Forces Involved Per Group	Average Losses Per Group
1786-1815	4	242	33
1815-1900	26	472	354
1900-1945	4	2102	675
1945-1986	39	765	589
All East Asia	64	740	469
All World	409	462	161

RUSSIAN WARS

Russia is, per capita, the most violent region.

Period	Wars	Average Combat Forces Per War	Average Losses Per War
1786-1815	6	548	67
1815-1900	9	622	26
1900-1945	7	3085	2400
1945-1986	9	4023	10
All Russia	31	2109	731
All Europe	46	595	105
All World	409	462	161

- India and its neighbors must be doing something right, as they have suffered the lowest number of wartime casualties in both absolute and relative terms.

- The Middle East was, until 1945, a quiet region. Oil money appears to have produced death and destruction.

- The Americas, next to the Indian region, have been the most peaceful.

- We have counted 1,011 participating groups, nations or other major organizations. Many show up in more than one war—there are over three hundred different entities. Some groups go to war much more frequently than others, and a handful of nations had the majority of the war losses.

- The nation most frequently at war was Britain, participating in 20 percent of all wars. Most were colonial, and resulted in a relatively low casualty count. British armed forces suffered less than 2 percent of the losses during this period. Russia fought in 9 percent of the wars but suffered over 25 percent of the losses (including civil terror casualties). Indeed, China and Russia account for over half the losses throughout this period, although these nations participated in less than 15 percent of the wars. Other high participation nations were Turkey, France and the United States. But none of these was involved in more than 6 percent of the wars, and usually half that number.

- Another part of the data base tells why the nations went to war. Long-standing grievances brought nations to the brink of war 40 percent of the time. A sixth of the time a sense of military superiority was the driving factor, while 39 percent of the wars internal disorder in one of the nations caused the hostilities. Less than 5 percent of the time, fear of attack was the primary cause.

- What kind of war? One percent was wars of civil terror, 42 percent were revolutions, 2 percent were secessions and 54 percent were territorial disputes. Most of the nations that engaged in territorial conflicts have below-average government stability.

- At what cost? Over one hundred fifty million people have died in wars since 1786. More than three times as many were injured by direct or indirect effects of the fighting. We compute the intensity of war by calculating the proportion of the population killed. We express this in terms of dead per 1,000 people. Many nations have suffered over 20 percent losses in a war. In most cases these nations were small, and were overwhelmed by much larger forces. Russia and Germany are exceptions, suffering nearly 20 percent population losses during World War II.

- When you are looking at a developing situation, look at nation size;

larger nations tend to fight larger, shorter, more destructive and more conclusive wars. Look also at size of conflict; larger wars are fought by nations with stable governments. It takes a lot of organization to get a large war going.

- The most warlike nation in the world? By every measure, it is Russia. Over the entire two-hundred-year period, Russia has been a leading participant in wars. Most other major nations went through intensive periods of warfare, with low activity the rest of the time. Russia has been at war for much of the two hundred years. Russia has fought larger and more deadly wars than any other nation. Russia's direct participation in wars has caused over fifty million deaths in the past two centuries. This has occurred because Russia has been invaded numerous times, has often struck out at its neighbors and has slaughtered its own people in the millions.

Most of these wars were fought while Russia was still a monarchy. Since Russia became a socialist dictatorship in 1918, there have been fewer wars, but far more deaths. Russia has fought these wars more intensively than most nations and has won 74 percent of them (versus the average of 46 percent for all nations). Overall, only 13 percent of nations fought their wars at maximum intensity; Russia has fought 74 percent of its wars this way.

Most of Russia's wars were territorial disputes (57 percent). The remainder were civil terrors and revolutions. Russia participated in some 9 percent of all wars, far less than Britain's 20 percent. However, while Britain incurred less than two million dead, Russia suffered over forty million. By maintaining the world's largest armed forces, Russia ensures that its military traditions are continued.

A close second to Russia is China. However, there are some important distinctions. China fought in only 6 percent of the wars. More of China's wars were internal conflicts and far fewer were attacks on neighbors. Still, China also lost over thirty million.

Between them, Russia and China participated in about 15 percent of the wars in this period and incurred over a third of all losses. If you include the dead of their opponents, this number more than doubles. Thus two nations were largely responsible for two thirds of the war deaths in the last two hundred years. The majority of the dead were Russians and Chinese.

For all this slaughter, Russia and China were more successful in defeating their opponents or resolving issues. Russia was victorious 74 percent of the time, the average for all nations is 46 percent. Overall, 66 percent of all wars fail to resolve their causes. Russia's percentage is 42 percent and China's 67 percent. These nations have paid a high price to resolve a few more disputes.

Many of Russia's wars were a result of the "Superpower Disease," otherwise known as a belief in military superiority and immunity from retaliation. This is an underlying cause of instability between nations 16 percent of the time. For Russia, this was a factor in 32 percent of its wars. The United States (68 percent) and Britain (59 percent) were worse. What makes Russia unique is its preference for attacking first (53 percent of the time versus an average of 44 percent for all nations). By contrast, America was the initial attacker only 5 percent of the time, Britain 5 percent and China 17 percent. Russia is unique among the major powers in looking for a fight, and generally being the first to start it.

Like most major powers, Russia is likely to fight its wars to a successful conclusion, even if it means exhaustion of the population and economy.

4. ISOLATE PATTERNS OF HOW WARS END

Patterns of wars ending can be easily seen by looking at the summaries from our study of 409 wars.

■ Once a war is under way, in most cases exhaustion (26 percent of the time) or a willingness to negotiate (18 percent) soon puts a stop to serious efforts at winning. In only 40 percent of the cases is the decision made to continue the war because victory is seen as possible.

■ For what final result? Two thirds of all wars do not resolve the issues that caused them. At the end of the war neither side has whatever was being fought over. When a war does not resolve the issues that caused it, the stage is set for further warfare. Some nations have been fighting for thousands of years over the same issues. Fighting a war until the fundamental issues are resolved is not exactly the solution either. By far the bloodiest wars are those that resolve the issues that started them. Wars unsuccessful in achieving goals were low-effort and small-scale affairs to begin with. Nations with low government stability and little support from major powers simply lack the means to fight a war to any kind of successful conclusion.

HOW WARS END

Read percentage total across (CS + MD + MS + MV + NC = 100%, DI + IR + NR = 100%)

Reasons for Deciding to End War	% Wars	Cause of War's End					Results		
		CS	MD	MS	MV	NC	DI	IR	NR
Exhaustion	3	2	98	0	0	0	4	0	96
Military Prowess	73	0	0	0	99	1	2	62	36
Negotiation	11	0	67	0	32	1	1	32	67
Stalemate	11	0	36	45	19	0	0	36	64
Surrender	1	3	94	0	3	0	11	3	86
Unresolved	1	0	0	97	0	3	2	32	66
Tot for Column	100	1	41	11	46	1			

The first column lists the reasons nations give for deciding to end hostilities. The next columns (CS, MD, MS, MV, NC) break out the event that caused a participant to leave the war.

CS—Collapse of Society. The stresses of waging war cause the nation to collapse economically and socially. The armed forces may still be intact, but no longer have much reason to continue the struggle.

MD—Military Defeat. A nation's armed forces are decisively defeated, thus making any further participation in a war impossible.

MS—Military Stalemate. Unable to achieve a military decision, both nations allow the war to taper off to something resembling peace.

MV—Military Victory. A nation's armed forces are decisively victorious, thus making any further participation in a war unnecessary.

NC—No Combat Between Nations. For one reason or another, a nation's armed forces are no longer involved in combat operations. The nation may still be officially at war, but has no problem in abandoning any semblance of warfare.

There are more victors (MV) than losers (MD) because many nations often gang up on one.

Exhaustion—The sides battle into a state of exhaustion. A form of peace follows. In this case, exhaustion usually means defeat.

Military Prowess is recognition, usually correct, that a nation has an overwhelming military advantage that will soon lead to victory.

Negotiation is not always a recognition of defeat, but usually it results in defeat.

Stalemate is sometimes recognized. Both sides abandon the struggle.

Surrender on short notice is often the result of internal political problems or simply a loss of heart by one side.

Unresolved wars are still going on.

The next columns (DI, IR, NR) look at the results of the wars.

DI (Destruction of opponent and Issues resolved)—Issues that caused the war are resolved through the destruction of the other nation.

IR (Issues Resolved)—Issues that caused the war are resolved without the destruction of the other nation.

NR (No issues Resolved)—Issues that caused the war are not resolved.

5. ISOLATE BEHAVIOR THAT AVOIDS WARS

Certain patterns of behavior exist in nations that have avoided war. These nations have:

- Accurate perception of other nations' military inferiority
- Control over grievances between themselves and opponents
- Willingness to negotiate
- Control over public opinion on grievances
- Historical willingness not to use force
- Accurate perception of the political situation in other nations

Each participant in a war was evaluated on a 1 to 9 scale for each of these characteristics. The nations examined were evaluated while participating in a war. In the data base we combined all of these factors into one value, which we call RISK. Interesting patterns emerge. For example, socialist dictatorships have an average RISK factor 27 percent higher than democracies. Even higher are insurgent groups. Not surprisingly, Russia's abundance of wars expresses itself in a higher-than-average RISK value. Some warlike nations are more warlike than others.

6. DETERMINE WHICH WAR-ENDING PATTERNS APPLY TO CONTEMPORARY WARS

We have found six general styles of wars ending.

TYPES OF WARS AND HOW THEY END

	Civil Terror	Revolution	Secession	Territorial
Percent of Wars	1	42	2	55
Reason for deciding to end war				
Exhaustion	40	29	35	22
Military Superiority	53	34	24	46
Negotiation	0	13	24	24
Stalemate	0	1	0	1
Surrender	7	3	0	3
Unresolved	0	20	17	4
	100%	100%	100%	100%
Type of War Ending				
Defeat	47	40	47	43
Stalemate	0	20	18	5
Victory	53	40	35	52
	100%	100%	100%	100%
Result of War				
Issues Resolved	47	25	24	36
Issues Not Resolved	53	75	76	64
	100%	100%	100%	100%

You can easily determine what type of war is going on. For some current examples of war types, we remind you of Cambodia in the 1970s (civil terror), El Salvador (revolution), Iran-Iraq (territorial dispute), Moslem Rebellion in Philippines (secession). There are many others.

Based on the historical experience shown in the chart above you can see what the most likely approach to ending the war will be. The above outcomes are the reasons a side uses to justify ending hostilities. Exhaustion will be the result if neither side is demonstrably superior to each other. Military superiority is a matter of who believes what. If one side can convince the other that it is superior in combat power, the war will quickly end.

All wars have some chance of achieving a negotiated settlement. If you add the number of wars that grind to a halt due to exhaustion, which is a form of unspoken negotiation, you can see there is always a good chance of getting the combatants to settle their differences without more combat. The unresolved wars are still ongoing.

One thing that should be immediately obvious is the large number of wars that do not resolve the grievances that began them. Wars that end in this way are simply laying the groundwork for another conflict. Ending wars like this does not end the fighting, it merely interrupts it.

While wars may begin with a certain degree of deliberation, they tend to end in a muddle of improvisation. Wars that do not end very quickly tend to go on for several years; the average is seven years. This leaves ample opportunity for intervention and early resolution of these wars. Once a war has begun, you have three choices:

1. If you control essential military supplies for one or both warring nations, you can withdraw or increase these supplies to control the fighting. This can have a dramatic effect on the fighting ability of the affected nations. Most of the Arab-Israeli wars were ended this way, as was the Greek Civil War in the late 1940s. The Iran-Iraq War that began in 1980 was prolonged because Iraq received copious material while Iran was largely cut off from such aid.

2. If you are going to intervene, prepare to do so with overwhelming force. Often, other nations, usually neighbors, will intervene. Examples are Zambia in Uganda, Vietnam in Cambodia and in Laos, the United States in Grenada, Russia in Afghanistan, Israel and Syria in Lebanon and so on. The list is long and the experience of the intervening nations is not encouraging. Stepping into the middle of someone else's war is similar to what happens when police are called to break up a domestic dispute. Both warring factions tend to turn on the peacemaker. Unless you can go in decisively, you are apt to find yourself in a long, somewhat hopeless, war.

3. Try to persuade the combatants to stop fighting and settle the dispute peaceably. This is the least likely method, but is always worth a shot. This is particularly true if the war persists and both sides are having a hard time of it. Often a combination of threatened intervention, halting of supplies and honest mediation will do the trick. The eternal problem, however, is to get the combatants in a mood for peace. Warfare generates strong passions for revenge and justification. Peace slowly emerges as an alternative to bloody triumph.

It is much easier to prevent a war than to stop it once under way. The risk factors of a potential war indicate where attention should be directed. But there are never enough diplomatic, military and political resources to attend to every potential hot spot. Simply choosing what area to pay attention to consumes a major portion of a government's time.

Unfortunately, in a democracy like the United States, the media often play a larger role in deciding where to focus attention than the appointed government agencies. The media in turn look to their public for direction. The media operate in a competitive environment; those that succeed best are those that deliver more of what their readers and viewers want. All of this is an endless circle, as the readers and viewers get most of their information from the media. Politicians, clergy, educators, traditions modify which causes the population will be more enthusiastic for.

Decisions are not made on any strictly rational basis. If the function of foreign policy were simply to save lives, the greatest efforts would be toward preventing, stopping or slowing down those wars that were killing the most people. In the early 1980s, most American attention was focused on South Africa, where the deaths were far fewer than in half a dozen other conflicts in Africa.

In our historical survey we found that 83 percent of all war participants had a RISK value of over 50, and 55 percent had a 100+ RISK value. The average RISK value was 99. Not surprisingly, the potential participants of wars that never happened had an average RISK of 74. The participants of potential wars have a RISK of 89. Several of these potential wars will become the real thing, which accounts for their higher RISK value.

Remember that a group that is indicated as violence-prone may not be in a position to attack anyone. For example, a revolutionary group may not possess sufficient military power to get a proper war going.

Future Wars and Wars That Never Happened also include one additional factor: Escalation. This rates the potential for a war spreading within a region. It covers such factors as superpower involvement, regional alliances and who has nuclear weapons. Two nations that are "closet nuclear powers" are most worrisome—Israel and South Africa. Both are under a considerable amount of pressure. If such pressure were to cause the use of nuclear weapons, the results could be far-reaching indeed.

Read the Future Wars Chart and make your own decisions.

Sources

One part of the research for this book was compiling data on wars since 1786 so that we can understand why wars have been fought and the effects of war. This essay explains how we did this research and the sources used so readers can see just how research on war is done.

For recent history, especially since 1900, we have lots of data on the major wars. Which nations or groups have fought wars, how many are killed, the approximate size of the armed forces and the duration of the war are known. While some details of specific wars remain murky, such as the exact reason for going to war, by and large wars since 1900 have been well documented by historians and journalists. But this is not so for wars in the 1800s, and even less so for many of the wars of antiquity.

Our first task was to compile a list of wars for the last two hundred years: big wars, little wars, even "wars" that did not happen. One source that was quite useful is *The Encyclopedia of Military History* (New York: Harper & Row, 1977) by R. E. Dupuy and T. N. Dupuy. The detailed accounts of wars provided a starting point for identifying wars.

For each war, we needed to know exactly which nations fought, when it began and ended, how long it lasted, how many died, the size of the forces that fought, the government and so on. An important reference was *The Wages of War, 1816–1965* (New York: John Wiley & Sons, 1972) by J. David Singer and Melvin Small. Singer and Small provide some data on the nations involved and the duration of the wars. It is also a good source of data on the size of the combat forces for each nation, and estimates of the casualties. Singer and Small, however, tend to generate statistics of dubious value, such as battle deaths per month of the war.

There is considerable uncertainty about the number of people who are killed in a given war, especially as one proceeds further into the past. Only during the last two centuries have nations begun to keep records, and unfortunately records often get destroyed in war. Singer and Small also provide comparisons of other authors' estimates of combat casualties. Some other sources for data on combat casualties are *Statistics of Deadly Quarrels* (Pittsburgh: Boxwood Press, 1960) by Lewis Frye Richardson; *Social and Cultural Dynamics* (New York: American Book, 1937) by Pitirim A. Sorokin; *Losses of Life in Modern Wars* (London: Oxford University, 1916) by Gaston Bodart; *Losses of Life Caused by War* (London: Oxford University, 1920) by Vedel and Petersen.

Military Balance (Letchford, England: The Garden City Press Ltd., 1985), which is published annually by the International Institute for Strategic Studies, is a good source for the size of armed forces in the contemporary period.

A useful source for the population of nations and tribes is the *Atlas of World Population History* (London: Viking Penguin, Inc., 1985) by Colin McEvedy and Richard Jones. It is difficult to estimate the population of political and ethnic entities, but the *Atlas* is the best reference we have on the historical populations of nations.

Our second general task was to compile more subjective data on the wars and their participants. We considered the stability of the government, the propensity of the government to settle grievances with violence, the intensity of the antagonisms that fuel the war, the quality of the armed forces, the willingness of the participants to negotiate and many other factors. We used numerous sources to piece together data on these soft variables. In addition to *The Encyclopedia of Military History,* we used *A Study of War* (Chicago: University of Chicago, 1942) by Quincy Wright, *History of Warfare* (New York: William Morrow, 1983) by Montgomery of Alamein, *A Dictionary of Battles* (New York: Mayflower Books, 1977) by Peter Young, *The Causes of War* (New York: The Free Press, 1973) by Geoffrey Blainey, and *War in the Great Power System* (New York: The Free Press, 1975) by Jack Levy. For recent conflicts, *A Quick and Dirty Guide to War* (New York: William Morrow, 1985) by J. F. Dunnigan and Austin Bay was useful. Obviously, this is not a complete list of all our sources, but it provides an important starting point for readers who want to study warfare on their own.

There is no single method for assigning values to the variables in historical events. We relied on our judgment for assigning a number to the stability of a government, or willingness to negotiate. But patterns do emerge. Some governments are involved in more wars than others, and some governments change more frequently than others. It is safe to infer that some governments are more stable than others. But there is no science of history. Studying warfare, which really is studying the combative side of history, is based in the end on judgment and reason.

Index